BEHIND THE SILICON CURTAIN

Behind the Silicon Curtain

The Seductions of Work in a Lonely Era

by

Dennis Hayes

South End Press
Boston, MA

Cover Design by Jocelyn Bergen and Chris Carlsson
Cover Photography by Dennis Hayes
Front Cover: Santa Clara County
Back Cover: Silicon Valley crowd cheers combat simulation with napalm July 5, 1985.
Production by the South End Press collective
Manufactured in the U.S.A.

Library of Congress Cataloging-in-Publication Data

Hayes, Dennis.
    Behind the silicon curtain.

    Includes bibliographical references and index.
    1. Computer industry--California--Santa Clara
County. I. Title.
HD9696.C63U5183227   1989   338.4'7004'0979473   88-35624
ISBN 0-89608-351-9
ISBN 0-89608-350-0 (pbk.)

South End Press
116 Saint Botolph St.
Boston, MA 02115
9 8 7 6 5 4 3 2   89 90 91 92 93 94 95

To Peter Zernitz,
wherever you are.

About the Author

Since 1984, Dennis Hayes has covered the Silicon Valley desk for the San Francisco-based magazine *Processed World*. Born in Sheboygan, Wisconsin, he studied undergraduate sociology, economics, and philosophy of science at St. Norbert College (Wisconsin) and graduate sociology at Carleton University (Ottawa, Canada). He received an M.A. degree from the University of Wisconsin in Milwaukee where he taught before moving to Silicon Valley in 1979 for a stint as a news writer for a socialist weekly. Since 1981, Hayes has worked as a receptionist, secretary, clerk, and technical writer in the civilian and military electronics industry. He currently writes freelance adcopy and specifications for computer and microchip firms.

Contents

Acknowledgements

Researching and writing this book began in 1985 and proceeded fitfully (in between jobs in Silicon Valley and issues of *Processed World**) over three and one half years. Because the project was neither independently funded nor a collaboration, the enthusiasm and support of my friends was especially crucial.

For sustaining encouragement and useful critiques I thank Tom Athanasiou, Chris Carlsson, Adam Cornford, Gary Cummings, Marcy Darnovsky, Matthew Holdreith, Wendy Johnston, Caitlin Manning, and (especially) Amelia Morgan. JoAnn Okabe-Kubo provided early support and faithful *San Jose Mercury News* archiving. I am also indebted to my fellow malcontents at *Processed World* for standing by this project. Thanks to David Noble for (rather suddenly) taking time out of an important schedule to read the manuscript and to write the introduction.

I am particularly grateful to Chris Carlsson, Todd Jailer (my editor at South End Press), and Amelia Morgan who read all the manuscripts; and to Caitlin Manning, Adam Cornford, and Shelley Diamond who read most. The text was much improved by comments from all as well as by copy editing from Adam (chapters 1 through 3, 5, and most of 7), Shelley (chapters 2 through 7), Jim Brook (chapter 7), and Todd (all).

Dan Sears consulted technically in the digital conversion of the manuscript. Pilot Dick Fugett took me up for the aerial photography that appears on the front cover; I am discreetly indebted to the Marine Corp guards who provided access to a roof vantage from which the back cover photo was taken during the Silicon Valley Air Show. Finally, I am grateful to Michael, Victor, Doris, Fred, Nick, M., Stony, and many significant others in Silicon Valley who took my interview questions as opportunities to candidly recount experiences (or lead me to those who would).

* Some of the material for three chapters appeared previously in *Processed World*.

Introduction
Sand Castles

by David F. Noble

Dennis Hayes has seen the future and it doesn't work. His disturbing account of the underside of Silicon Valley provides a powerful and
much-needed antidote to the print-out panaceas purveyed by today's
born-again progressives, the false promises of Yankee enterprise in the
computer age.

Evoked every day by promoters, prophets and politicians, the
images abound of a harmonious and prosperous future, a bright, bucolic
and beneficent new world created and sustained by the market magic
of unbridled entrepreneurial elan and the impetuous spirit of invention.
"It's time to rekindle the American spirit of invention and daring,"
high-tech candidate Michael Dukakis declared; "A new era is about to
begin."

The hallowed site of this modern miracle is Silicon Valley, California, microchip mecca, where the future is now. Silicon Valley is the point
of departure for all of today's disc-driven dreamers—at once a sign of
and a guide to our computer-based salvation. The symbol for this new
world is the silicon chip, patterned bits of hardened sand which carry
the electronic intelligence of computers and microprocessors into the
myriad machinery of modern life. Silicon is the material substrate upon
which the high technology culture is being etched. As the technological
titans of ages past have left their imprints in stone, bronze, iron, and steel,
so those of this new age will leave theirs in silicon. Strength in silicon,
we are told, is thus the key to our continued greatness; it is here that the
reality and the fantasy converge. For, if the material foundation of this
new world is built upon sand, so too are its dreams. This is the unsettling
moral of Dennis Hayes' story.

A century and a half ago, at the dawn of America's first industrial
revolution, publicists for a powerful group of Boston manufacturers
portrayed their new textile town of Lowell, Massachusetts in much the

same way as today's high-tech progressives portray Silicon Valley. Lowell too was a pastoral paradise touched by the miracle of enterprise and invention, a showcase of the promise of industrial society, a living utopia. Unspoiled nature here joined with innovative spirit to yield not satanic mills, poverty, exploitation, and social strife, but material abundance and social harmony.

The image of Lowell, glorified by promoters, prophets, and politicians, and celebrated by distinguished foreign visitors, centered on the wholesome vitality of the mill girls. Neatly dressed, well-mannered, self-reliant, and cheerfully optimistic, these young women fresh off the farm embodied the promise of the new industrial era. They flocked to the machines in their garden to weave not just cheap cotton cloth but a new social fabric for an emergent empire. Paternalistically preserved from idleness and its attendant vices in their well-kept and sternly supervised boarding houses, the "Lowell girls" wrote poetry and essays for their own publications, attended Lyceum lectures, enjoyed a modicum of social respectability, and, for a time, relatively high wages. They were also able to move back and forth between farm and factory, as the needs of their family required. The Lowell girls were living proof, in short, that industry in America would escape the ravages of Manchester, and they became, accordingly, the symbol of the beneficence of the new order.

The romance of Lowell, however, was short-lived. By the time the mythology became common gospel, the reality underlying it had all but disappeared. Once the Lowell manufacturers became able to recruit immigrant labor at subsistence wages, the paternalistic paradise evaporated. No longer required to recruit young women from the farm, appease their anxious parents, and appeal to their ambitions, the mill owners were able to create a permanent factory workforce, reduce wages, and extend the working day. For the veteran Lowell girls, accordingly, poetry gave way to poverty, respectability to rebellion.

Sarah Bagley had worked in the Lowell mills for eight years, roughly the same period of time that Dennis Hayes has worked in Silicon Valley. After her early paeans to the "pleasures of factory life," Bagley grew skeptical of the blessings bestowed by big business and she resolved to expose and resist the abuses of the textile barons. Together with some of their sister mill girls, she spelled out their grievances about working conditions in the industrial utopia: the endless 12- or 13-hour days, the constant deafening noise, the lack of ventilation (windows were nailed shut), the discomfort and health hazard of lint flying in the air (resulting in the disease today known as brown lung), speed-ups in production with no increase in pay, the lack of bathing facilities, the crowding in the dormitories (two to a bed, six to a room), and the lack of vacation time.

Having seen the harsh reality behind the tinted image of Lowell, Bagley decried "the driveling cotton lords who arrogantly aspire to lord it over God's heritage." A born leader, she soon became America's first woman trade unionist. She organized and became president of the Female Labor Reform Association, an organization which numbered some 600 members in its first year and quickly spread to the mill towns throughout New England. As the plutocratic publicists continued to testify to the miracle of Lowell as a sign of industrial salvation, Bagley and her colleagues gave testimony to the state legislature on the life-depleting working conditions in the mills. These Lowell women failed in their efforts to shorten the working day—the legislature was dominated by the textile magnates—and their union was effectively destroyed in a few short years. Nevertheless, their experience, their words, and their deeds laid to rest for a time the fantasy of an industrial utopia.

Today the Silicon Valley fantasy of a postindustrial utopia is likewise being laid to rest. Just as the creation of a permanent workforce of immiserated immigrants shattered the illusion of Lowell, so capital flight, speculations, and mergers and their attendant disorders are shattering the illusion of Silicon Valley. However much the propagandists for yet another generation of industrial lords peddle their paradisiacal palaver, the brutal realities of life in the vaunted valley are becoming increasingly apparent. And as Sarah Bagley and her sisters strived to expose these harsh realities in their day, so Dennis Hayes does in ours. The technology of production aside, not much has changed. Like the earlier reformers, Hayes knows first-hand of what he speaks, as he describes the pursuit of wealth, power, and technical enchantment on the one side, and the human degradation on the other.

Taking the reader behind the promotional veil of the engineers and entrepreneurs, Hayes calls our attention to both the natural and human costs of their driving ambitions. He describes the cruel irony of the so-called "clean rooms," the fume-filled chip processing facilities where workers are "packaged to protect the product" rather than the other way around. And he explains how the clean room casualties multiply beyond the factory gates, as processing chemicals seep into the valley's air, water supply, and food chain.

As the desperation of Irish immigrants depressed wages and working conditions in Lowell, so that of Asian immigrants, and undocumented and temporary workers does the same in Silicon Valley. Cynical hiring policies and corporate complicity with immigration authorities keep these most vulnerable employees in line and belie the enlightened new age image of employee-centered management. As the textile magnates thwarted efforts at reform and unionization, so too have the silicon magnates; established unions have abandoned the valley of the future. Meanwhile, the high-tech firms, corporations-without-a-country, flee "off-shore" in search of profits, leaving behind industrial ghost parks, unemployment, and dislocated lives. Always prepared to move, valley firms keep investment to a minimum in their pre-fab factories, leasing facilities and workers alike on a temporary basis. Little wonder that Silicon Valley has the highest job turnover and highest industrial vacancy rate in the country.

Behind the Hollywood set of Silicon Valley, Hayes finds the wizards of this Oz, the alchemist investors who want only to turn their sand into gold, and the manchild engineers who want only to be left to play in the sandbox. Socially and morally irresponsible or incoherent, both are sustained less by the noble spirit of enlightened enterprise than by the war games of military contracting—the real mechanism behind the miracle. In the military half of Silicon Valley, the manchildren are cloistered in their cubicles by vows of obedience and ignorance. Whereas Sarah Bagley and her co-workers lost in the factory system all control over the products of their labor, these modern workers are deprived by official policy and a "culture of collective avoidance" of even knowing what their products are. Such alienation and the sterile social deformity it engenders are the most disturbing aspects of the Silicon Valley Hayes describes.

The desperation and alienation that characterize the Silicon Valley workplace carry over into the anomie of an atomized society beyond the workplace. This "processed world" has been best described by the San Francisco-based magazine of that name, for whom Hayes writes, and his analysis here reflects an accumulation of experience and insight. Hayes recounts the social erosion in the valley, the closing of schools, the escalating housing costs, the inadequate child care. He vividly describes the banal horrors of the two-hour commute, the loneliness of lives. He probes the spirit of the new era and finds it dissolving in the solvents of Silicon Valley, leaving up to three-quarters of the working population victims of substance abuse, over half in therapy, and the highest divorce rate in the nation.

With the deterioration of all social supports, Valley people are compelled to turn to individualized regimens of "self-maintenance" to allay their anxieties. Some are seduced into seeking redemption through work; aided and abetted by corporate compulsory overtime policies, they turn their neuroses into product and sublimate their desire for love and community with hackers' highs. Those less technically inclined or without a Protestant alter ego, turn to diets, exercise, or the ultimate solution, shopping. "Whenever I get depressed, I buy shoes," sings the Impossible Theatre; compulsive consumption competes with obsessive fitness as the therapy of tomorrow today.

For all the similarities, the contrast with Lowell is striking. Drawn to Lowell by the fairy tale and the temporarily attractive conditions, the mill girls rather quickly saw through the publicists' propaganda. Before long, they had aired their grievances, forged an organization, and collectively fought back against the depredations of the textile lords to retain their dignity and their humanity. Many such struggles followed in the wake of industrialization and continue today. But the resolve for such collective action is noticeably absent in Silicon Valley. Notions of human dignity and a shared future have been forgotten in the silicon gold rush. Whereas Sarah Bagley was joined by hundreds and then thousands of mill workers, Dennis Hayes is a lone observer. This apparent obsolescence of social purpose is the most telling casualty of the emergent era. Amid an ocean of human debris, the sand castles of Silicon Valley stand firm, testimony to a desperate belief in miracles. Illusions of technological transcendence, they testify less to a rebirth of spirit than to a loss of will.

1

Mutation

The Electronic Colony

People were looking at this as an area where the American dream could still be realized.

Silicon Valley industrial psychologist, 1985

Official proposals to spend billions of federal dollars to revitalize the [U.S. microchip] industry could well be too little—and even too late.

The Wall Street Journal, 1987

Dream Boost

Rarely has one location, one industry inspired dreams among so many. In the decade following the American Quarter Century (1950-1975), a Pacific coastal valley on the western shores of San Francisco Bay became the hub of a global industry. The tidings of its prosperity encouraged imitations from Jerusalem to Tierra del Fuego and attracted immigrants from Islamabad to Pittsburgh. More than this, Silicon Valley—or the mythology constructed on its behalf—stirred dreams that the world had come to identify with some essential part of the U.S. character. The most remarkable of these dreams struck transcendent themes: material salvation through migration and work as a spiritual haven. These merged into a grand social vision of a new technology making life better and creating jobs lost to obsolete industry. Like their nocturnal counterparts, the dreams blended less-than-conscious hopes and fears.

15

It should not have been too surprising, then, that as the dreams came true they entailed something other than fairy-tale endings. The fairy tale had become the stock literary device for the authors and journalists who named this land of enchantment "Silicon Valley" and chronicled its fortunes in articles, interviews, and books that celebrated the entrepreneurs and the technologists.[1] As a result, a sort of truth-by-anecdote had been allowed to accumulate in which social history was quietly suspended. This oversight affected nearly everyone's vision, including that of investigative journalists, whose custom is to disturb the projects of business enterprise. Lulling critics, pushing dissent well off the pages of acceptable inquiry, the fairy tales transformed skepticism into adulation.

In 1983, a prominent investigative-reporting magazine praised the paths taken by the "microchip moguls" of Silicon Valley and urged popular support for them—as if any such urging was needed. Two years later, another investigative reporter balanced his ebullient book on the Valley with anecdotes of drugs and espionage, but continued to recite the now familiar litanies: "Sunnyvale...has more millionaires per capita than any city its size in the world. The result is the overnight-wealth story played out scores of times every month."[2] The spell cast by the prosperity was such that each new forward twitch of technology appeared as a social advance.

Before long, the dreams assumed a millenarian stature, lifted by the conviction that history was in the making, that a new stage in civilization was at hand. Who would deny that the Information Age moved with the same unyielding destructive sweep of the Industrial Revolution? In the semi-rural communities that began to model themselves on Silicon Valley, enigmatic urban habitats evolved, marking a visual and cultural rupture with the cities and towns that grew up with Industrial America. In Silicon Valley, there occurred a confusing but inexorable transformation from apricot orchards, Main Street, and ranch hospitality to "smart" missile labs, theme malls, and residence hotels. It was reminiscent, in its thoroughness and abruptness, of the enclosures of the English Commons and the rise of the urban "manufactories" that thrust the Industrial Revolution upon the world. But the epochal metaphors were also inspired by an unspoken desire to transcend the bleakness of Industrial America circa 1975.

By 1980, references to the coastal valley evoked the vital categories of adolescent capitalism: entrepreneur, venture capital, technological innovation, upward mobility. Outside corporate fitness centers, underneath the canopies of *al fresco* cafeterias, the computer professionals could be seen eating salads, browsing through survival-gear catalogs, gazing at digital wrist stopwatches, and sporting the most sophisticated running shoes, as if personally embodying the leanness, adaptability, efficiency, and power of the new technologies. Thus conceived, "Silicon Valley" was like a tonic for the muddled—some said geriatric—U.S. capitalism of the times. It consoled and provided dream material for those who still believed the United States was the land of opportunity. By the early 1970s this belief had been thoroughly shaken by the economic "restructuring," oil price scandals, mergers, and financial speculation that marked the end of the post-World War II national prosperity. A "motivation crisis," panels of scholars and consultants agreed, had been weakening the U.S. will to work and cultivating resentment.

Within Silicon Valley, a politics of hope emerged to compete with the resentment. The United States now looked to the electronics entrepreneurs for deliverance. Around them, economists and politicians formed something of a cargo cult. It was within this context of deliverance that the dreams were subjected to the nuance of many interpretations.

The dream boosters championed a populism whose symbols were the computer and the entrepreneur, and whose opportunities were limitless. Management consultants hailed the "practical autonomy" of the Valley's corporate cultures, which were said to thrive like the potted ferns, rhododendrons, and *benjaminus* ficas that appointed the new "employee-centered" workplaces.[3] The computer's capacity to transfix the new worker was becoming legendary: Silicon Valley worked overtime and its professionals found work meaningful at rates that soared far above national averages.[4]

Spokespeople for the young computer hobbyists, whose inventions made electronics commodities accessible and increasingly affordable, espoused a more radical populism, one that viewed personal computers as anti-corporate tools and a franchise for democracy in the Information Age.[5] The disciples of electronic convenience rose up to praise, in advance, every innovation. Futurists, entitling their treatises in the millennial idiom—*Megatrends, The Third Wave*, etc.—competed with each other in predicting the details of the computer's liberation of work, shopping, and homemaking from drudgery.[6] Economists characterized Silicon Valley as an enclave of "flexible specialization" and "yeoman democracy" that would propel U.S. industry into a new Golden Age.[7]

If the dream boosters' interpretations were diverse, even a little preposterous, they shared a vision of computers and electronics as an essentially progressive force. This diversity freighted the dreams with a pluralist appeal, while technological positivism swept aside the critiques that had shadowed the debut of computers in the 1950s and 1960s.[8] Dreams and hopes, however, were grounded in the prosperity of Silicon Valley and that of the other Silicon terrains that had become, by 1980, the featured topics at Chamber of Commerce luncheons and of U.S. urban planners everywhere.[9] Silicon was the modern stake everyone had been waiting to claim.

The Return of the Repressed

By 1986, the prosperity that had nourished the politics of hope was shriveling. Ed Zschau, one of the most visible and vocal dream boosters, also an electronics entrepreneur and U.S. Congressional representative from Silicon Valley, campaigned for a Senate seat. He lost.[10] In Silicon Valley, capital flight, unemployment, speculation, mergers, and talk of "revitalization" were rife. It was the return of the repressed—the industrial era symptoms from which the electronics industry was supposed to provide refuge.

The notorious Christmas parties—the feasts at which companies thrust shellfish, champagne, big name entertainment, and bonuses at employees, the grand occasions where entrepreneurs recalled their humble origins and proclaimed to the world that Silicon Valley worked hard and played hard—were scaled back so drastically that it seemed that the firms' generosity had been drawn from tanks that had suddenly run dry. In place of the company-wide affairs planned by professional consultants, employees now organized department-wide holiday pot-lucks.[11]

On the eve of Independence Day, 1986, a local business columnist could observe glibly that "almost every week some Silicon Valley electronics company decides to move its production overseas." The assembly areas, clogged during the prosperity with bench workers, clerks, technicians, and their managers working overtime, were empty-ing abruptly at the rate of 1,000 employees per month.[12] Against the advice of management consultants, several companies removed the potted ferns, rhododendrons and ficas from cubicles—scorning the plants' production of negative ions that were said to soothe the harried computer worker.[13] It was as if a film recording the years of mass hirings, frantic expansions, and stock-offering celebrations was rewinding at high speed, reeling in frame after frame of prosperity and its pretensions.

Few expected it to last forever; but it had been so brief, so quickly undone. The swiftness with which the firms freed themselves of workplace and worker should have been disillusioning. In the industrial East and Midwest of Goodyear, Carnegie, and Chalmers, factories and warehouses were accorded respect as part of a firm's fixed assets and amortized over several decades. The electronics industry, in contrast, had treated such industrial era assets as liabilities. More often than not—certainly more than in any other U.S. manufacturing industry of comparable size—the landscaped office malls, misshapen labs, jerrybuilt assembly areas, potted plants, cubicle walls, modular desks, phone and computer networks, shipping and receiving racks, satellite dishes, and so much else had been leased.[14] "It makes very little sense to build your own production facility," explained the president of a chipmaking firm.[15] As a *Newsweek* reporter observed, in Silicon Valley, "All an entrepreneur really needs is an idea and a telephone," and through technology-licensing agreements, even ideas could be leased. With less "deadweight," the electronics firms—like the healthy computer professional, jogging, going to therapy, and avoiding cholesterol—could stay in fighting trim to move quickly to new opportunities.

As never before, the workers, through temporary agencies and job contractors, had also been leased. Some contended that Silicon Valley employed a larger concentration of temporary workers than anywhere else in the country.[16] This practice was viewed without skepticism; a certain culture favored it. Job-hopping was commonplace, voluntary as often as not, and widely supposed to be upward in trajectory.[17] "In a start-up, where the risks and rewards are higher, people don't expect to achieve that womb-to-tomb security that larger organizations represent," explained a computer firm's marketing director.[18] But the "larger organizations"—IBM, Hewlett-Packard, Control Data Corporation—were also the largest employers of temporary workers, whose unstable assignments served as a buffer for its full-time employees.[19] Many full-time workers played a version of musical chairs inside the same company, wandering from project to project and from building to building. Workers didn't expect "womb-to-tomb" stability, no matter how many may have longed for it.

During the prosperity, leasing was regarded as a shrewd way for management to anticipate and accommodate the cycles of innovation and obsolescence that struck computer firms so quickly and so often. With the onset of bad times, however, the borrowing of workplace and worker could be seen in a new light, one that revealed widespread leasing as a plug that could be yanked quickly, an emblem of a firm's vulnerability.

Yet it was far from certain that these conclusions were being drawn. The signs of a flagging prosperity were everywhere. A bleakness had begun to touch many lives. But there was little evidence that the spell cast by the dream boosters had been shaken.

Had commuters begun to wonder at the stillness that fell over the construction sites, at the fading "For Lease" bunting that was draped across evacuated workplaces? The Valley had, without anyone noticing, accumulated the nation's highest industrial vacancy rate; nearly 40 percent of its workspace, new and used, was empty in 1986 (several times that of Houston and Detroit combined). Real estate speculators were sitting on top of 32 million square feet of sheltered Valley air that was depreciating by the minute. One of the nation's largest realtors concluded that filling the Valley's empty buildings would take nearly three and one half years of boom, something no business columnist was predicting. Other electronics industry regions, such as those near Boston and Phoenix, were likewise glutted.[20] The glut was written off as a classic, if extreme, case of overdevelopment.[21] But there were other views.

The vacant office malls and their unblemished asphalt skirts inspired material for a Japanese comic strip which depicted the President of the United States walking steadfastly through a windswept ghost town. *Kudoka,* the Japanese were calling it, the "hollowing out" of the United States by corporations who liquidated their manufacturing core or exported it to sites offshore, leaving behind a shell of lawyers, accountants, marketing specialists, and, in the Silicon Valleys, design, development, and support staff as well.[22] By its example and through its products, the U.S. electronics industry, more than any other, had promoted and accelerated *kudoka. Kudoka,* in fact, had been at least as crucial to the industry's prosperity as had the technical ingenuity of its entrepreneurs.

During the 1960s and 1970s, U.S. semiconductor firms took full advantage of the lightweight nature of microchip assembly and packaging to establish more offshore manufacturing operations than domestic ones.[23] By 1987, chip makers had only one-third of their wafer fabrication facilities in Silicon Valley.[24] Inside the United States, the industry filled its clean rooms mainly with Latin American, Asian, and Pacific Rim emigrés. With labor gathered from the lands of the least paid, the industry helped create satellites, global inventory networks, robotics software, and all manner of international data links. These established an infrastructure that encouraged other U.S.-based industries to operate their manufacturing from afar.[25] If *kudoka* was luring the electronics industry's production base away from the United States, the Valley's development and design achievements encouraged a different sort of *kudoka* in less developed countries. From Taiwan, China, the Philippines, India, Pakistan, and Iran, middle- and upper-class emigrés came to Silicon Valley to pursue computer occupations, while many more prepared for degrees in U.S. technical schools.[26]

The *kudoka* interpretation challenged the notion of a *U.S.* electronics industry. Another development threatened to make it nostalgic rhetoric. The U.S. electronics firms were shedding their distinctness, like the Asian, Latin, African, and Anglo women who, inside the delicate chip fabrication environments, wore identical surgeon's gowns that blurred ethnicity. The roadside signs above the firms' landscaped embankments—signs that once evinced anecdotes of fabulous wealth and Yankee know-how—continued to display the familiar names and logos: "Fairchild Semiconductors," "Amdahl," "Syntex." But it was widely known that finance capital from Bahrain, France, Germany, Great Britain, Holland, Japan, Korea, Saudi Arabia, Taiwan, and elsewhere was flowing into the Valley, changing the firms' national configurations. Within the United States, insurance, real estate, banking, and holding companies began to purchase interest in the electronics firms, imbuing them with unknown but vaguely distrustful motivations, and diluting further the confidence that marked the years of prosperity.[27] It was the scarcely visible, thoroughly modern, global migration of speculative finance capital.

Then came the revitalization schemes. These began as monthly and, by Christmas 1986, became almost weekly media items. The once fiercely *laissez faire* industry, now led by a somber collection of conglomerates, was engaging in a scandalous blackmail. No longer promising prosperity, but merely survival, the largest electronics firms—IBM, Intel, National Semiconductor and many others—demanded millions in government grants, exemption from antitrust laws and special protection for their diminishing trade. The projected ransom was antithetical, some said, to the very principles for which the Valley stood. But the large firms warned that the measures (and the mergers they allowed) might be too little, too late. "We're past the point where the industry can take care of itself," declared an emigré-entrepreneur-turned-executive at one of the largest Valley chipmakers. "This isn't the eleventh hour, it's 12:01."[28]

The Pentagon, in a special report, announced that the United States had forsaken a "vital capability": its electronics industry could no longer produce the chips on which the country's launch consoles, battle control systems, and war-making decisions now depended. The very military electronics firms that shared and helped conceive the Pentagon's technology-dependent future had been, in a related but not well-known scandal, increasingly unable to deliver reliable components. Somehow—few were saying just how—huge portions of the tacitly protected military electronics markets had slipped through the fingers of U.S. firms and into the clutches of what a Defense Science Board panel called "foreign powers." The Pentagon seconded the electronics industry's survival plan, proposed a $2 billion federal ante, and announced that the Joint Chiefs of Staff, if necessary, were prepared to take over segments of the electronics industry.[29] The generals and admirals may have contemplated this contingency nostalgically, since it recalled the protracted incubation and delicate birth of the U.S. electronics industry, which had never fully weaned itself from military spending.[30]

So it was that no sooner had accolades for Silicon Valley and the electronics industry christened a new era of prosperity than warnings and epitaphs were heard, at first quietly, then with increasing rudeness. It was as if the youthful industry had contracted *progeria,* a rare disease that struck down toddlers with the infirmities of advanced age. Prosperous times would return. Certainly, the pace of innovation and the proliferation of new electronics products had never really slackened. But the U.S. electronics industry had changed, just as inexorably and confusedly as Santa Clara Valley had transformed its apricot orchards into groves of silicon. Though emigrés to the Valley continued to invest fresh hope in them, the dreams of work, prosperity, and social progress were undergoing metamorphosis.

Misgivings

Critical voices, returning from the margins to which a prosperous Silicon Valley had consigned them, were now heard in public. Stories about the drugs that sustained the Valley's working people, about the "new poor" and homeless, about the fractured families and about the chemicals that were leaching from unsafe equipment and tanks into drinking wells now made headlines in the local and national media.[31]

By 1987, the citizens of San Jose spent $500 million each year—or over $700 for each man, woman, and child—on illegal drugs. The San Jose Police Chief estimated that, at some firms, more than eight out of ten employees, from assemblers to top executives, were taking, buying, and/or selling drugs *on the job.*[32] The highest divorce rate in the nation was creating one of the densest concentrations of lawyers west of Manhattan and filling the Valley's apartments, tract homes, and fern bars with a special sadness which no amount of work or shopping could alleviate.[33] With the pause in prosperity, work itself, like drinking untreated Valley tap water, had become an uncertain activity.

Silicon Valley, which, above all, had promised work to all comers, could no longer come across. By 1985, 60,000 people over the age of 50, many of them former middle managers earning between $35,000 and $75,000, had been laid off, fired, or forced into early retirement. These people were now looking—anywhere—for work, their resumes languishing in the files of personnel departments all over the country. "They're not bag ladies and men; they're briefcase ladies and men," quipped a job counselor.[34] Collecting at dusk in shopping mall parking lots and outlying parks, some of the not-quite-elderly jobless were living out of cars and trailer-campers. Others had taken month-to-month leases in mobile homes (with views of vacant office malls). They lived a shabby compromise with the residences many of them were accustomed to, houses (with views of the coastal hills) whose median price had risen well above $200,000. It was then painfully recollected that most Valley electronics firms had offered stock options instead of pension plans.[35] Of course, these 60,000 were only one segment of the "new poor." From 1984 through 1987, by several estimates, from 5 to 10 percent of electronics employees had lost their jobs.[36] No one was calculating joblessness among the variously estimated 150,000 to 200,000 undocumented immigrants.[37]

Others pointed out that the electronics industry had been fouling air, soil, water, workplace, and worker all along. With the belated official recognition of these problems, a reservoir of misgiving and grudge was surely building.

The daughters of the migrant farm laborers who once planted, harvested, and packed Valley fruit had taken jobs inside the fluorescent hothouses amid the chemicals that yielded electronic life. The orchards were paved over and the canneries torn down or auctioned off, reminders of the finality with which the new technology entombed the old. The new work, however, was as tedious and often as migratory and poorly paid as the old; it was more dangerous, for its dangers were far more subtle.

The women labored hard and long—up to twelve-hour shifts. They required regular overtime, or other incomes, to make ends meet; the wages were so low, in fact, that working mothers qualified for welfare assistance.[38] The wages reflected the terms set by a global electronics labor market.

The gases and acids, against most of which the firms protected neither worker nor environment, laced the water supply that once nourished the orchards, converting one of North America's most pristine aquifers into one of the nation's most perilous and puzzling contaminations.

Most of the chemicals left no scars, were unseen, unfelt. Unleashed under names and in combinations that workers couldn't understand, the solvents and etching compounds were confusing the immune systems and altering the chromosomes of many of the farm laborers' daughters, who now left the new work to preserve their health, or, like the mothers in surrounding neighborhoods, miscarried or bore malformed babies in numbers and at rates that could no longer be ignored.[39]

In May 1988, a three-year California Department of Health Services study found that pregnant women who drank tap water in Silicon Valley and environs (Santa Clara, Alameda and San Mateo Counties) had significantly higher rates of miscarriages and birth defects than those who drank filtered or no tap water during their pregnancies. *Up to twice as many miscarriages and nearly four times as many birth defects occurred.* The report was a follow-up to an earlier study that was prompted by the controversial Fairchild-IBM contaminations.[40]

Who would repair the addled immune systems of the many women laid-off, fired, or no longer able to work in the chemically profuse environments of the Valley's misnamed "clean" rooms? The chipmaking firms denied responsibility for workers' injuries, and, when necessary, paid doctors by the hour for their testimony at workers' compensation hearings, "expert" testimony that discounted as "psychosomatic disorders" the workers' seared lungs and enduring bronchitis, the chronic nose-bleeds and headaches, the AIDS-like pan-allergies. Who would repay the women whose babies were delivered to them stillborn, or with impaired hearts, lungs, and livers? Not the State of California, whose industrial hygienists confirmed high rates of miscarriages and birth defects in neighborhoods surrounding IBM and Fairchild Semiconductor, but dismissed the apparent connections. Not the industry, which assisted IBM and Fairchild in contesting the class action suit brought by parents whose grieving had given way to anger. Although IBM and Fairchild Semiconductor admitted that chemicals, apparently, had leaked, and were still migrating from their storage tanks, IBM and Fairchild purchased releases from liability, settling the suit secretly and out-of-court.[41]

Who would console the survivors of the 57 people each year who, by 1986, were dying as a result of airborne pollution, mainly from the Valley's congested freeways? Not the Valley's county and city planners, who granted subsidy after subsidy for the overdevelopment, apologized for zoning violations, and proposed special taxes to fund widened freeways and more commuting corridors. Not the voice of Silicon Valley, the *San Jose Mercury News*. Although it broke the story with the banner headline "Santa Clara County's Killing Air," its management had secretly exposed the *News'* press operators to PCB-laced ink day in, day out, for months.[42]

Who would comfort the Vietnamese, Laotian, Cambodian, Indian, Filipino, Pakistani, Iranian, and Hispanic refugees and immigrants, harassed by "racial incidents," their car tires slashed at night, their children beaten coming home from school, their parents underpaid and distressed by the threat of deportation?[43] Not the INS (the dream interpreter of last resort for immigrant families), whose agents welcomed Eastern bloc engineers hired by the military electronics firms, denied Latin American emigrés fleeing regimes allied with the West, and collaborated with sweatshop computer entrepreneurs who trafficked in the resulting underground labor market, scheduling pre-payday raids and separating husband and wife, parent and child, unofficially adding immigrants to the Valley's already high family separation statistics.

Who would calm the families of the commuters and bicyclists maimed and killed by cars that swerved as their drivers, bored with weekday and weekend traffic jams, reached for cassette tapes, struggled to open beers, fumbled in ash trays for yesterday's marijuana ? Not the mall and condominium developers, whose projects pushed sidewalks onto the streets and made shopping, schooling, dining out, dancing, taking piano lessons, fetching an ice cream, and almost every trip and errand contingent on access to a car. Not the convenience marts, the fast food outlets, or the discount pharmacies whose franchises saturated the Valley in a frenzy of consumer homogenization.

The evaporation of good will and innocence extended even to the entrepreneur. His success—and it was invariably his, which became yet another charge hurled at the fraternity of electronics industry leaders— now required more than perseverance in service of a new product, more than "an idea and a telephone." More than ever, "entrepreneuring" demanded substantial startup funding and a mean-spirited zeal to subdue competitors. A rising Valley entrepreneur, the subject of a 1985 *Esquire* interview, surveyed a competitor thus:

> He'd stick me in five nanoseconds if he could, but he can't—because I've got big guys behind me...So he leaves me alone only because he has to, and I leave him alone only because I can't get as close as I'd like to. And that's okay! But one of these days we'll ride into his village, we'll burn his huts, we'll rape his women, and we'll dance on the bones of his children![44]

So many had seemed so confident of the destination. Careers had been launched, commutes tolerated, consumption patterns altered, personalities adjusted. The artifacts of a less constricted, slower era (lawn mowers, badminton nets, garden tools, extra bedroom sets) had been stowed away in the mini-storage lockers that pocketed Silicon Valley. Others with no such possessions, who instead had risked long, dangerous passages from equatorial hovels and shanty compounds, had arrived only to suffer new risks, unknown exposures, a modern loneliness. So much had been invested, put on hold, even sacrificed to the dreams of work and prosperity. Where were the dreams leading? What, other than the dreams, connected each to all?

The quiet microtechnologies, the verdant ferns, and the well-lit "employee-centered" workplaces had promised a departure from the noisy tools, dingy sheds, break whistles, and time-clocks of the industrial era. Though it had not quite escaped, Silicon Valley had thrust its communities of work into a modern dimension where problems defied conventional explanations, even when the problems appeared to be of industrial era vintage. This failure was more profound than the belated recognition of problems obscured by prosperity, or the mean-spiritedness engendered by austerity. For all the limelight, all the futurist prose, all the fairyland anecdotes, Silicon Valley and the electronics industry were running aground on a historical reef that confused even the most imaginative dream booster.

The entrepreneur-turned-executive, who claimed the industry couldn't survive without swift and prodigious government intervention, now likened Silicon Valley to Detroit, claiming an essential historical similarity in their rise—and, by implication, their decline.[45] This analogy fit nicely, since the government intervention demanded by the electronics industry and the Pentagon recalled the millions of dollars in credit the Treasury Department had extended to Chrysler in the 1970s. The comparison, however, turned on the belief that Silicon Valley, like Detroit, "is first and foremost a center for manufacturing activities." But manufacturing capital had been taking its leave of Silicon Valley. The proposed ransom could be viewed cynically as a bid to subsidize capital flight from Silicon Valley, just as the earlier ransom had given wing to the Detroit automobile plants.

U.S. chipmakers, like Detroit automakers, also called for trade protection from foreign competition. But this amounted to raising prices for foreign-built microchips and components. And the U.S.-based computer makers, to the Pentagon's dismay, had become dependent on foreign chips, just as the U.S. consumer had become addicted to the ever swifter and more fanciful stream of foreign-made consumer electronics.

By raising foreign chip prices, the protectionist lobby proposed to chastise the consumer, to artificially tax the local electronics producers, and, in so doing, urge *kudoka* upon them, since the price increases could be averted by moving production offshore. Besides, given the global commingling of capital in the electronics industry, skeptics could legitimately ask the protectionists: what exactly *was* a U.S. electronics firm?

More immediate concerns informed interpretations at the other end of the political spectrum. Chemically injured workers, union organizers, activist lawyers, and environmentalists continued to call for collective bargaining, investigations, and protective legislation. During the prosperity, their appeals failed to generate community support. With the slump and the depletion of good will toward the electronics industry, a constituency for reform, if not rebellion, seemed plausible. But where were the communities that would no longer tolerate the social costs that had accumulated over the years, the communities that might have supported the simple demand to clean their tainted drinking water? Where were the workplace organizations that might have rallied opposition to the inadequate wages, to the layoffs and plant closures, to the alarming rates of tragic and enigmatic workplace injuries, and to the chipmaking firms' denial of damages to injured workers?

With exceptions too few to mention, the working-class communities, as Industrial America thought of them, had never congealed in the electronics industry. So dull were the prospects for solidarity in the workplace that the largest unions in Silicon Valley observed an unofficial moratorium on organizing. The unions had given up, without really trying, on the possibility of organizing Silicon Valley; they had discouraged—and in at least one case, transferred—those within their ranks who had persisted.[46] A frustrated IBM production worker, whose phone calls to a union business agent for assistance went unanswered, concluded that there simply was "no heart in organizing." The traditional view that those most affected by social ills would organize against them no longer held.

The Information Age was proving a regime of technological, not economic or social, enlightenment. Its turbulent U.S. course was astounding the world and provoking a rash of reevaluations. To some, it must have seemed that the dreams were fading. After all, where work was increasingly doubtful, there could be neither material salvation nor spiritual haven. But who, among those who remained in Silicon Valley, could stop dreaming?

The dreams had articulated the aspirations and staved off the fears of a people whose identity, tied to larger economic fates, was always in question. The unraveling of prosperity revealed the devotion to dreams as the thread that held Silicon Valley together. Unhinged from the prosperity that had seeded them, however, the dreams had run amuck, dissolving into grotesque parodies of themselves. The dreams were mutating.

On the Frontier: Mass Transience

Midway through the 1980s, the geographic center of the U.S. population was moving west by 58 feet and south by 29 feet each day.[47] This measured a convergence of emigrés from the eastern United States as well as the accelerated arrival of Asian and Central and South American refugees. California, especially Silicon Valley, became a global population and financial magnet.

Once again policymakers debated the "American Frontier," whose western boundaries Frederick Jackson Turner pronounced closed at the end of the nineteenth century, but which had reopened time and again, in cities such as Detroit and Chicago, and then in urban habitats, like Greater Houston and Silicon Valley. A conventional wisdom attached purpose to the migration, seeing in it opportunity for new waves of immigrants and a renewal of capitalism's rhythms, proof that having shed its worn-out industrial coveralls, U.S. industry was donning a leaner look appropriate to some new role.

In 1979, a controversial White House report, *Urban America in the Eighties: Perspectives and Prospects,* urged acceptance of the death of the industrial east, and offered the solace of a historical perspective on the new migration west and south, which, the report suggested, involved "simultaneous painful growth and shrinkage, disinvestment and reinvestment." James Fallows, *The Atlantic's* eloquent economist, asserted that migration was what U.S. prosperity was all about, that "through most of American history the factories have constantly been closing down—and opening up—and people have been moving from declining areas to those on the rise." But the new industries were unlike the old in unanticipated ways.[48]

Many migrants to Silicon Valley never stopped migrating—from workplace to workplace. Engineers, electronics trade magazines complained, were changing jobs every two years.[49] Production workers and word processors might work overtime on projects for months, then receive furloughs, hire on elsewhere, or sign up for temporary labor through a "job shop." Shrinking product lifetimes and merger-related job relocations eroded the occupational stability of electronics employees.[50] A new group of "business service" entrepreneurs, the largest number of which were in the temporary help and job placement business, capitalized on the mass transience. By 1985, the growth of this industry outpaced that of every electronics industry segment.[51]

Silicon Valley unsettled its settlers with one of the highest job turnover rates in the country. In 1980, electronics workers vacated their jobs at twice the national average. Yearly job turnover rates for production workers approached 50 percent.[52] The rate had declined somewhat by 1986, but it was now supplemented by layoffs and a growing proportion of "permanent" part-time and contract positions. The employee leasing, part-time work, and layoffs reflected the fickleness of electronics capital—capital that had always been transient, in contrast to the relative permanence of capital in steel, coal, auto, rubber, glass, machine tools, and railroads. These were the U.S. industries whose tradition the White House report, James Fallows, and many others expected the upstart electronics industry to carry on.

What was emerging was a less purposeful, and quite new, migrational pattern—the flow into and out of the new electronics jobs. Workers came and went with such frequency that workplace acquaintance was too short-lived to sustain a class bond. The growth of part-time positions, even when these reflected a marriage of convenience between capital and labor, likewise diluted the workplace as a focus for human connection. Many of the "permanent" part-time jobs were temporary arrangements, since, in practice, the partially employed, no matter how satisfied with their positions, were spending non-work hours preparing for a career or caring for infants who would soon be old enough for a childcare center.[53]

A modern heartland was palpitating to new and relentless rhythms, inhabited by an emigré workforce that couldn't seem to settle down. The aimlessness and occupational motion bequeathed fragmented cultures of work, shifting occupational itineraries, and a new isolation. This elicited the labor leaders' instinctive reluctance to organize electronics workers, since even the bureaucratic, dues-broker union relies ultimately on a collective identity that had eluded the electronics workplace.

The new transience was infectious, and the carrier was the insurgent electronics industry. On the one hand, job turnover rates and part-time positions were rising in the information "processing" and point-of-sale jobs that electronics technology made possible.[54] On the other hand, electronics products (robotics stations, global manufacturing systems) helped automate, simplify, and routinize production labor, effectively lowering wages, creating layoffs, and closing plants. These effects combined to create the framework for mass transience among wage workers in goods and service industries. Childlike and full of wanderlust, the U.S. electronics industry had confused those dream boosters who took the industry's growth for the first tugs of a longer wave of frontier expansion like those that previously had shaped eastern and midwestern America. There, despite wars and depressions, despite "factories...closing down and opening up," prosperity had brought more than a semblance of community and stability. The United States, led by its impetuous electronics industry, was becoming a land of transient workers and moveable workplaces.

The New Enclave

If the electronics industry was diminishing the connections that the workplace once extended to workers, it also stimulated a new regard for work itself.

Movies and novels celebrated the lust for computer work; comic strips and TV sitcoms annexed it. Through these media, the socially inept computer devotees became articulate, complex 1980s heroes who tripped their foes with electronic snares. Invariably, the computer heroes—the *nerds* and *hackers*—were, like the new professionals, fanatic workers, for it was at and through work that they derived their power.

The new regard for work was genuine, and this warmed the hearts of management consultants and their patrons. It seemed not only to resolve the employee motivation crisis of the 1970s, but also to confirm the theories of "corporate culture." The electronics firms, apparently, had successfully challenged their employees to "excellence."[55]

Although management consultants (supported ironically by one of their critics[56]) took responsibility for work's "re-enchantment," their claims were hard to credit. Did workers accept at face value the allegedly employee-centered "corporate culture"? Or were high job turnover and frequent layoffs teaching workers a different lesson—to regard their employers as fickle and calculating. A *San Jose Mercury News* survey, taken in 1984 during the height of the prosperity, found that while Silicon Valley was working overtime and prizing work at rates well above national averages, over a quarter of its production workers expected to be laid off "soon."[57]

There were more credible explanations for work's rehabilitation. Salaried professionals and their managers comprised the majority (56 percent in 1984) of the Valley's electronics workers.[58] Among them, the cold logic of career and the allure of intriguing technical problems created an independent, narcissistic attraction to work.

Job counselors, community college teachers, headhunters, and occupational self-help literature invited the new professionals to view each passing job as one logical step in a career that no personal matter was too pressing to derail. Jobs and employers merely provided access to work, or, more precisely, to the technologies that were new and in demand. This outlook transcended work's traditional loyalties of employer and job. It established access to new technology as the link between the professional's technical fascination and material self-interest. Creative and well-paying work—this was the private agenda that subverted loyalty to specific employers, and thereby uncoupled renewed interest in work from the corporate motivations fantasized by the "excellence" consultants.

Above all, the new worship of work amounted to a movement to *personalize* it, to take on as one's own the absorbing challenge of computer work, and thus to become an intimate part of something larger, something meaningful. It was the practical response of isolated people to the vacuum of community, the erosion of traditional ties, and the suspension of social coherence—the prices exacted by the impersonal bargain the emigré struck with the Valley. They might live in overpriced apartments or shrunken condominiums surrounded by traffic's glutted arteries, but there was always the relative constancy of interesting work. Despite their "corporate cultures," the electronics firms had done little more than indulge and channel the curiosities and material motivations of technically-inclined people. This created something of an oasis amid the loneliness.

For the itinerant computer professional, portable, lightweight electronic commodities announced the possibility of communing with work away from the workplace, and thus achieved an almost erotic cachet. A spread in *California* magazine entitled "Working Vacation" suggested that if "business is your pleasure, getting away from it all isn't half as much fun as taking it all with you." The display showed a world time clock, a cordless battery-run phone, a laptop computer, a compact faxphone (with "autodial"), a digital "diary" pocket computer, and a microcassette recorder all strewn about a poolside table—for that "office-away-from-office ambience anywhere, anytime." The display caption concluded with a paradox Silicon Valley could appreciate: "So relax, and get to work."[59] The computer professional's relationship to work approached the compulsive masochism of the athlete in training: pain and the lonely allure of an endorphin high.

While management consultants and their critics debated the corporate role in motivating the computer worker, no one bothered to examine a consequence that overshadowed all others in its peculiarity. Amid all the reveling in work, there flourished an equally remarkable indifference to work's products. Computer work was becoming a new enclave—comparable to the fragmented hobby and lifestyle enclaves that British and U.S. sociologists had identified in modern leisure activities.[60] Among computer professionals, work was so self-referential, so thoroughly personalized, that it no longer required a public rationale in order to yield meaning. No one seemed to care about who purchased the product or what purposes it served. What mattered was the product's capacity to provide more interesting work—a capacity that usually dovetailed with the corporate concern for profitability.

The special alienation of electronics workers from their products was not hard to trace. Computer products were baffling, microscopic, and bore mysterious names. They were infinitely more complex than, and at least as ambiguous as, other commodities. Their ambiguity derived from their role as components—chips, boards, kits, and black boxes—that were incorporated into a wide array of commodities from kitchen appliances to missile guidance systems. Where was the engineer who really knew, or cared about, which products would incorporate the microchips he designed? And computer products were also ephemeral. Volatile markets beckoned, were saturated, overrun, made obsolescent, and forgotten as quickly as new product releases, or new markets, were created. In this way computer work became more and more detached from social contexts. A culture of product indifference and ignorance had engulfed the computer sophisticates.

It was not always so. In the 1970s, a visible faction of inventor-entrepreneurs spoke of their brainchildren—various prototype personal computers—as educational tools, as entertainments, as harbingers of household convenience, and as checks on a corporate computer monopoly.[61] Some corporations, including older ones such as Control Data Corporation and younger ones such as Apple, donated computers to schools and community groups. Electronics innovation, however implausibly, was linked to the public good.

By the 1980s, the perceived need for public rationales had all but vanished. The computer entrepreneurs and technologists advertised computers as productivity- and profit-enhancing tools, appealing to the increasingly nonpublic realm of work.[62] But even this inward, productivist rationale was actively suspect from a public point of view, since computers were in fact displacing workers and heightening instability by facilitating more automation, encouraging *kudoka,* and placing weaponry on an inherently more dangerous footing. The ideological association of computer innovation with convenience and social progress was, evidently, fallible. How was society using computers? The electronics industry didn't know. Its think tanks described markets as outlets for electronics sales, not as workplaces employing people and creating social goods and services that would be more or less drastically changed by computer technology. No one, in fact, seemed to know much about the broader uses and impacts of the computer.[63]

The electronics industry had made possible financial networks where none had been.[64] Banks and savings and loans now featured automated tellers, innovative consumer credit lines, and rapid access to expanding financial services, but all banks large and small were less stable and their services more expensive for the consumer.[65] Meanwhile, the wages, benefits, and health of banking, telephone, and airline employees were not improved by the introduction of computers into the workplace. In fact, workers' pay, health, workplace productivity, and product and service quality fared poorly in the most heavily computerized industries: services and retail sales.[66]

As the evidence of dubious progress accumulated, the grand social dream was mutating. Just how computers were enriching civilization became difficult to say unequivocally. All of this inconclusiveness and misgiving made it easier for computer workers not to examine too closely the social impact of their labors.

Their ignorance was most explicit and cunning inside the military electronics workplace. A rigid subdivision of labor, reflecting a mandate to maintain design secrecy, meant that workers weren't apprised of the precise applications of their labor. They were also forbidden to discuss the work among themselves and with their families. As a result, they could maintain a plausible innocence about their responsibility for the hostile technology they built. Secrecy created an intellectual gulag, depriving military electronics production of the collective oversight of fully informed workers. The vaunted "feedback" sought by the "excellence" consultants was stifled. This, given the immense complexity of the work, increased the probability that the military's high-tech future wouldn't function as planned, if at all. The public was spared this little-known but potentially far-reaching scandal; the media elected to underpublicize it, even when "incidents" (the space shuttle Challenger fiasco, the sinking of the U.S.S. Stark, and the downing of Iranian Flight 655) suggested otherwise. The evidence of shoddy guidance systems, operational component failures, and radar misreadings was growing so rapidly that the Pentagon accelerated plans to censor it.[67] In the military as well as the civilian electronics workplace, the lust for work merged vocation with avocation, which might have made many people happy. But a notorious loneliness—a local therapist called its symptoms the "Silicon Syndrome"—stalked the new enclave.[68] Relationship counseling, stress management seminars, and a variety of therapies, new and old, comforted the computer professionals. Their project deadlines, career strategies, and investment decisions were stacked too tightly, leaving little room, and often little desire, for other people. The stories of tragic attachments to work became commonplace, but the social costs were rarely reckoned. Electronics workers were uniquely well-placed to reject or subvert the socially hostile or ill-considered technologies that depended on their imagination and creativity. Seduced and blinded by their work, the computer workers disavowed any such role and eagerly prepared the instruments of war, the levers of speculation, and the tools of *kudoka*.

The Coordinates

Silicon Valley, like the new habitats that were growing furiously outside of Atlanta, Portland, Phoenix, Denver, and elsewhere, did not appear to equal more than the sum of its isolated parts. For this reason, perhaps more than any other, no one could conjure a name for the habitats that stuck. An *Atlantic* feature suggested "Urban Villages," but the habitats lacked the warmth of a village.[69] *The Wall Street Journal* proposed "Mini-Cities," but they were far from mini; in fact, they constituted the fastest-growing population centers in the country.[70] In William Gibson's future-fiction, cities had evolved into the "Sprawl" or "Metropolitan Axis," extrapolations that captured the "feel" if not the logic of aimless urban compartmentalization.[71] Yet as early as 1966, novelist Thomas Pynchon had invented "San Narciso," which better characterized the West Coast habitat. "Like many named places in California," Pynchon wrote in *The Crying of Lot 49*, San Narciso "was less an identifiable city than a grouping of concepts—census tracts, special purpose bond-issue districts, shopping nuclei, all overlaid with access roads...a vast sprawl of houses which had grown up all together."[72] Silicon Valley, like San Narciso, was a lonely outpost, a collection of monuments to work, technology, and shopping assembled on the rough edges of civilization. The electronics industry had comported itself like a colonialist power, exploiting and disfiguring its holdings with disregard for posterity, concerned only with the cash crop whose cultivation was polluting the resources on which cultivation depended. This ecological burn, like the diminishing cotton yields in the antebellum U.S. South, may have been inevitable. But the cycle was exceedingly short in Silicon Valley, as if there the process had skipped the stages between frontier and decadence during which communities emerge to assert control over the ravages of capital, if only to ameliorate its impact. Too much uncertain motion—volatile work, unstable capital—and a tremendous constriction of the time available after working, shopping, and commuting, stripped community feeling from the repertoire of daily experience.

The emigrés, more out of circumstance than choice, had sided with the industry. In doing so, they declined the stabilizing roles of missionary and settler, apparently having neither spiritual nor material wherewithal to sustain such roles. They talked to each other like strangers in a train station. They complained about superficial friendships, about not having time to stop after work for drinks with fellow workers, about work's intensity and uncertainties, about the strangeness of their habitat. But hadn't they come for the work, to do what work required of them? Hadn't they left friends and communities behind? Where else could work be had in the 1980s if not in Silicon Valley? Where stability, communities, sidewalks, and now (for many) work proved elusive, there was a torpor of social conscience, a political lethargy inflicted by the stark terms that the Valley continued to dictate to its scattered inhabitants.

With glacial force, *kudoka* was enveloping the U.S. character, hollowing out features of its social substrate. In Silicon Valley, loyalty to work and its shifting locations was fragmenting people and the effects could now be seen in the quality of indifference to human misfortune. This process was evident not only in the sparse provisions for human casualties, but even more clearly in the elaborate personal strategies that emerged spontaneously to filter raw social experience.

Subdivided into over a dozen municipalities, additional unincorporated districts, and housing developments, Silicon Valley's political landscape reflected the rashly conceived needs of expanding capital and thus defied coherence. Funds for the Valley's indistinct municipal infrastructures had been sacrificed to the development subsidies. Among countless oversights, there were no plans to buttress the growth or to accommodate the losers.

For lack of foresight, the largest municipality (San Jose) suffered a fiscal crisis that stopped just short of bankruptcy.[73] For lack of funds, the largest school district filed for bankruptcy (the first in the United States to do so since the Great Depression), schools continued to close or were consolidated throughout the Valley, and in one district, high school drop-out rates exceeded 50 percent.[74] For want of teachers, the Valley's largest public school of engineering, whose salaries couldn't compete with industry's, nearly closed its doors.[75] For lack of summer recreation programs, the shopping malls and the Valley's amusement theme park (the theme: "Great America") teemed with adolescents squandering allowances, seeking adventure and intrigue in the clashing gangs and cliques of their respective ethnic and class subcultures.[76]

A safety net of welfare services had neither time nor resources to develop. When the prosperity began to vanish, few of the subsidized housing projects had vacancies. In Sunnyvale, where investigative journalism identified "more millionaires per capita than any city its size in the world," the waiting lists for public shelter were one and a half to two years long.[77] Even the Valley's jails were crowded, so much so that a federal judge, citing evidence of "cruel and unusual punishment," cited five county supervisors for refusing to add cells.[78] The price of childcare (of special concern to the mothers that disproportionately worked the jobs that pay the least) was scandalously high.[79] In this regard, many extended Asian and Latin families fared better than those of Anglo parents who were more accustomed to the nuclear family arrangement.

There were sporadic displays of community politics, but these were invariably fragile, short-lived, or expressive of fear rather than hope.[80]

The most predictable, frequent, and effective displays of community politics involved homeowners. Homeowners banded together to oppose almost anything that threatened to depreciate the inflated values of their properties. This was endemic to the new habitats, from Georgia's Gywnn County to Oregon's Beaverton technology parks.[81] School closings were tolerated, mediocre grade school curriculums accepted, fouled water and air ignored, but plummeting property values could not be endured. The houses and condominiums, for those who could afford them, were purchased as assets as much as selected for neighborhood, schools, or even proximity to work, since these might change to accommodate more development and since the purchasers did not know where they might be in two or three years. These calculations conspired to assign a lasting and profound importance to property values, the denominator to which community feeling sank. In Silicon Valley, where a housing crisis sustained some of the highest median property (including rental) prices in the country, homeowners organized against multifamily and elderly people's housing, and against senior life-care projects.[82] The field of conventional politics, aside from the influence-harvesting of the electronics entrepreneurs, the developers, and the new ethnic (Hispanic, Vietnamese, Japanese) chambers of commerce, was likewise practically barren of grassroots activity.[83] By 1987, it was left to a TV station to organize a "town hall" meeting. About one hundred Silicon Valley residents, in the manner of a syndicated afternoon talk show, upbraided officials and an industry lobbyist and applauded environmental and welfare leaders. As a result of the show, a developer was temporarily blocked from bulldozing an elderly woman's home. But the meeting was a media-managed charade, an event sponsored by retail tire stores and furniture outlets; it had no popular energy behind it, and therefore no future.[84]

The Fix

The fix emerged from the fragmented moral and social coordinates of the habitats. The self-centering New Age ideologies of the 1970s had anticipated it. The social psychologists of consequence—U.S. market researchers—now articulated its logic.

A fix was a consumption pattern that offered relief from, or supported survival in, the habitat. The plausibility of a fix did not rely on a rational scrutiny of its capacity to succeed or on its staying power. Rather, a fix embodied the pursuit of something that, for a few days or weeks, "gave shape to the longing of the moment."[85] A fix, like any consumption trend, was immediately revocable; the more a fix was subject to fashion and whim, the more attractive it was likely to become.

The logic of the fix approximated that of physical and psychological therapy. In response to environmental degradation and atrophied social cohesion, an emphasis on physical health and self-control blossomed. In Silicon Valley, these became the reigning modes of self-expression, cinching the personal, introspective experience cultivated so relentlessly in the post-Vietnam United States as the realm in which individuals reacted to the Valley's malaise. People were not, as cynical dream boosters concluded, indifferent to social problems, but rather to social solutions which, in the context of the habitats, simply didn't occur to them.

A consensus to purge the computer workplace of toxics never emerged, and the Valley's drinking wells, aquifer, and air continued to absorb acids, solvents, and petroleum distillates. So people purchased (presumably clean) bottled water or (presumably effective) filtration devices for kitchen faucets and companies supplied water tanks at department coffee stations. Armed with these purchases, people—and companies—could express therapeutic disapproval of the pollution, enjoy the appearance of doing something about it, and at the same time hope to survive the immediate consequences of doing nothing to prevent its spread.

Amid unchecked spoiling of land and water all around them, there rose up an unquenchable appetite for survival gear and health gadgetry—from camouflage and safari "activewear" to digitalized car-key alarms, from all-terrain vehicles to athletic straps with LED pulse displays. Engineers hung posters depicting wildlife and uninhabited beaches on their cubicle walls. Programmers booked exotic treks to under-travelled seas and mountains. Electronics professionals displayed a preference for natural fiber clothing, and project teams conferred naturalistic titles—"Sierra," "Redwood," "Peregrine"—on conference rooms, hallways, and products. The accents on naturalism, health, and survival highlighted the fields in which individual effort and discipline could make a difference. The accents suggested the merger of scientific technology with a vague Rousseauian contempt for dense population and excess fat, if not for progress itself. It seemed to matter little that the real expressions of this merger resided in the consumption habits and daydreams of the electronics professionals more than in any practical reproach of their technology's grim impacts.

With less and less evidence of hope for the Valley's ecology, there were health fads on a scale for which no one could recall precedents: vitamin treatments, life-extension newsletters, health spas, low-impact aerobics, jazzercize programs, "wellness" regimens, and every manner of diet—liquid, fiber, vegetable, meat, carbohydrate, and hypnotic. Outside, the air thickened unhealthfully with particulates and carbon vapors; inside, by overwhelming consensus, the smoking of tobacco was banned in common work areas, in cafeterias, and in ever larger sections of restaurants. In defiance of the smog, exercise stations studded cor-porate landscapes, showers appointed salaried workers' washrooms, and Silicon Valley became one of the running capitals of the world, with many firms sponsoring five and ten kilometer and marathon runs.

The lengthening commutes and the ways Silicon Valley workers chose to deal with them were emblematic of both the style of the fix and the reasons for its popularity.

The habitat defined a genuine rupture with the older urban center (which the emergence of the suburbs in the 1950s supported). Silicon Valley was unlike the older urban cores where paved footpaths, trains, and buses brought people within intimate proximity, confronting each other's smells, sighs, poverty, wealth—a forced sharing of immediate, unmediated experience. From this, a culture of compartments now offered daily and prolonged retreats.

The automobile and its private commute were phenomena with more than a quarter-century of U.S. history. Unlike the postwar traffic patterns and predictable rush hours between suburb and urban center, however, traffic now flowed from suburb to suburb, from work suite to shopping mall to housing development, so the traffic was itself aimless, the rush hours less distinct. The new patterns, as well as the flexible work arrangements and chronic overtime, extended the commutes and subverted traffic's predictability. The result was the modern commuter's deepening self-absorption, a persona hardened in the powerlessness each experienced, almost daily, in a mobile solitude.

Individuals leased or purchased (on credit) high-performance cars, off-road vehicles, excursion vans, or fuel-efficient compacts. In jammed traffic, these could travel no faster, nor very efficiently, but they constituted evidence of attempts to assert self-control, to surround oneself with comfort, to economize, or simply to exhibit good taste (no matter how obviously taste was commercially derived). To release themselves from the stalls and carbon monoxide, commuters acquired expensive car stereos on which they indulged their musical tastes, "listened" to books, and attempted (or pretended) to learn other languages. Some leased cellular telephones (real and bogus) and thus remained plugged in to work. Others dined in transit. For an untold number, marijuana, cocaine, or alcohol suspended the special pain of not getting somewhere fast. These were the elaborate yet, by unspoken consensus, popular ruses by which commutes were endured. Thus did Silicon Valley announce the triumph of the privatized thoroughfare, the filtered social experience; its inhabitants were predisposed to the therapeutic allure of the fix.

The home also became an increasingly lonely haven. Video cassette outlets and cable television—the consumer electronics services in hottest demand—secured the victory of the living room and the TV (the "monitor") over the public gatherings and cinema screens of the older cities. While Silicon Valley breadwinners spent less time at home, TV viewing time grew longer, and new modes of isolated consumption unfolded. Multiple TV sets per household allowed a division of viewing within families, while the spread of consumer videotaping offered to insulate TV programming itself from the mass culture of coast-to-coast network broadcasting.

Second to TV viewing, strolling in the sealed-off, thematic shopping mall had become the most popular leisure "activity" in the United States.[86] In court rooms (based on an incident in Silicon Valley), the sidewalks and parking lots of the malls were declared private property, sanctuaries in which free speech was suspended, displays of poverty or extreme behavior cause for expulsion at the discretion of the mall's proprietors.[87] In the new habitats, capital was contriving to mediate, and thereby isolate, human contact in unprecedented fashion.

A surrogate social discourse began to revolve around therapy and consumption, the two becoming less distinguishable than ever. From a Silicon Valley think-tank, a pathbreaking series of studies examined unabashedly and minutely the consumption-as-therapy connections. The result—psychographics—became a catechism for marketing and advertising. Psychographics attempted to characterize and order social values, beliefs, fantasies, and dreams to better attach these ideologically to commodities. It reduced people to an amalgam of consumer lifestyles and urged advertising that associated commodities not so much with ideas ("convenience," "economy") as with experiences and emotions that evinced contemporary values and lifestyles.

Like that of any advertising, the success of psychographics depended utterly on execution. It could not settle the misconstrued debate on whether "advertising really works." Psychographics did, however, reflect and reinforce the spirit of the times. It was a dubious alliance of therapy—once restricted to upper and middle classes—for the masses with a credit card-based discretionary consumption.

A therapeutic allure imbued shopping and the lifestyles that shopping supported with new meaning. U.S. shoppers, their embrace widened by an apparently infinite line of credit, showed a practical indifference to price and an absorbing attraction to the baroque abstractions that passed for product usefulness. The urge to purchase overwhelmed the consumer's perception of need. In 1987, a marketing-research firm surveyed 34,000 mall shoppers and found that only 25 percent had come to purchase a specific object. The same year, a *Wall Street Journal* reporter found shoppers in "total fulfillment" even though "they don't even know what they're after."[88]

It was only a matter of time before individuals would explicitly seek out therapy as a surrogate politics. This was the path blazed by a group of electronics businessmen and their wives in Silicon Valley, who disavowed political activism, yet sought to resolve, through "positive thinking," the dilemma of nuclear arms—as well as the equally pressing problems of guilt-ridden military electronics professionals. They found fertile soil in Silicon Valley for their faith that if only humanity changed its outlook, the new technology's manifestly evil application, nuclear weapons, might evaporate (without any loss of income or convenience). The success of this movement in Silicon Valley and beyond marked a growing constituency for therapy as a substitute for the community-based politics that didn't emerge. In the meantime, the new movement proposed no practical alterations to the Valley's essentially political agenda of producing the weapons and tools of social control and financial gimmickry.

By making endurable the social loneliness of Silicon Valley, the fix proved indispensable to the electronics industry. By postponing the confrontation between the isolated creators of powerful technology and society, it did incalculable harm.

A semblance of prosperity returned to Silicon Valley by 1988, the year presidential politics reaffirmed the electronics industry as our national salvation. But locating social progress was more difficult than ever.

Where prosperity visited an electronics firm, it was often the paper prosperity of a recent merger or that of a modest recovery from record losses. On the financial markets, "technology" issues tottered. They were so overvalued and fragile that a report of poor earnings from one firm could trigger a selling off of others deemed relatively sound. Where the outlook for professional computer occupations was declared a bright one, electronics firms continued to move thousands of manufacturing jobs out of the area and the growth of minimum wage service and retail sales jobs outpaced all others. The cost of living in Silicon Valley rose so high that $13 per hour was declared a substandard wage.[89]

What had become of the dream of material salvation through migration to the new industry? "A lot of our workers obviously are earning the second or third or perhaps fourth income in their family," observed a Valley employer. A Filipino emigré (earning minimum wage) depicted his interpretation of the American dream circa 1988:

> Imagine, one room for six people in a family and they are sharing a kitchen with many other families. They still manage to survive here, though not comfortably, and many of the people go to the Salvation Army to buy their clothes secondhand.[90]

The computer professionals fared better—materially speaking. Careers advanced. Work, although unsteady for so many, remained for some an endeavor of great personal meaning, individual achievement, and intellectual fascination. Sustaining work as a haven, however, perpetuated an entrapment: work's discontents, the sharp, frequent turns of the electronics industry, and the loneliness of habitat living buffeted the computer professionals, who sought temporary relief in traditional therapies and in the compulsive lifestyles and often destructive habits of daily life.

These tainted the grand vision; how was the new technology making life better, more convenient, more comfortable? In Silicon Valley, the vision corresponded less and less plausibly to the lengthening traffic commutes, the drinking water advisories, the teenage homicides, the toxic industrial fires, and the budding awareness of the electronics industry's leading role in shredding the ozone.[91] The pursuit of American dreams had become a prelude to nightmares.

2

Lonely Trails, Itinerant Cultures
Work's Diminishing Connections

It's really inconvenient to carry on much with my fellow workers
socially...it's not even practical for me to stop for a drink on the
way home after work.

Silicon Valley worker[1]

The United States electronics industry cultivates the fabric cubicle
partition. Rising to the height of stockyard pens, the partitions, in all
shapes and colors, intrude nearly everywhere. They connect and isolate
circuit-board assemblers, shipping clerks, systems programmers, and
marketing analysts. Alongside windows, even managers and vice-presidents sequester themselves in the fabric corrals.

Enclosing assembler and executive alike, the partitions confer the
appearance of classlessness and suggest unity of entrepreneurial purpose. But the impermanence of the partition design—its quick assembly
and disassembly—reveals deeper meaning. Expanding and contracting
with the fortunes of each company, the partitions shape the fragile
edifice of Silicon Valley. They are an emblem for the transience of its
workers as well as the profound loneliness of so much of its work.

The industry has adapted the partitions, and those who work
within them, to its volatile project—making new technologies for which
there often is neither precedent nor market.[2] Small or large, the
electronics firm must cope with disruptive forces: instant success, ill-
fated market debuts, compressed development schedules, sudden

product obsolescence, unexpected and unrelenting competition, unforeseen "bugs," and disloyal financial sponsors.[3] These erratic forces prompt each firm to insist on flexible constellations of workers and managers—in effect, to pass on its instability to the labor market.

The expansion and mid-1980's contraction of "Silicon Valleys" in California illustrates the point: In 1984, Xerox subsidiary Shugart closed its Roseville floppy disk assembly plant, idling 400 workers. The same year, on International Workers Day (May 1), Fairchild closed its Healdsburg facility, idling 200 workers. Also in 1984, Scotts Valley electronics companies laid off 2,200, about 50 percent of the 4,300 electronics jobs there. In 1985, Hewlett-Packard shelved plans to boost employment at its Roseville plant from 1,600 to 5,000. In many cases, the small towns are burdened with sudden high unemployment, municipal bond shortfalls, and a late twentieth century Potemkin village of abandoned electronics facilities.[4]

Electronics employers are fickle. They fire and hire to automate a labor process here, relocate a plant there, work overtime on a product today, cancel or postpone it in favor of another product tomorrow. It is as if America's largest manufacturing industry,[5] after decades of development, still cannot make up its mind what it will make, how and where it will make it, or whether it is in it for the long run. This is why electronics firms favor the impermanence of the cubicle partitions.

Volatile Capital, Transient Labor

The volatility of electronics capital is in step with the lurching rhythms of contemporary capitalism. The industry came of age during the restructuring of the U.S. economy from manufacturing to service-based industries, especially retail sales and financial services. Electronics firms reflect this shift.[6] The industry's products have made it possible.[7]

An abiding design objective of electronics technology—ever faster data transmission—mirrors the priorities of an economy that now prefers to enlarge itself by accelerating the circulation of capital rather than by manufacturing it anew. After the electronics industry itself and the military, the swelling "industries" of retail sales, financial, insurance, banking, brokerage, and business services absorb most new U.S.-made computer products.

It is amazing that, by 1988, there is still no systematic data available that show the purchase by economic sector of electronics products. Market researchers, who sell "trend" reports to the industry, instead rank electronics firms' shares of artificial market categories such as "corporate resource systems," "large department systems," "work group systems," etc. This serves the needs of electronics firms but avoids larger questions such as where, as a society, are we deploying computer resources and how are we really using them? These concerns were echoed by Census Bureau researchers in the first study of computer use in the U.S. Writing in 1988, the researchers noted:

> While some manufacturers provide estimates of how many computers they produce or sell, no overall market total exists...Also, it is not known how many of the small "personal computers" that have been sold are in homes, as opposed to offices...If computers are becoming more and more a part of our lives, we need to know how they are distributed, who uses them, and how they are being used. This report provides a first attempt at providing this information on a national level.

The report found the highest workplace use of personal computers in "finance, insurance, and real estate."[8]

As it is, only 15 percent of the U.S. microchip market "is geared to consumer products (compared to 55 percent of Japanese semiconductor sales)."[9] The largest markets for made-in-U.S.A. electronics are the military ($56 billion, or about 25 percent of total electronics sales) and the U.S. computer industry. A market researcher "[a]nticipated double-digit growth in the U.S. computer and military electronics markets, the largest consumers of U.S. made chips..."[10]

In fact, non-manufacturing enterprises are among the fastest growing parts of the civilian economy.[11] Their growth depends largely on the speed with which they provide their services. Brokerage firms attract more business by allowing clients on-line access to market trading. Banks make float profit by processing outstanding checks and notes faster. Corporations enlarge "idle" cash assets via rapid currency and portfolio transfers. Restaurant chains boost sales by delivering fast food faster during peak hours. So profitable, and thus crucial, is the demand for faster computer processing that electronics products now rapidly become obsolete. Electronics firms used to make products with average market lifetimes of five years. As of late 1986, it was 1.5 years and shrinking.[12] This makes the entrepreneur wary. His product lines—and his assembly lines—are always changing.

We think of Silicon Valley as a manufacturing center. As it exports more and more of its manufacturing jobs offshore, much of Silicon Valley has come to resemble a sprawling product design-and-development service for Japanese, Korean, and other Asian-based manufacturing concerns.[13] By the late 1980s, Silicon Valley journalists acknowledged the changing scene:

> Chip makers long ago moved the latter stages of chip production—assembly and testing—to low-wage areas overseas. But they kept the most costly and complicated part of manufacturing—wafer fabrication—here in the United States. By 1981, however, chip makers had only half their wafer fabrication capacity in Silicon Valley...Today that figure has shrunk to only one-third.[14]
>
> Silicon Valley shouldn't be viewed as a home of electronics production. Rather it's a place with a variety of R&D activity and where lots of startups are trying to make it, and it's where the marketing brains of high-tech are based."[15]

By 1984, managers and salaried professional and technical workers accounted for 56 percent of the Valley's high-tech workforce, while production workers accounted for only 30 percent.[16] This is lop-sided compared with the 70 percent figure for production workers in U.S. manufacturing as a whole. The relatively fixed, and thus long-term, investment required for domestic manufacturing is not favored in the boardrooms of the conglomerates and venture capital concerns that increasingly control the Valley's electronics industry and its entrepreneurs.[17] The entrepreneurial spirit that is widely believed to animate Silicon Valley is evidently an incarnation of the gambler's lust that has seized the U.S. economy.

The short-sighted quest of its financial sponsors and the fluctuations of its markets make the electronics business inherently unstable. Like the nervous contestants in a vaudeville amateur show, electronics entrepreneurs must line up for the chance to make their sponsors' money dance. In place of the hook that yanks ill-starred performers from the stage, a standard clause in a startup contract allows those who provide the capital to fire the startup firm's president at any time, for any reason.[18] According to an ongoing Silicon Valley survey, less than one in four firms survive the rigors of startup—the rest either fail or are "acquired."[19]

Instability imbues the computer-building workplace with an urgency that outsiders interpret as inspired effort. There are sublime moments of excitement, of unity between workers and their work; but they are the momentary excitement of frenzied effort, the soldierly unity of a military campaign. Volatile circumstances create and dissolve, more than sustain, the fabled communities of work in Silicon Valley. Suddenly or gradually, temporarily or permanently, the firm's growth slackens, the market evolves away from its products, the work subsides, and the workers are reassigned or withdrawn from the front. The ephemeral fabric partition ebbs and flows while, expandable and expendable, the itinerant worker comes and goes.

Following the trails blazed by electronics capital, the itinerant worker travels from one company to another, finding work where it can be had and working fiercely until a layoff or another job looms. The itinerant worker spans the occupational gamut from microchip fabrication operator to systems analyst, from assembler to engineer. The itinerant's working conditions, status, pay, and workday culture vary widely, too. His or her immediate guises include the temporary worker, the immigrant worker, even the skilled "professional." Some move from project to project and building to building within the same company. Many are likely to quit, transfer, or be laid off within a year or two— provided their department, division, or company lasts that long. Those who remain watch a revolving door of new workers arriving and old ones exiting.

The motivations that impel workers along an occupational itinerary are as varied as the itineraries themselves. Many workers attach a coherence to their workplace transience, regarding job changes as the logical steps of an unfolding career. Salaried professional employees with skills in high demand can do so plausibly; the less-skilled production worker cannot.

Doris is a single, 38-year-old working mother who grew up in Silicon Valley. In twenty years, Doris has worked as a circuit board assembler and production expediter in eight jobs with half a dozen Silicon Valley electronics firms. Though her Fortune-500 employers have been among the most stable,[20] Doris has been laid-off twice, fired once, and has collected unemployment three times. (She qualifies for, but declines, welfare assistance, a common occurrence for working women heads of households in Silicon Valley.)[21] Her longest stint at one job lasted nearly four years; her shortest, several weeks. The day after our interview, she lost her most recent job, which had lasted nine months. Doris is an itinerant worker.

Silicon Valley Gross Wage Compensation[22]		
Occupation	**Entry Level**	**Experienced**
Semiconductor Processor	$ 9,000-$12,000	$12,000-$18,000
Electronics Assembler	$ 9,000-$13,000	$12,000-$18,000
Electronics Technician	$14,000-$20,000	$18,000-$28,000
Secretary/Word Processor	$13,200-$20,400	$16,800-$25,200
Computer Operator	$14,400-$19,200	$18,000-$25,200

Victor is an itinerant worker, too. Victor is a single, 30-year-old systems programmer who moved to Silicon Valley from New York in 1980. Victor's first electronics employer "flew me out to California and shipped my car in a big moving van." Since then, according to Victor, "it's been one new company to get in bed with after another." In less than eight years, Victor has held four jobs. Unlike Doris, he has never been laid off or fired. Instead, he has carefully picked his next job on the basis of his technical interest in the projects offered. His latest employer has sold his department to another company. Victor's interest in his current project is waning, and so he contemplates his next move.

As with Doris and Victor, expendability affects the forms a worker's transience assumes; in Silicon Valley, the Dorises are laid off much more often than the Victors. Programmers' and engineers' career-hopping is more likely voluntary—planned to minimize financial and emotional trauma. When salaried workers move on, it is typically through a placement agency or through a web of "professional friends," a far-flung network of instrumental acquaintances who are periodically consulted and polled for access to new jobs. Firms encourage the networks (which sometimes include wage workers), offering bonuses to employees who bring new workers "on board." (The network bonuses are a bargain for employers, who otherwise pay much higher bounties to placement agencies.)

Among workers, the professional etiquette of networking and the cavalcade of changing jobs dilutes interest in the enduring connections of class. Why bother cultivating them? For better or for worse, a group of workers is no longer "stuck" with each other at a workplace year in, year out. Instead, a wandering occupational itinerary fragments and truncates shared experience. In the shifting soil of short-lived employment, the itinerant worker's roots must be shallow, retractable.

When I asked Doris if she kept up with workers from previous jobs, she was mildly surprised by my question. "Not really," she replied, adding that she would "occasionally get a call" from a former fellow worker. Regarding her current workplace, she complained, "I have no friends." She didn't really mingle much with workers during nonwork hours because she was so busy. Victor is less isolated from past and present workmates, though he recalls that at two of his four jobs, he did not mix socially. Work cultures separate Doris, a wage worker, from Victor, a salaried professional, but their occupational transience imparts a common perspective of detachment from the workplace and its circle of acquaintances, neither of which, after all, they can take with them to their next job.

Itinerant workers in the electronics industry are distinct from migrant farm workers who travel together from job to job, whose work follows predictable seasonal rhythms, and who often speak and act as members of a community more or less conscious of itself. The modern itinerant worker may be fired in groups, but does not travel, find work, live, or act with others as part of a community, despite sharing similar burdens. The burdens are many and not strictly peculiar to Silicon Valley: the frequent, unsettling motion in and out of work; the deprivations of prolonged overtime; the anxiety of little-known workplace dangers; the shocking cost of housing; the fatigue of withering commutes to work, to childcare centers, to shopping centers; and the stress of juggling it all. The itinerant tends to perceive these burdens less as the common problems of a group of workers and more as individual dilemmas to be ignored or suffered before moving on. Work's larger purposes—if we can still speak without cynicism of its capacity to provide for a sense of connection and contribution to society, for satisfying and healthful lives outside of work, and for security upon retirement—recede before the immediate prospects of finding work and, once found, before the press of work's daily demands.

Job turnover rates—the percentage of full-time employees who resign or transfer each year—provide a glimpse of the furious labor migration within the electronics industry. In 1980, an American Electronics Association (AEA) survey covering over one thousand member firms reported an industry average turnover rate of 26 percent[23] —twice the national rate.[24] The following year, a Dun's Review report put the Valley's turnover rate at over 30 percent. Engineers, it was said, were "averaging a mere two years at any one company."[25]

The turnover estimates are based on nonexhaustive surveys and should be taken with the precautions that all statistics require. But the numbers suggest a common plight: workers were not staying long at the new jobs they were finding in the electronics industry. Job insecurity casts doubt on the electronics industry's heralded role as a refuge from Rustbelt unemployment.

The electronics industry turnover rates have slackened, according to the AEA. Thus, 1985 yielded the lowest-ever industry turnover rate— just under 18 percent (still well above the national average).[26] But the apparent trend toward employment stability is bogus. The turnover rates *exclude layoffs*, and layoffs have made frequent copy in business columns during the open-ended electronics recession of the 1980s.

If job turnover rates establish the presence of itinerant workers, layoffs augment their number. Just how much so is difficult to say with certainty. Layoffs may or may not be permanent, and are not always announced (for every five publicly disclosed layoffs, a sixth layoff probably occurs behind closed doors).[27] For years, IBM has hidden layoffs by downgrading employees, selectively applying performance standards, and demanding frequent or unpalatable transfers. "There's a lot of turnover," according to an IBM-San Jose production worker, who added that workers who fall from grace with their superiors are "pushed" into resigning when high production swings wind down.[28]

Excluding the large military contractors, Silicon Valley saw a loss of at least 5 to 7 percent of its electronics industry jobs from spring 1985 through autumn 1986.[29] A comparable job loss occurred throughout the industry. (It is not known how many of these jobs were transferred offshore.) To these statistical casualties must be added the thousands of early retirements—10,000 at IBM alone, beginning in late 1986—the periodic furloughs,[30] and the forced unpaid "vacation" days, all of which increased the instability of electronics jobs.

Taken together, turnovers and layoffs probably separate at least one quarter of the electronics industry's permanent workforce from their jobs each year. But even this calculation, which is above the national average, is wanting. It excludes the part-time, the outside temporary, and the legions of undocumented immigrant workers with which the electronics and related firms supplement their payrolls. The temporary and the undocumented immigrant worker constitute the most under-privileged substrata of the itinerant workforce and illustrate the separate-ness of transient cultures.

Permanent Temporary Workers?

Emerging in Silicon Valley, perhaps with more intensity than anywhere else, is the *deployment of temporary workers as a substitute for permanent workers.* "When you're dealing with volatile industries like semiconductors and electronics," explained the head of the Valley's temporary agency trade group, "the role of the temporary has changed to a detached workforce actually planned for by personnel depart-ments." A Silicon Valley worker is more than three times as likely to be a temporary worker than elsewhere; within the computer-building and related industries, this figure rises. "The general consensus for a lot of high-tech companies is to have 10 to 15 percent of their labor force temporary," according to a Valley agency spokesperson. One computer maker, Convergent Technologies, uses temporaries for nearly 30 percent of its work force. The temps' assignments include the traditional ones of filling in for full-time clerical/secretarial workers on vacation or sick leave. But far more often, "temps" are electronics assemblers and other production workers as well as programmers, accountants, technical illustrators, and writers.[31] The assignments can last weeks or months, but increasingly are open-ended in accord with the inconstant demands of the computer corporation.

Permanent workers may be dragooned by their employer into the ranks of impermanence. In a practice known as "employee leasing," Corvus, a computer-storage firm, fired its technical writers and then offered to "rehire" several of the now jobless ex-employees at lower expense as temporary workers.[32] Still other firms displace permanent employees with part-time staff.[33]

Startup computer companies, liable to expand wildly but tentative about their future, are a natural employer for the easily-riddanced temporary worker, who supplements a core of dedicated "founder" workers. But large, mature computer corporations also rely heavily on temporary workers as well as "supplemental" workers—part-time personnel hired directly by the employer. Hewlett-Packard (H-P), IBM, and Control Data Corporation are among the largest users of temporary and supplemental workers. H-P maintains its own temporary agency and also contracts with nearly a dozen outside agencies, spending millions to keep temporary workers on its payroll, mainly for production and clerical work, but also for programming, technical writing, and other esoterically skilled work. The rationale? When there is a slowdown, as one agent put it, "you don't have those layoffs that put you on the front page"—merely the orderly and predictable release of temporary workers. According to a full-time production worker, for example, IBM-San Jose, quietly laid off "several hundred" supplementals in autumn 1985.[34]

The statistical fictions of the Department of Labor have been compounded by both IBM and H-P's claims of "never having a layoff anywhere," since the hundreds of temporary and supplemental workers each employs and dismisses every year are not, strictly speaking, employees, and thus are not counted by these clever firms as layoffs. These unannounced dismissals are no less tragic for going untallied in local and national media, and for eluding those who calculate official joblessness; on-again, off-again temp workers cannot always petition successfully for unemployment compensation or simply do not bother.

The advantages of employing temporary help are not reducible merely to greater labor flexibility. As the executive president of the National Association of Temporary Services explained about the booming Silicon Valley temporary market, the temp "provides a buffer zone" to a company's full-time workers, "shield[ing] them from the ups and downs" of the economy.[35] This observation, really a recommendation, is saturated with paternalism, but it also locates the temp worker in an economic class that is well beneath that of the permanent worker. The temp's pay and benefits, with which the agencies are notoriously stingy, are far less than that of nontemporary workers performing similar work. The economics are straightforward. Employer contributions for disability insurance, unemployment compensation, and benefits constitute up to 40 percent of a payroll.[36] This percentage inclines steeply for employers—such as the computer-building firms— who offer attractive benefits to entice skilled labor in scarce supply and who lay off workers frequently and in large numbers (and thus must contribute proportionately higher unemployment compensation deductions). Enter the temporary worker.

When firms "hire" temps, the wages and overhead—as well as the associated bookkeeping—are picked up by the temporary agencies, who are the real employers and dispatchers of most temporary workers. The agencies typically charge firms seeking temporary labor a 35 to 45 percent markup over and above the wages paid the temp. The temp's pay and benefits, however, are generally lower—much lower—and of poorer quality than those paid by most computer corporations to their permanent employees. As a temporary clerk for a microelectronics firm, I received $4.50 an hour without medical insurance, vacation benefits, or pension plans; later hired directly by the firm, I earned $6.25 plus extensive benefits (but none of the premium advanced by the firm to gain my release from the agency). One observer estimates the temp/permanent pay differential at $2.50 per hour.[37] The contrast in pay and benefits suggests the privileged culture in which the permanent worker is placed relative to the temp.[38]

The temp's relative power and control over a job is also badly compromised. Some workers envy the temp's mobility and detachment. With few exceptions, however, the temp is viewed by management and workers alike as a mercenary whose allegiance to the company, and thus to the job, is actively suspect. No amount of reassurance and advertising by the larger temp agencies seems to have changed this prejudice. There is a conceit regarding the temporary worker, as if this status reflects an inability to hold down permanent work, rather than the plight imposed by a volatile labor market. In consequence, the temp suffers special indignities.

As a rule, the temp is hired to do the most boring or physically demanding jobs on the slowest, clunkiest equipment under the least comfortable conditions. Thus situated, temps are expected to perform to the exaggerated standards advertised by their agencies and to exude the unctuousness of the cheerful subordinate. To make matters worse, the temp is often exempted from informal work rules and rituals, such as the permanent worker's longer lunch breaks, late morning arrivals, early Friday afternoon departures, and extended breaks. Moreover, the temp may be an unwelcome guest at the usual gossip and *kaffee klatsches*. This is the special "detachment" of the temporary worker, whose natural allies, fellow workers, are often unapproachable at first.

The infringement of the temporary worker's rights is perhaps the greatest injustice. In a practice known as "payrolling," employers may screen prospective permanent employees sent to them by a temp agency. As one employer put it, payrolling "allow[s] us to test someone in place of a probationary period." Payrolling may or may not lead to a permanent job for the temp. The important difference is that firms can dismiss temporary workers without even the minimal notice or explanation given fired probationary workers. As it is, employers are discouraged from hiring temps by the substantial "release" fees charged by the temp's agent.

"Payrolled" or not, when problems do emerge, temps cannot, according to many agencies' policies, deal directly with an on-site manager. Instead, the temporary worker must appeal to the good graces of the temporary agent to represent him or her in a dispute with the agency's "client." Without so much as an exit interview, fired temps may find out only that "there were problems" or that their performance was "unprofessional," generalities that are impossible to defend against. Nor are the agencies reliable defenders of their temporary employees. Temps are usually easily replaced. Also, an economic interest predisposes the agencies to accept the firm's version of things; the firm is a potentially greater and certainly more stable source of income for the agency than the offending temporary worker.

Some observers, especially those riding the waves and charting the trends of the future, put the best face on the emergence of temporary workers, depicting them as an innovative and happy medium for labor and capital.[39] Here it is imagined that temporary work fulfills the avocational aspirations of students, retirees, the unemployed-in-between-jobs, and others who scorn permanent work. There's no denying that impermanent and part-time work is well-suited to many schedules. But the sanguine appraisals apply mainly, I suspect, to the minority of well-paid, highly skilled temps. This is small consolation for the majority of disenfranchised temporary workers whose ill-paid and unstable assignments more accurately reflect the unilaterally determined needs of increasingly volatile capital.

The enduring tragedy is the temporary worker's isolation not only from the permanent worker, but also from other temps, who are freshly dispersed with every assignment. No one is better suited to ameliorate the temp's abused status than temp workers themselves. Within this fragmented itinerant culture, there is great potential, but little occasion, for solidarity. Divided, they cope.

In the tumult of the electronics industry as well as the tentative atmosphere of the economy at large, the temporary agency offers transient labor on good terms, and is therefore a growth industry.[40] (The Conference Board of New York estimates that the number of part-time or temporary workers, the self-employed, and people who work at home constitutes 34.3 million people, or almost one-third of the labor force.[41]) This offer is secured by the isolation of the temporary worker from mainstream work cultures.

Undocumented Workers: Here Today...

The least publicly acknowledged itinerant culture is that of the undocumented immigrant.[42] No one knows with certainty how many undocumented workers reside and work in Silicon Valley, officially home to 220,000 Hispanics and 100,000 Taiwanese, Vietnamese, Filipinos, Chinese, and other Asian and Pacific Rim peoples.[43]

Biased estimates abound. In 1984, the Immigration and Naturalization Service (INS) opened a special branch office in Silicon Valley, claiming that 25 percent of the workforce—nearly 200,000 workers—were there illegally, that more were on the way, and that it was high time something was done about it.[44] This was a staggering calculation and a threat of wholesale inquisition; both were inflated, probably deliberately. A year later, *The Wall Street Journal* put the numbers slightly lower, between 10 and 20 percent.[45] But by then, the INS, as it has nearly everywhere, had capitulated to a familiar bloc of Sunbelt political and corporate interests who traffic in what the *Journal* calls the "cheap, docile, and abundant" undocumented worker. Despite the fair play pretense of the recent "amnesty" legislation, the traffic continues, pushing the terms and prices of the United States labor market downward toward the subsistence levels of the Third World.[46]

As it is, the law creates what *The Wall Street Journal* called "a subclass of illegals bound to their bosses and vulnerable to abuses." This subclass, which may include as many as one million immigrants (based on Census Bureau and INS data), arrived after 1982, and is therefore ineligible for amnesty. But their current employers can legally retain them indefinitely if employment precedes November 6, 1986, the date President Reagan signed the legislation. As Jorge Bustamante, a researcher at the University of Santa Cruz Diego Center for U.S.-Mexican Studies put it, "Immigration obeys the law of supply and demand, not the laws of immigration."[47]

Since the early 1970s, the U.S. semiconductor and electronics firms have been among the biggest employers of Third World labor in the United States and abroad. By the mid-1970s, for example, the five largest chipmakers collectively had over 60 production facilities abroad—*more than these firms maintained in the United States.*[48] Many a firm has shifted work from Sunnyvale to Manila as the fidgeting of accountants dictated. Former computer game *paterfamilias* Atari relocated its entire production facilities from the Valley to El Paso, Texas and then to Hong Kong and Taiwan; before it was through, 4,000 Valley workers were permanently disencumbered of their Atari jobs. Through such arrangements, north and south, east and west are meeting, and not only on the payrolls of the global computer-building firms. Nowhere is this more apparent than in the bargain basement of the itinerant labor market in Silicon Valley—the life of the undocumented immigrant worker.

My most frequent contact with undocumented workers came while I was a temporary clerk making pickups and deliveries for a digital camera maker that subcontracted work to metal shops in Silicon Valley. Inside one of the shops—a dirt floor quonset hut in Santa Clara—were Hispanic workers in rubber boots, gloves, and aprons, and without respirator masks. They moved about quickly, stoking fires beneath vats of chemicals, climbing up and down the jerrybuilt platforms which gave access to the vats. Some of the vats boiled; others, untouched by the fires, yielded the smoke of chemical reaction. The first time I delivered there, the workers regarded me suspiciously. They may have taken my tie, twill slacks, and sunglasses for the accoutrements of *La Migra* travelling incognito. Then, after my pick-ups and deliveries at the metal shop became commonplace, their suspicion gave way to silent, grinning salutations.

Into the vats the workers dipped the unfinished alloy chassis panels, nuts, and screws I would drop off from the digital camera factory. The foul metallic odors made me want to hold my breath. The twirling bulb-shaped fans on the roof provided little ventilation. After I stopped making deliveries there, someone in a position to know confirmed my suspicions: most of the metal shop employees were undocumented workers. I wondered how much they were daunted by their "alien" status from speaking out against the fumes.

Much of Silicon Valley, as well as huge swaths of the U.S. south-west, has become a *de facto* Export Processing Zone (EPZ)—an entrepreneurial no-man's land where the civilized pretensions of the above-ground labor market are checked at the shop door. In EPZs in Malaysia and the Philippines, or in the *maquilladoras* along the Mexican-U.S. border, an electronics firm escapes taxes, enjoys the presumption of abridged labor organizing and safety precautions, and employs young, mainly female, first-time wage workers for as little as 70 cents an hour. In the United States, by informal decree of the INS, the same firm, or its subcontractors, receives similar advantages. In the Valley, the small-to-middling shops of metal plating, printed circuit board assembly, landscaping, and janitorial service muster the undocumented worker for $2.50 an hour or lower. Even the *Journal* noted that "10,000 illegals [are] estimated to be manufacturing printed circuit boards in Silicon Valley, often at below the minimum wage." Without them, *The Wall Street Journal* speculated, the local economy "might collapse."[49]

The parallels between the foreign EPZs and the underground neo-serfdoms being carved out in the Valley run long and deep. For speaking out against workplace dangers, company-store markups, or a foreman's sexual advances in the Philippines, a worker risks both current job and general blacklisting within the EPZ. Not only can dissident undocumented workers in Silicon Valley be summarily fired; they must also be wary of the dogs, handcuffs, and searches of immigration police agents. At intervals dictated by the complex politics of immigrant labor, these agents may suddenly round up hundreds of hapless workers, preventively detain them, and dispatch many of them to the unfriendly or indifferent governments of their homelands. The raid, like the EPZ blacklist, severs the workplace connections to the immigrants' potentially most helpful companions—resident fellow workers. Even the rumor of a raid can result in preemptive withdrawal from one's job so as to avoid arrest.

The temp's workplace rights and conditions are shabby, confined by once-removed ties to the labor market; the underground immigrant electronics worker's rights are nonexistent and workplace conditions generally much worse. This is despite the frequent deduction of worker's compensation, job disability, and unemployment contributions from the immigrant's pay—for benefits he and she will never see. As one employer put it, "Whenever there's an accident...the Chicano [Mexican-American] will stay home and ask for worker's compensation. The Mexicans, they work."[50]

Undocumented immigrant workers are so important to the Valley's electronics-based economy as to be tolerated (but, to date, only in their current subclass status) by a revealing alliance of interests. During its first week of business in 1984, the San Jose INS raided several electronics workplaces. San Jose City officials, sensitive to the importance of "illegals" to the local economy, adopted a resolution against "the unwarranted disruption of the business community" as well as the affront to resident Chicano workers being shaken down by INS agents.[51] The City Attorney explored means to prevent the raids. The Police Chief instructed his minions not to cooperate with raiding INS agents. Within months, a federal judge issued a local injunction against the open-ended INS raids, ordering its agents to notify employers or to describe to them each suspect before a raid. Chastised, the INS relented, but not before installing a resident alien database against which employers can check the validity of workers' "green" cards. Under this *pax laissez faire,* employers decided when and against which employees to apply INS heat; when INS agents came calling, the employer could schedule raids to coincide with a week's "vacation" for their undocumented workers—or hand over the names of troublemakers.

It is too early to discern the impact of the new immigration rules being gradually introduced. The laws appear to offer hope to those immigrants both willing and able to provide proof of their residency. Most immigrants are skeptical. Some, in Silicon Valley, can recall previous amnesties: National Semiconductor workers tell the story of their employer's promise of diplomatic and legal assistance to its immigrant employees. When some of the latter then revealed their improper documents, National Semi ordered them to provide proof of legal status within 72 hours. In the doldrums of a sales slump, National Semi fired those who couldn't produce appropriate visas and escaped liability for unemployment compensation claims.[52]

In the shadow of official disavowal, little light is shed on undocumented immigrant workers' jobs. No one, except the odd underfunded legal defense fund or parish food kitchen, ventures to tally their layoffs, injuries, illnesses, or wages. Stuck in subcontracting electronics shops or even smaller cottage-type operations, undocumented immigrant workers are physically, as well as culturally, removed from the legal workforce. Without legal status, without a voice, and without the active sympathy and support of resident workers, they remain vulnerable in the worst ways. Silicon Valley indeed might "collapse" without them, but their lives remain hidden, and they are ill-placed to help themselves.

The Diminishing Connections

The urge to quantify the itinerant worker phenomenon is difficult to resist. But lumping the temporary and undocumented workers together with the previously estimated 25 percent of workers separated from their jobs each year by turnover and layoffs is ill-advised, even as an approximation.[53] What can be said is that transient cultures saturate the electronics industry, creating an atmosphere of impermanence among its workforce.

That electronics is now our largest manufacturing employer may be prophetic. Thanks in large part to the electronics industry, job descriptions near the end of the twentieth century read like recipes for workplace transience.[54] Electronics products play a crucial supporting role in the growth of service-based industries that offer low-wage, part-time jobs as well as automation technologies that reduce the manufacturing workforce. According to a Joint Economic Committee of Congress study by Barry Bluestone and Bennett Harrison,[55] more than half of all new jobs pay less than $7,000 per year, a disproportionate number are part-time, most are unchallenging to jobholders, and many are vulnerable to automation. These are the conditions that favor workplace transience, as rising service sector turnover rates and manufacturing layoffs will likely confirm.

Some workers, even in Silicon Valley, manage to stay on at firms year after year. But permanent workers cannot escape the consequences of a transient workforce around them. If their fellow workers are forever shifting, the complexion of their departments, shops, or labs can change significantly within a year. Transience may not affect every worker, but, as with the quarantined survivors in Camus' *The Plague,* life is not the same for those who remain.

The itinerant worker is as restless as the microelectronics industry is volatile. The mobility—even by U.S. standards—is often dizzying and causes immense, if little noticed, social changes.

Itinerant workers are, by tenure, less informed about a specific shop or office, its management, labor relations, problems, and history. By that measure, itinerants are less effective in speaking out with the authority of experience on workplace problems. It is perhaps too early to pronounce with certainty, but the itinerant perspective of a large and growing proportion of workers probably reduces pressure on firms to correct problems, to invest in and implement safety procedures, or to chastise or remove offensive managers. This helps explain why itinerant workers have proven elusive targets for electronics industry union organizing, such as it has been.

Compared to organizing fellow workers, changing jobs is a less cumbersome means of resolving an intolerable workplace problem. Workers' transience, however, cannot explain the nearly total absence of unions in the electronics workplace where some of the most dangerous conditions, lowest wages, and worst job security in the United States suggest fertile soil for organizing. Organized labor, whose ranks dwindle every year to new post-World War II lows, is ostensibly in need of new unionists.[56] Vulnerable to the myriad corruptions and corporate logic of a labor brokerage, however, U.S. labor unions are in fact among the least effective allies of electronics workers. The unions' conservative and meager organizing efforts, in the words of two electronics labor organizers, have "proven to be spectacularly unsuccessful."[57]

Like an artless cardsharp holding bad cards, the U.S. labor leader is often reduced to bluffing. Late in 1985, the Communications Workers of America (CWA) announced the first 'serious' organizing drive at nonunion IBM. Ken Major, a CWA Northern California spokesperson, said he was answering calls from several production workers at non-union firms in Silicon Valley. The announcements, perhaps intended for consumption at the CWA's annual conference, surprised IBM workers (in Silicon Valley and in Endicott, New York) who had been organizing themselves informally—and independently.[58]

"Sounded to me like it was off the wall," according to M., an IBM-San Jose clean room worker who helped publish *Workers Voice,* a dissident IBM shop floor newsletter. Shortly after the CWA's proclamation, M. recounted the following:

> I've called the local head of the CWA; she doesn't even return my calls... We have put out requests to the [Santa Clara] Central Labor Council to do just very low-level funding and provide a phone and so on, which they have not done. Then I was referred to someone in San Francisco named Ken Major with the CWA and told he could answer my questions and he hasn't called back. So they're obviously not serious. It's really arrogant I think.[59]

Like M., we needn't support the Valley's corporate anti-union agenda[60] to see why the CWA and other AFL-CIO affiliates are unlikely saviors of electronics labor. In 1982, when rumors of massive Atari layoffs began to circulate, Atari workers approached a union. A year later, the union was defeated by a five-to-one margin. As the business editor of the *San Jose Mercury News* gloated, "many workers at Atari questioned what a union could do for them... What they emphasized was job security. But Atari workers, who work in Milpitas, realized that strong unions up the road at the Ford and General Motors plants didn't prevent the elimination of thousands of jobs at those facilities."[61] Likewise, the CWA announced its IBM drive amidst the worst ever slump in Silicon Valley and when job security, even at IBM, was again a major issue.[62] At the time, AT&T was laying off thousands of CWA rank and file nationwide with no effective resistance from that union.[63]

Another source of bad feeling toward U.S. unions is often overlooked. Most electronics production workers are minorities. Many are recent Asian and Central American immigrants. Racist and anti-foreigner sentiments run as deep in the U.S. labor movement as they do in other sectors of U.S. society; nor is the AFL-CIO's record in immigrant workers' homelands likely to inspire faith in Silicon Valley organizing efforts. AFL-CIO dues, plus once-removed congressional and federal agency monies, fund the quasi-secret activities of AIFLD and AAFLI (Latin and Asian American "Free Labor" Institutes). These august bodies actively support U.S. State Department policies and, as required, pro-dictatorship "unions" in South Korea, El Salvador, Guatemala, and elsewhere. In a characteristic act of solidarity with Filipino workers, AAFLI channeled money into a government-organized union that defended the mass arrest of workers by the now-deposed and then-despised Marcos regime.[64]

Explaining the unions' dilemma by citing workplace transience as well as the prevailing "anti-union" environment hides a telling fact. Unions are not organizing. In the electronics industry, they have rarely done so.[65] In 1982, during the Atari organizing drive, a representative of the AFL-CIO's Santa Clara Labor Council admitted, "Frankly, the whole thing about organizing [in Silicon Valley] is a media hype. There is no concerted effort."[66]

Among the unions actively not organizing in Silicon Valley is the International Association of Machinists and Aerospace Workers (IAM). Years ago, the IAM contracted with the two biggest employers—missile-maker Lockheed and tank-maker FMC. These, plus nuclear weapons contractors Westinghouse Marine and General Electric—both also IAM-organized—comprise the only industrial union shops of consequence in the Valley. The IAM Lockheed local president told me that his union's executive board has imposed a moratorium on organizing in Silicon Valley.[67] In a background report, Silicon Valley labor organizer Michael Eisenscher notes, "IAM continues to show no interest and has done little in the past despite its considerable base."[68] Labor organizer Rand Wilson, whose activism led to a parting of ways with the CWA, summarized the situation in 1986:

No union—large or small, progressive or conservative, acting alone or in concert with others—has been willing or able to provide consistent support for efforts to organize high tech targets that do not offer the prospect of immediate membership gains. As a result, organized labor has—for the time being—abandoned the field in high tech.[69]

In the current period of mass transience, an organizing strategy based on industry-wide unions that extends protections to workers regardless of employers (rather than organizing a single workplace where workers come and go) could be effective. It is a strategy that eludes the AFL-CIO, which, ironically, has come to blame its failures on a bad image.[70]

Lacking responsive workplace organizations, transience continues to shape the forms employee resistance assumes. When management policies do inspire resistance, its collective character is often preempted or aborted in favor of individual measures. For example, at a computer graphics company in the Valley, several technical writers, including myself, quit as a result of an overbearing manager. The departures were staggered, and came after the foundering of rebellion against the manager's crude wielding of authority. The failure reflected our inexperience in collective resistance, but also the less troublesome option of finding another job while biding our time as best we could. This escape route was conditioned by the availability of jobs and high demand for our labor, but also by a shared itinerant perspective; none of us had planned on staying with this company. No one really *plans* on staying with an electronics company indefinitely, even when one would like to do so.

Whether our jobs are taken from us or whether we leave them voluntarily, we may or may not improve our lots by finding work elsewhere. But by looking elsewhere, we are less and less likely to address work problems collectively, an option that is fading from the realm of the familiar and feasible. It's not that collective undertakings are spurned, but more that they're difficult to imagine while in the flow of an itinerant culture. Transience is difficult to share.

3

Above the Crescendo
Cleanly as Deadly

What is it like to work in a "clean room"?

In cramped locker rooms, the women enjoy their last chatter before the crescendo. They snap on vinyl surgeon's gloves and don white and pale-blue dacron: hoods, jump suits, veils, and booties. As they shroud themselves in nearly identical *bunny suits,* the workers, or rather the images they present to one another, shed their distinctness.

They walk through a narrow vestibule with a grey sticky mat on the floor. Abruptly, the crescendo begins its deafening ascent; they barely hear the stripping sound of the mat cleansing their soles. Along the vestibule walls, crooked plastic tentacle stumps pour a continuous fusillade of air at them, removing dust flecks and lint from the dacron. The roar submerges normal conversational tones—all but shouts and sharp sounds.

Passing through the vestibule to the clean room[1] or *aisle,* the workers take up their positions to new tones at different pitches: the dissonant arpeggio of rapidly moving air and loudly humming machines. From ceiling to floor, the forced air of the *laminar flow* blows dust particles larger than quarter-widths of human hair. This protects the even smaller circuitry that blots the wafers. But the air flow merges acoustically with the dull whir of the processing equipment. The consequence of this merger is a cacophonous, low boom—a crescendo that peaks but never falls off.

Above the crescendo, casual conversation is difficult and the distraction often dangerous. Their mouths gagged and faces veiled (often above the nose), phrases are muffled, expressions half-hidden. The customary thoroughfares of meaning and emotion are obscured. Do furrowed eyebrows indicate pleasure or problem? Like deep-sea divers, the workers use hand-gestures, or like oil riggers, they shout above the din created by the refrigerator-sized machines and the hushed roar of the laminar flow. But mainly, the crescendo encourages a feeling of isolation, of removal from the world.

What is a "clean room"?

In the calculated isolation of the clean room, workers fashion the most sensitive and inscrutable computer components: a variety of chips, disk surfaces, and disk-drive heads. Their microscopic scale and their metamorphosis from mere sand and gas fall plausibly within the realms of revelation and magic, even among the engineers who design and control the transubstantiation.

Managers compare the clean rooms they supervise to the conscientiously scrubbed intensive care units of hospitals. Both are micro-environments requiring special gowns, face masks, and artificial atmospheres. Both connote protection from unseen danger. Even the paths danger stalks are similar: the particles that destroy microchips and the viruses that infect ICU patients are measured in *microns* (millionths of a meter). The analogy conceals a horrible irony.

Engineers design clean rooms to protect modern machine parts—the inanimate "patients" workers nurse to support electronic life. But clean rooms are neither clean nor safe for workers. The irony is easily lost in the loneliness, fatigue, and dull ritual of work. But the undetected dangers produce human suffering that is no less palpable for going unexamined by industry, unreported in local media, and often unattributed by the victims.

Columnists and congressional committees perennially brood over the military's stockpiling of nerve gases. No such brooding accompanies the mundane exposure by electronics workers to arsine, phosphine, diborane, and chlorine, the latter internationally abhorred over 60 years ago after its use as a weapon on the Western Front. These gases are prized by the semiconductor industry because they impart electrical properties to microchips. They are among the most toxic substances in the biosphere. When mixed and released under pressure at high temperatures and in extreme environments, they combine to hazardous effect—effects modern medicine studiously ignores.[2]

The chemicals deployed by the semiconductor, printed circuit board, and disk-drive industries include life-altering mutagens and carcinogens, as well as less mysterious gases and acids that sear and disfigure human tissue on contact. Many elude detection, despite the criminal reassurances of clean room managers, one of whom (with a

PhD in chemistry) told me that workers can sense chemicals "below the level of harm."[3] Poor warning qualities make most of these chemicals dangerous in a particularly sinister way. Still other qualities simultaneously enlarge and hide the danger.[4]

Chemical injuries are confusing. They may not announce themselves immediately; trace toxins can accumulate in fatty tissue for years before a weight loss releases them into the victim's system. The symptoms induced by chronic exposures often are indistinct, masquerading as those accompanying common illnesses. Chemicals also can spontaneously create harmful compounds. One of many evacuations at a National Semiconductor clean room began with leaking silicon tetrachloride.[5] Silicon tetrachloride emits hydrogen chloride fumes, which, when inhaled, react with moisture in mouth, throat, and lungs to form hydrochloric acid that dissolves living tissue.

Semantic conventions celebrate the confusion. In electronics workplaces, workers see and hear the industry's neutral designations: "agents," "chemicals," "gases," or perhaps "aggressive fluids." When encountered in soil, in ground water, or in sewage effluent, the same substances are identified by hydrologists and environmental officials as "contaminants," "poisons," and "toxic wastes."

How dangerous is "clean room" work?

In any honest estimation, electronics production work must be counted among the most dangerous of occupations, though this statement might clash with the daily perceptions of workers and certainly with those of managers. By 1980, the occupational illness rate for semiconductor workers was over three times that of manufacturing workers; all electronics workers experienced job-related illnesses at twice the general manufacturing rate.[6] Yet workers are denied even these abstract reckonings of the dangers they face.

In the early-1980s, the industry simply changed the way it recorded injuries and illnesses. The result was a two-thirds drop in the occupational illness rate. To this day, the Semiconductor Industry Association's (SIA) "adjusted" data collection system projects a safe picture of the clean room. At all levels, government agencies have supported this fiction by failing to investigate.[7]

The SIA's revisionism killed two birds with one stone. It allowed the companies to avoid legal obligations to report many work-related illnesses—redefined as injuries—since firms are required to report all job illnesses, but are only required to report injuries that result in lost work time. This helped establish a trend of declining occupational illness data that could later be used as circumstantial evidence against disabled workers' claims of *chronic illnesses*. Secondly, as long as SIA firms' injury rates didn't soar, they would attract less attention from government inspectors. Under the Occupational Safety and Health Administration's (OSHA) new role as "cooperative regulator," initiated during the Reagan administration, if an employer's injury rates remain below the national average, OSHA inspectors examine employers' logs of on-the-job injuries rather than inspect their workplaces, ask workers questions, etc. The upshot was a cleaner bill of health for the semiconductor industry— from "wafer fabrication to health fabrication" one observer quipped. Furthermore, employers now could cite statistics in support of their boast of being the nation's third safest industry. Bureau of Labor Statistics officials told one journalist that semiconductor companies throughout the U.S. are following California's lead in changing the way they record on-the-job injuries and illnesses.

At about the same time the SIA was revising its workplace safety records (1981), the Reagan Administration also cut funding for the Project on Health and Safety in Electronics (PHASE). PHASE was an outreach program that, as its meager budget allowed, collected and publicized information for electronics workers on the chemicals they used. At one point, PHASE was getting 60 calls a week from worried Silicon Valley workers. (PHASE research contributed to the description of chemical dangers appearing in this chapter.) The same year, a controversial Cal-OSHA study found "no evidence of chronic health hazards" in the semiconductor industry. Critics found the study limited in scope and cursory. Mike Williams, the study's principal author, found a job as chipmaker AMD's director of health and safety. Subsequently, the planned NIOSH study of electronics workplaces was dropped, as was a workers' compensation insurance investigation.[8] Until 1983, not a single study of electronics workers' health was completed.[9] When preliminary results of the first U.S. study underscored the dangers, the industry downplayed them, sought to protect itself legally, and promised, someday, to launch its own study.

Preliminary results of the Digital Equipment Corporation (DEC) study of several hundred Hudson, Massachusetts plant workers attracted national attention in December 1986. The focus was on workers who process microchips. Summaries of the study were released to DEC and the *Boston Globe*. The study, according to *Globe* reporter Bruce Butterfield, found "double and higher the incidences of worker-reported rashes, headaches, and arthritis" and, among male workers, "significantly higher incidences of nausea." The most publicized finding, however, was of a twice-normal miscarriage rate—39 percent—among workers in wafer-etching areas. An alarming 29 percent miscarriage rate was found among wafer photolithography workers.

Liable for damages from injured workers' lawsuits, the industry responded by denying, as it has for years, a causal connection between clean room chemicals and fetal damage. Amid much dissembling over the study's results, some firms adopted "precautionary" policies that appeared to deal with the problem. DEC promptly banned on-site interviews with workers at the Hudson plant, and then announced a policy of free pregnancy testing and job transfers for all women of childbearing age who worked in the high-risk areas. AT&T went furthest, mandating job transfers out of controversial clean room work for pregnant women. Despite evidence that clean room chemicals (such as glycol ethers) cause shrunken testicles, not to mention a variety of disorders in male and female laboratory animals, none of the chipmakers would guarantee transfers for exposed male workers, who, the industry explained, weren't having the miscarriages. The industry refused to consider replacing the toxic chemicals, instead of the workers. On the contrary, SIA spokesperson Sheila Sandow responded to the DEC-sponsored study by noting that women working in certain chipmaking areas have a "personal responsibility" for their health and pregnancy.[10] The industry's statistical sleight of hand, censorship, and press agentry support a milieu of contrived ignorance about clean room work that multiplies the dangers workers face.

Difficult to detect, camouflaged by indistinct and time-released symptoms that afflict workers unevenly, the hazards of clean-room acids and gases are dismissed even by most workers.[11] Vigilance is uncommon (as if the decision to live and work near the San Andreas Fault, which promises one day to violently sever and collapse much of Silicon Valley, impairs sensitivity to danger). A psychology of indifference emerges, encouraged by jammed production schedules, supported by a distracting focus on chip yield, and reinforced by the energy-sapping inertia of workplace ritual in a surreal environment. The cues that should alert one to danger instead bolster indifference.

Gowning up in outfits that outwardly resemble protective clothing provides the vague sense that we are preparing *ourselves* for another environment, much like putting on boots, coat, and hat for a winter outing. But the bunny suits provide no protection from the chemicals; rather they protect the clean room from *us*—the invisible particles our bodies throw off with every slight movement. Yet more than once have I heard workers (and in one case, a manager) speak of the bunny suit as if it guarded against danger.

The laminar flow also imparts a false sense of safety. Laminar flow and air filters are designed to extract particulates only, not dangerous fumes, traces of which can circulate undetected for hours, especially in older fabrication areas. In some clean rooms, the forced air can "kick up" toxic fumes, spreading them outward and upward toward noses and eyes. Still, the sound and feel of flowing air lends a deceptive "cleanliness" to the ambience. The ambience is misleading in a distinctly modern (i.e., ambiguous) way.

What sorts of dangers are workers exposed to?

The human nose cannot detect arsine (gaseous arsenic) until it reaches a concentration twenty times the established—and probably understated—danger threshold; likewise with phosphine until it reaches a concentration six times the danger threshold, and diborane 33 times the threshold. Heart palpitations, pneumonia, anemia, skin cancer, and damage to the liver, kidneys, spinal column, and eyes are among the milder symptoms that we know these chemicals induce.

Hydrofluoric and hydrochloric acids are used to harden and etch microchips, in electroplating processes common to the computer industry, and by assemblers outside the clean room to retard oxidation of the solder that attaches chips to boards. Like the gases mentioned above, hydrofluoric acid cannot always be felt immediately. But even a diluted concentration can seep through the skin, destroying tissue in its wake and causing extremely painful, slow-healing ulcers. The damage is not always easily or immediately reckoned. The same acid may eat away at the calcium in a worker's bones, especially the lower back and pelvis, thus preparing the possibility years later of a fracture, not ostensibly linked to the occupational environment.

Repeated exposure to hydrochloric acid irritates the skin and the upper air passages. The resulting symptoms—laryngitis, bronchitis, dermatitis—double as those from a cold, hay fever, or other allergies. This resemblance makes it possible to dismiss the occupational connection, a resemblance electronics firms take systematic advantage of during injured workers compensation hearings.[12]

Trichloroethane (TCA) and methylene chloride, chloroform, and carbon tetrachloride are used as solvents to clean the chips, disk-drive actuators, and computer boards. They contain cancer-causing stabilizers. In small amounts, they too are undetectable and cause dermatitis, depression, and mental dullness.

Many of these substances induce "sensitization" or "chemical hypersensitivity," a dread condition that multiplies the harmful effects of even small exposures to chemicals. This disease is easily the most controversial, confusing, and alarming for all involved, including the medical community, among whom immunological knowledge is in a state of primitive accumulation. This condition is known variously as "environmental illness," "twentieth-century disease," or "chemically induced T-cell inadequacy." Company lawyers and doctors dismiss it as a "psychosomatic disorder." But by less biased accounts, the diagnosis reads like a technical description of AIDS, acquired immune deficiency syndrome.[13]

"Chemically-induced AIDS provides a picture similar to virally-induced AIDS," according to an immunologist who has treated over 400 cases of T-cell inadequacy, half of them Silicon Valley workers.[14] The AIDS-phobic American public knows nothing of its *chemically induced* relative, even though it is transmitted at workplaces where hundreds of thousands of women and men work.

The immune system is a crucible of microbiological war and peace. Whether incited by a perceived or real threat (a psycho-somatic border the immune system straddles), it acts as both sword and shield. But its sentinels are confused and deceived by a world where substances tinker with the immunological balance evolution has struck. A plethora of new chemicals and viruses generates immense pressure to adapt, and to do so quickly. Apparently, this pressure pushes our immunological resources to the limit to preserve health in the interim.

This pressure to successfully adapt and preserve is played out microscopically. Essential to the body's immune system are the T-cells that detect disease at the cellular level. The sentinel T-cells sense an offending virus or chemical as it enters the body, and then dispatch B-cells, the antibodies or cellular foot soldiers, to dispel the invading substance.

Research suggests that virally-induced AIDS tends to *deplete* T-cells in its victims. In contrast, the limited and contested evidence available suggests that chemically-induced AIDS may render T-cells dysfunctional, rather than deplete them.[15] When chronically exposed to one or a combination of toxic substances, an electronics worker's overstimulated T-cells may simply fail to regulate the B-cells properly. B-cells—and accompanying allergic reactions—are unleashed at the slightest provocation. The confused and overworked immune system fails and in some cases never recovers. As this occurs, mere traces of toxic substances can induce violent and life-threatening allergic responses. Workers who bring a history of allergies to the clean room seem to be predisposed to this condition.

The clean room is a chemical cornucopia. The chemicals it pours forth are found in products that occupy the aisles of pharmacies, hardware stores, automotive shops, and supermarkets and thus find their way into the cabinets and cupboards of kitchens, boudoirs, and bathrooms. These become quarantined territory for many chemically injured electronics workers. For example, workplace exposures to chlorine gas can result in allergic reactions even to mild laundry bleaches at home. Clean room exposure to the fetal toxin glycol ether may not only cause miscarriages, but may also induce hyperallergic reactions to the traces of glycol ether in printing ink, paint, perfume, cologne, and oven and glass cleaners.

With a weakened immune system, the injured worker is prey to a host of opportunistic infections and viruses. The list of symptoms and conditions is long and painful to contemplate: chronic headaches, hyperventilation, colds and influenza, short-term memory loss, laryngitis, eye, bladder, lung, breast, and vaginal infections, menstrual problems, inability to conceive, and spontaneous abortions, some of which have occurred in company washrooms. So insidious is the immunological damage that it may also compromise the effect of antibiotics and conventional treatments. Victims typically require a variety of expensive physical and psychological therapies.

Rivaling the physical misery of chemical injury is the isolation to which it banishes its victims, who now must avoid casual contact with chemicals that are everywhere. This can mean a forced and open-ended retreat from society—friends, lovers, parties, dining out, even walks or shopping trips.

The only feature *San Jose Mercury News* article on this topic provided a glimpse of a chemically-injured clean room worker's modern hermitage:

> She doesn't venture out much beyond her house, which she cleans with nothing stronger than Ivory soap…She no longer keeps pets. She can't bathe her children: chemicals in the tap water make her sick. A trip to the grocery store means a raging headache and a nosebleed by the time she's through. Before she worked at AMD [Advanced Micro Devices], she reacted only to tomatoes and penicillin; her current list of allergies extends from auto exhaust, beef, and chlorine to wool.[16]

Another disabled and now socially isolated worker told a *Ms.* journalist, "I used to have so many friends. I used to have parties." Violently allergic to hair spray, perfume, cigarette smoke and plagued with ever present headaches, she has difficulty concentrating and remembering things. "I want to be sharp like I used to be. I want to be interesting."[17]

In the constricted world of the chemically injured, we find the tragic apotheosis of the crescendo—the sense of isolation and removal from the world that the clean room imparts to its workers.

Why do firms choose women to work inside clean rooms?

In deference to the fragile wafers—rather than to the dangers that loom everywhere—the workers move in eerily cadenced motion that resembles the tentative movement of astronauts slightly free of gravity. Sudden movements raise eyebrows and suggest accidents. This restrained, unspontaneous motion is the preferred body language. It is a language not everyone can speak, and one which managers bear in mind when screening job applicants. They select women, disproportionately recent immigrants from Central America, the Pacific Rim, and Asia, for the most tedious clean room jobs.[18]

"Men as a group do not do as well" at the lonely, detailed, and monotonous tasks, confides a male clean room manager. "I'm not talking about [women's] little fingers being more agile [than men's]. That's bullshit. But just the way our society trains women and the [lack of?] opportunities that they have, cause them to be more inwardly directed." The same manager applauds the suitability of maternal instincts to clean room work. "A lot of the dealing with children gets transferred to dealing with wafers: [the wafers become] 'my babies, be careful.' "[19] Perhaps these observations are rationalizations for management's *primary* attraction to women (low pay) and recent immigrants (gullibility). But more than a semblance of truth clings to this rationalization.

The Latin, Asian, and Pacific Rim countries from which so many clean-room women hail are experiencing rapid, if uneven, modernization. So the comparison to middle-class American culture—the culture of permanent modernization—is not always a stark one. But by differences of degree, the more traditional Latin and Asian cultures impoverish a woman's expectations for herself, binding her more tightly to the world of child-rearing, housekeeping, subservience to men, and poverty-level wage labor. In its traditional or modern versions, it is a world that supports virtues esteemed by clean room managers: diligence to demanding work, humility before male authority, and a halting estimation of self-worth. The women earn between $4.50 and $10.00 per hour—pay that requires regular overtime, or other incomes, to constitute a living wage in Silicon Valley.[20] Many of the women are not wise to the traditions of American wage labor and workplace rights. This is disadvantage enough. Many, however, suffer a special anxiety: they are here without immigration cards and stand to lose everything at a moment's notice. Some have applied for amnesty. All are victims of a humbling sociology of approval.

By dint of time, attention, and pampering, clean room work approaches that of a 24-hour nursery. For six to seven days a week on eight to twelve hour shifts around the clock, the women move gracefully from process to process, gently bearing *cassettes* or *boats* of delicate wafers from the photolithography of the *steppers,* to the arsine and chlorine doping of the *ion implanters,* to the acid baths and gas clouds of the wet and dry *etchers.* Even gloved hands are too rough for the brittle wafer; workers use vacuum wands, plastic tweezers, or custom pronged tools to "handle" them. Drilled by management in misplaced priorities, many women perceive the most demanding aspect of their work—wafer handling—as the most dangerous. This is because wafer accidents are not easily forgotten, by anyone.

Stamped on each wafer are dozens of microchips. Workers learn quickly that the boat of 25 wafers they load and carry may represent thousands or hundreds of thousands of dollars. To most of the meagerly paid clean-room workers, that is like holding the world in your hands, which are soon putrefying in clammy surgical gloves. And the wafers must be loaded into the boats, carried, and unloaded often; each is resurfaced, doped and etched up to twelve times, microscopically scrutinized more than once, tested, and *back-plated* with gold. Wafer handling requires a sharp burst of concentration and worry, punctuating a routine of machine-tending that even clean room managers characterize as "dull" and "boring."[21]

The pampering prevents accidents to the vulnerable wafers, but it abets fatigue, which many clean room workers relieve with nicotine. On breaks in company lunchrooms they can be seen sitting together smoking cigarettes with almost tribal formality. "It's a ritual you can do quickly and yet it will allow you to relax," observes a clean room manager who doesn't smoke.[22] But you cannot smoke inside a clean room, where you may be stuck for hours at a time. To cope with the tedium and frequent overtime, a few succumb to the allure of amphetamines, though these are not favored as they are on computer assembly lines, probably because they tax patience too severely for clean room work.

One of the most fatiguing and other-worldly tasks falls to those who sit atop stools and peer through German microscopes or into Japanese X-ray scanning screens. Through these portholes, strained eyes seek misalignments and patterns of light, invisible to the untrained, that indicate scratches or particles on a wafer. These discoveries may spell disaster for the company's chip yield and usually set in motion a micro-detective story. The investigation generates paranoia among workers who may be implicated, reassigned to another shift, or laid off during a *blind prevention*—the closing down of the clean room until technicians determine the cause of the *yield bust*. When the cause is detected, there is blame to assign, and temporary layoffs can become permanent. This is one reason yield figures are always on the minds and tongues of clean room workers, much in the way the latest stock market quotations preoccupy speculators.

Other concerns cement the clean room's attention to yield. Yield figures are how clean room managers gauge work performance, how vice-presidents gauge clean room management, and finally, how boardroom executives reckon cash flows in the heat of production. In pursuit of a quarterly quota or a new product release, clean room managers may set entire shifts against each other in competition for the best yield. A surprisingly good yield may precipitate bonuses, free lunches, or spontaneous celebration. It may even temporarily relieve tension in executive stomach linings, bowels, and necks. High or low, the yield functions as a barometer of pressure felt by all. It is a fickle arbiter of human fate and perhaps the most conscious common frame of reference in the clean room. Like Odysseus and the Sirens' song, it focuses attention away from danger.

How often are workers exposed to dangerous substances?

The answer must be reconstructed from scattered clues that occasionally slip through a tightly meshed net of secrecy shrouding the labor process.[23] Pleading the sanctity of "trade secrets" in a highly competitive market, the semiconductor industry's production techniques, chemicals—even the brand names of its clean room equipment—constitute "proprietary information." In Silicon Valley, local fire departments are the only outside force privy to the chemicals unleashed by these firms. Daily logs that list evacuations and their effects, tapes from fume detection systems, injured worker dismissal memos—these clues are closely guarded by a handful of clean room and plant managers and the vice-presidents to whom they report. During injured worker compensation hearings, the clues are withheld by obliging lawyers and judges, or otherwise simply evaporate, like the volatile gases they point to.[24]

With hundreds of clean rooms in Silicon Valley, evacuations probably occur weekly, though they are rarely reported. A San Jose IBM worker told me of chemical leaks causing evacuations in his clean room on an average of once every three months; he had personally experienced twenty evacuations.[25]

Evacuations imply major exposures. These are likely outnumbered by chronic minor exposures of the sort that occur daily: leaky processing equipment that spews chlorine or silane clouds into the laminar flow, acetone-laced freon that blasts the faces of workers lifting wafers from ultrasonic vapor-cleaning equipment—the equivalent of sniffing airplane glue. Even *hooded* (ventilated) processing equipment leaks. A "state-of-the-art" dry-etching machine designed for inherently more dangerous gallium arsenide wafers comes equipped with its own laminar flow, but access windows and cracks in the transparent plexiglass doors provide an escape for chlorine vapors. And with most sealed and hooded equipment, the chambers that seconds ago contained arsine, phosphine, and xylene are opened by clean room workers removing a treated batch of wafers and inserting a new one.

Many—perhaps most—workers believe that compensation for on-the-job injuries and illnesses is covered by law. They see, in California and other states, regular paycheck deductions for "job disability" insurance. But this deduction is for disabilities sustained *off-the-job;* workers' compensation insurance covers those suffered *on-the-job.* The law compels employers to pay for and carry workers' compensation insurance or be "self-insured" against job-related damages, but it does not preclude firms from contesting workers' claims. On the contrary, employers are invited to do so.

The invitations issue from some familiar dynamics. Workers' compensation operates like most private insurance policies: premiums rise in relation to the amount of claims actually paid out by the insurance carrier. Since employers pay the piper, naturally they want to call the tune. Most of the larger semiconductor corporations (AMD, National Semiconductor, Intel, Fairchild, to name a few) *are the piper*—i.e., are self-insured. "For self-insured employers," according to Mandy Hawes, a Silicon Valley attorney and counsel for dozens of chemically disabled workers, "the relation between 'successful' claims and the corporate treasury is even more direct; if the employee wins, the employer [not an outside insurance carrier] pays." Self-insured or not, the firms see in disabled workers' claims something other than reflections of human tragedy.

The plaintiffs—workers claiming on-the-job injuries or illnesses—often face unemployment, lifelong medical bills and incalculable personal trauma. *Temporarily* disabled workers stand to win two-thirds of their average weekly pay (tax free)—after an uncompensated waiting period—and reimbursement for medical bills. A *permanently* handicapped worker's compensation claim may take years to be adjudicated. Attorney Hawes observes sardonically, "tremendous resistance to claims is commonplace [such as] paying outside counsel by the hour to throw blockades in the way of claimants." When injured claimants finally do get their day in court, they confront scales of justice weighted heavily in favor of the corporation.

To deny the plaintiff damages, the firms often respond at hearings in a manner that suggests they are the injured ones. Corporate experts exonerate themselves with testimony of "excellent safety records." Corporate lawyers block access to records, logs, etc. sought by the injured worker to establish a claim. Corporate doctors, also paid to wait in the wings at hearings, take advantage of the obscurities of chemical afflictions. The doctors take the bench to stare down the plaintiffs and conclude "the injuries are psychosomatic [i.e., imagined]," or contracted "off the job."

"Benefit schedules" in the workers compensation system limit the amounts for which the carrier may be liable. By the modern world's standards, the schedules offer very little, even in cases of total disability, for which the injured seldom receives more than $25,000-$30,000. This form of "pay out" supplements a two-digit monthly pension, vocational rehabilitation if applicable, and not a penny for reproductive or other "noneconomic" damage. All told, the penalties equal sums of money a semiconductor corporation might spend on a few days' supply of toxic chemicals.

Frequently the denial of claims borders on the ludicrous. For example, former high school gymnast and runner Anita Zimmerman suffers now from a pulmonary disease that makes it difficult for her to breathe—the result, she contends, of chronic exposure to leaking chlorine-based gas while working at AMD. AMD is contesting her claim, now several years old, and contends that Anita's problems are caused by asthma. As a child Anita was diagnosed as having asthma, but for fifteen years showed no symptoms until exposure to the chlorine leaks that took her job—and her breath—away.

Are "clean room" injuries preventable?

The industry claims that it is installing air monitoring systems in clean rooms, that these systems preclude the possibility of harmful exposure, and that as a result, clean room air meets threshold limit values (TLVs) for hazardous substances. The question is, what, exactly, do air detection systems detect? Industry must set the alarms at the TLVs cited by public officials. But public officials—local fire department, OSHA, and NIOSH inspectors—receive almost all TLV data from outside contractors, such as the fifteen-member committee of the American Conference of Governmental and Industrial Hygienists (ACGIH). A professional organization, ACGIH insists the TLVs "are not standards, but recommendations." This is because the ACGIH committee, according to a Cal-OSHA inspector, *does not itself conduct any substance testing.* Instead it reviews literature—literature that may reflect industry-sponsored research—and then makes recommendations.

As it is, a TLV, according to the ACGIH, is a "time-weighted average concentration for a normal 8-hour workday and a 40-hour work week to which nearly all workers may be repeatedly exposed, day after day, without adverse affect." The TLV is not weighted explicitly for fetuses of pregnant workers, for chemically "sensitized" workers, for workers with allergies, or for the overtime workers regularly log in Valley clean rooms. Moreover, the TLVs measure hazardous exposures for discrete chemicals: TLVs do not take into account the so-called "synergistic" effect—*the harm inflicted by simultaneous exposure to a variety of chemicals.* Although such concerted exposure is routine in many clean rooms, there is, in effect, no safe or permissible exposure level. "We don't have complete knowledge," acknowledged a Cal-OSHA hygienist who asked to remain anonymous. "We don't know the health hazard of a combination of toxics." The inspector's concern was echoed in a three-year National Research Council/National Academy of Sciences study. The study probed "the status of toxicity-testing" for a variety of chemicals. Its authors found no toxicity information available, and thus no solid basis for recommending TLVs for 78.6 percent of 48,523 workplace chemicals it considered. "This is of particular concern," the study observed, "inasmuch as the primary motivation for testing chemicals in commerce is their potential for environmental and occupational exposure."[26] Because of the dearth of social medicine in the United States, our modern air detection systems are working from an inadequate data base.

Air detection systems are long overdue and a step in the direction of improved safety. With alarms set at thresholds for deadly gases, the systems can warn workers to evacuate as dangerous exposures occur. Unfortunately, they are no panacea. According to Santa Clara Fire Department chemical specialist Campbell, the technology is too new— none of the systems have U.L. (Underwriter Laboratory) listings and "we probably won't have authorized specs" on the systems "for five to ten years." More troubling questions linger.

How often are the air detection systems functionally tested? Fire officials inspect Valley clean rooms infrequently—once per year at best—and do not, as a rule, administer such tests. Because the systems do not contribute directly to the production process, full and frequent testing may be overlooked. Some company officials have complained that the air detection systems, by sounding alarms with such frequency, interrupt production. In at least one AMD clean room, workers obtained evidence that a chlorine monitoring system was turned off—allegedly to save energy. Chlorine gas exposures ensued, prompting evacuations and injuring several workers. Are system sensors placed in the most dangerous areas? I have heard from more than one source anecdotes of sensors placed in corners, well away from potential leaks. According to fire department inspectors, many workers aren't aware that air detection systems have been installed, even though they often are in the best position to know where to place sensors. A combination of operator and maintenance engineering expertise is needed to properly deploy and frequently test the air detection systems. Unfortunately, poor communication and conflict between operators and their seniors is notorious. An industry sponsored clean room worker survey found that "Operators consistently complain that there is little useful communication between themselves and engineering, maintenance, or even managerial personnel. This problem is exacerbated by the operators' feeling that they are on the bottom of the work-force hierarchy and enjoy little respect from those above them."[27]

Even when public officials, freed from the task of examining electronics workers' health and workplaces, learn of a problem, their response is often dismal. On December 6, 1984, a Silicon Valley clean room worker called Cal-OSHA complaining that fellow workers couldn't hear the evacuation alarm signal, that evacuated workers weren't properly accounted for, and that fire precaution was wanting. The company, National Semiconductor, refused to grant entry to a Cal-OSHA inspector. Its spokeswoman Linda Baker explained, "We feel we don't have a problem." Baker added "our policy is to require [inspectors] to have a valid complaint to come in because with the kind of work we do, it is difficult to have any kind of disruption." Though such inspectors don't need warrants to enter most San Francisco Bay-area industrial premises, Cal-OSHA beat an obliging retreat from National Semiconductor's doorstep. (Two months later a court awarded Cal-OSHA its warrant.)

Finally, the unsavory fact is that most clean rooms were not equipped with air monitoring technology until the law compelled them to do so. By the "cost-effective" calculus in which both industry and government officials tend to assess human safety, air detection systems competed poorly against the latest productivity-boosting processing equipment, even though the latter may have cost twice as much as an air detection system, and even though it may have been scrapped in less than six months for a newer machine. How many workers suffered exposures as a result?

Are clean rooms the creations of evil men?

It is an old story. It recalls the maiming of meatpacking workers chronicled in Upton Sinclair's *The Jungle* or the stealing of breath from miners described in Orwell's *Road to Wigan Pier.* In those times, public pressure and direct action by enlightened and outraged workers and their allies prompted attention and redress, albeit too little and too late. Then the unambiguous evidence of industrial barbarism was forgotten.

The carnage in the electronics workplace is rarely scored in spilled human blood, more often in the invisible world of corpuscle and chromosome. It may have to grow considerably before the negligence is appreciated and acknowledged. Perhaps half a dozen magazines have run stories on the chemically injured workers of Silicon Valley; some of these deftly avoid obvious conclusions, diffuse responsibility for the atrocities, take corporate denials at face value, or conclude, as clean room managers often do today, that times have changed, that the dangers are no longer with us.[28] Others conclude that more study is required before the danger can be properly understood. This last conclusion is probably correct, though inadequate. Unfortunately, only a handful of people not employed by or beholden to electronics corporations understand the issues, and their suggestions of preemptive measures—protection that gives workers' health the benefit of the doubt—go unheeded.[29]

When one considers that many of the dangers are avoidable—that existing toxic monitoring technology remains unsold for lack of demand; that installed monitors are turned off to save energy or tampered with to allow higher exposures; and that public officials fail to enforce existing laws, deny funding for potentially revealing studies, issue toothless warnings and not even token fines—then the oversight escalates into criminal negligence.[30]

The industry's willingness to accept risks—albeit unknown ones—on behalf of its workforce might be less reprehensible if it lacked the resources to evaluate those risks. It doesn't.

At industry conferences and trade shows, exhibitors cite the latest studies and quote the last word on microchip contamination but are manifestly ignorant of human safety issues, or even that safety is an issue in the clean room. At one of the industry's largest trade shows, SEMI-CON/West, I wandered from booth to booth, inquiring about the safety aspects of the new technology on display. A few exhibitors expressed discreet alarm about the dangers, how glad they were that they "only sold the stuff." But many shook their heads, wrinkled their brows, and, disingenuously or not, suggested that safety was not their concern, or that they knew of no manufacturer of safety equipment.

The show's sponsor is the Semiconductor Equipment and Materials Institute (SEMI), which serves as liaison between vendors and consumers of the industry's technology. It also coordinates and publishes extensive and elaborate chemical, equipment, and process guidelines on the industry's behalf. Seventeen years passed before SEMI planned publication of a single safety standard for clean room substances or equipment. In Volume One of the *1985 SEMI Standards for Chemicals,* the following perfunctory disclaimer is the only mention made of safety:

> Because of the continuing evolution of safety precautions, it is impossible in this publication to provide definite statements related to the safe handling of individual chemicals. The user is referred to product labels, product data sheets, government regulations and other relevant literature.

In trade magazines such as *Microcontamination,* scientists, engineers, and chemists write treatises on "wafer ecology." They dissect the world class clean room and the objects of its managers' paranoia: particles. Graphic charts display statistical analyses of the average particles-per-breath that seep through workers' face masks and onto valuable chips. Ads purvey the latest device to cope with product contamination, like one which warns, "The Average Storage Box Can Hold 50 Wafers—And Over 4,000,000 Particles." A maker of clean room garments displays its slogan: "Packaging People to Protect Products." The articles and ads christen a lop-sided fascination with product contamination to the exclusion of human health. The articles and advertising reflect and reinforce the fetishized culture of engineers and managers with corporate treasuries to spend. Industry associations and trade journals are not encouraging corporations to spend in ways that are kind to the lives and genes of their workers.

The negligence of the industry is no less criminal for being the opaque product of essentially economic and bureaucratic forces, rather than that of manifestly evil men. The distinction is an instructive one. Clean room managers may genuinely care about their workers' health. But a low chip yield is a more likely source of insomnia because it is the more decisive force in the daily scheme of things. Privately, corporate executives may feel badly about the injuries inflicted by their ventures, but they comfort themselves with the notion that safety costs workers' jobs by diverting funds away from "productive" investment.

And what of workers? Although no one wants to blame the victims, their ignorance and inaction can be excused only so long. How many of their sisters must be stricken, fired, and denied compensation before workers take heart, reject the divisive calculations of job security, and act accordingly?

This controlled chemical catastrophe reflects a conspiracy of unexamined faith in the pursuit of profitable technology. This pursuit girds the entire high technology project and prompts corporations to charter themselves in ways that preclude all but inhuman concerns: their product's margin, its market, and above all, its competition. Competition is the Sirens' song. Inside the clean room, its rhythms score the hellish din of the crescendo, above which we hear so little.

4

Computer Builders & Hackers

Neurotic Romance?

The current computer and software development situation is like building bigger, more powerful cars while the world is running out of gas.

Computer marketing manager[1]

Put a pacifist to work in a bomb factory and in two months he will be devising a new type of bomb.

George Orwell[2]

Hacking had replaced sex in their lives.

Steven Levy[3]

We are awed by computer builders because we have succumbed to a conception of life in which the computer is nearly sacred. In the American office the computer is pronounced a necessity, even when corporate productivity and computer workers' health deteriorate as a result of its use.[4] At home, the personal computer is purchased in the heat of widely presumed need, though most gather dust from neglect.[5] Despite these misgivings (or perhaps because they are so rarely acknowledged), there is a firm sense that, as the businessman declares, "the single most important reason to have a computer at home today is for the future of our society."[6]

Like the rest of us, the computer builder rarely pauses to debate the politics of our national affection for the computer. He is too busy filling orders, and preoccupied with improving the product. As George Orwell observed in 1936, "the faculty of mechanical invention has been fed and stimulated 'til it has reached almost the status of an instinct." With remarkable prescience Orwell anticipated the contemporary milieu of electronics programmers and engineers: "People invent new machines and improve existing ones almost unconsciously, rather as a somnambulist will go on working in his sleep."[7] Today we can add nuance to Orwell's insight. Behind the cold logic and discipline implied by their "faculty of mechanical invention," the programmer and the engineer's relationship to work is intensely emotional, as are all creative projects. Programmers especially seem driven by an urge to indulge an erotic or child-like fascination with work and its tools. For many of them, work becomes play. Some proclaim it "art."[8] A vocal minority of computer journalists identify a highly evolved morality and politics among software and hardware designers: *hackers* in league against the bureaucratic, corporate, and police forces of the world. There are few more misleading notions.

The creative and complex labors of computer building resist management efforts to "automate" and de-skill the electronics design and programming occupations. This constitutes a tactical defeat for twentieth century capital. But it is hardly a political victory over work's sponsors. If the computer-skilled occupy a strategic corporate footing, they embrace corporate and military projects as their own; many know but few care how their products are used or who uses them.

The Seductions

Like much contemporary science fiction, the novels of William Gibson share a dystopian context. In them, scientists and computer engineers have complied with a corporate evolution of technology that corrodes civilization and cheapens daily life, often transforming entire regions and leaving inhabitants in retreat to a new dark age. Gibson's fiction is intriguing because he extrapolates from the present as imaginatively as he projects from an alien future.

In *Neuromancer* (1984) Gibson introduces his protagonist in "Night City," which (shades of Silicon Valley) "wasn't there for its inhabitants, but as a deliberately unsupervised playground for technology itself." Case, Gibson's drug-addicted, drifter-hacker, "saw a certain sense in the notion that burgeoning technologies require outlaw zones."[9] It is a corrupted world: computer experts are bio-electronically-aided mercenaries, information pirates, or charmed junkies. In Gibson's *Count Zero* (1986), a pubescent hacker, emotionally abandoned by his single-parent mother, assists underworld experts who bring gifted scientists in and out of global biotechnology conglomerates.[10] In both novels, youthful hackers barely survive a Faustian flaw: their deep attachments to ethereal computer networks. The networks, suspended in a semi-autonomous *cyberspace,* offer transport through an intuitive realm of carnal stimulation *(simstim)* and psychedelic constructs *(ice).* At times, Gibson is fatalistic about this romance of the "neurons"—the hacker's erotically-charged attachment to tools and "missions"—as well as the hacker's tacit collaboration with a corporate-dominated world.

For all its remarkable fantasy, Gibson's fiction betrays a grasp of the character and politics of computer builders that eludes the non-fiction of others.

In *Techno Stress,* therapist Craig Brod suggests that some computer specialists suffer symptoms of a "techno-centered state," a "form of over-identification with computer technology." Brod continues, "At its most serious, this form of techno stress can cause...the inability to think intuitively and creatively."[11] But the addictive kick for many computer workers is precisely the intuitive, creative, and emotional states they achieve at their terminals.

"Rapture. Epiphany," insists Michael, a system utilities programmer who claims that "the high that I'm getting out of it has very little to do with working with computers *per se,* but...with the kind of problems. I'd say it's really very creative."

"A feeling of total absorption. A feeling of, like, oblivion," says Victor, also a systems programmer. "I used to do drugs a lot, when I was in college. And when I started working with computers, my drug use was cut drastically." Steven Levy suggests that the programmer's "trials and tribulations" are rewarded by an "addictive" sense of "control," a "feeling you get...unlike any other feeling in the world. It can make you a junkie."[12]

Michael describes the flipside of his rapture: "You're bugged when it doesn't work. Profoundly bugged. Like, I'm disturbed. And in a really foul mood for a day or two when I'm working on something that I can't fix in an hour." Victor acknowledges the "depression [that] ensues after you finish writing a large project." Away from the lash of a deadline, some grow listless, others are like sailors on leave. And in between projects, many do leave. Loyal to projects and technologies more than to employers, programmers and engineers switch jobs with alarming frequency.[13]

The dark, brooding side of the computer builder is sometimes self-destructive. Computer journalists rarely dwell on it. In *Hackers,* Levy mentions in passing several suicide attempts by the Massachusetts Institute of Technology (MIT) Tech Square "hackers"; in *Star Warriors,* William Broad remarks that the California Institute of Technology "has academic pressures unmatched by any other school in the country... it has one of the nation's highest rates of suicide, almost every class losing several members over the course of four years."[14] A project manager in Tracy Kidder's *Soul of a New Machine* recalls that hiring for the computer-building project "was kind of like recruiting for a suicide mission. You're gonna die, but you're gonna die in glory."[15]

The volatility of the computer building workplace helps create the emotionally-charged atmosphere. Short product cycles and unsteady markets generate enormous pressure. Indeed, Michael's workplace ambience was like a "pressure cooker" in which programmers discouraged themselves from helping each other, from taking computer courses as a means of acquiring fresh skills, or even from "asking questions" of more experienced workers—all to avoid openly acknowledging their ignorance.[16] This "puts you on a footing of always having to go through the most tortuous route," according to Michael. This machismo creates an atmosphere of one-upmanship conducive to boosting productivity and corrosive of the solidarity that otherwise might flower amid such high-pressure work. In *Soul of a New Machine,* for example, Kidder documents Data General's ploy of competitively assigning to each of two programmers the task of building separate software emulators—only one of which was desired—to speed work on a new minicomputer.

"Testosterone-oriented people...are not bad necessarily; it's important to have that impetus, the push," says Victor. "The push" is not lost on project management, who, along with senior engineers, often encourage and exploit programmers' machismo. It is a delicate thing. Again, from Michael:

> My sense is that, if I work 18 hours a day for a week and...took a couple of days off, well, no one would tell me I can't take the time off. But no one would tell me to take the time off. There's a sense of "We'll cog as much work out of you as you are willing to give."

But Michael, who enjoys work immensely, does not condemn his company's exploitation: "It happens to be a happy medium."

"Brooding," "passionate," and "macho" are missing from the list of personality traits assigned to engineers and programmers by Silicon

Valley therapist Jean Hollands. In *The Silicon Syndrome,* Hollands' "Sci-Tech Man" is "coldly logical," "cautious," "dependable," "often aloof," "literal and logical vs. the imaginative and emotional."[17] Hollands' "Silicon Syndrome" afflicts mainly male computer professionals who find themselves unable or unwilling to communicate emotionally with spouses. Hollands' therapy may help couples, but her "Sci-Tech Man" is too glib a diagnosis. The "Silicon Syndrome" more likely stems from the ardor reserved for work and its tools—an emotional attraction so consuming and irresistible that, like the junkie's lassitude between fixes, the computer builder's interest in the outside world and others becomes tentative or withdrawn.

Capital and modern technology apparently have seduced the computer builder with rare privilege: a genuine excitement that transcends the divide between work and leisure that has ruptured most industrialized civilizations. If Gibson's science fiction provides any clues, the computer-addictive persona is unlikely to protest his corporate- and military-sponsored projects, even when these threaten civilization. When computer-building becomes an essentially creative and emotional outlet, any politics larger than those governing access to work and tools seem distant concerns.

The Ghost of Charles Babbage

The canny Englishman Charles Babbage was a visionary and perhaps the original computer hacker. The mechanical circuitry of his "analytic engine" proved too subtle for the lumbering metallurgy of the nineteenth century. But the blueprint for his computing machine had all the markings of a forerunner. This earned Babbage a mantle in the pantheon of the computer's founding fathers.

Babbage's passion for control and manipulation animated other projects. In *On the Economy of Machinery and Manufactures* (published in 1832), Babbage encouraged capitalists to break up the labor process into ever-simpler tasks. In this way, Babbage argued, workplaces might engage less-skilled employees. Profits would rise because employers could pay common-laborers' rates instead of the higher craft rates. Babbage illuminated a perspective from which capital could actively reshape the "labor process."[18] The disquieting solitude of the assembly line was barely a scientific manager away.

Honored by computer history, reviled by social history, the career of Charles Babbage reflects contemporary tensions in the electronics industry. Computer builders today create "analytic engines" that help routinize and simplify many workers' labor—usually to management's specifications (if not uniformly to its advantage). The results would probably please Babbage.[19] If the intricacies of Babbage's analytic engine defied his era's technology, however, the mysteries of modern computer-building stymie Babbage-like campaigns to routinize the computer expert's labor. It is the growing complexity and innovative context of the computer-building project that seduces the computer builder and frustrates his managers.[20]

Computers are among the most complex and short-lived commodities ever created. Their escalating complexity is something of a riddle: as today's computers become more powerful, more specialized, and easier to use, computer hardware and especially software become more complex to design, develop, and support.

The size of computer operating systems provides a clue to the growing complexity. One release (4.1 BSD) of the widely-used UNIX operating system consisted of 33,000 lines of code. The subsequent, more sophisticated release (4.2 BSD) leaped to 70,000 lines—more than double the size and intricacy of its predecessor. Another much-used operating system—VMS—has grown to 2 million lines of code. To these sums must be added application program and communications code. Modifying a system of this size—or integrating it with another system— becomes an increasingly unwieldy task.

A parable from the annals of Apple corporate history also illustrates the trend. In 1976, Steve Jobs and Steve Wozniak hand-assembled the first Apple computers in a Silicon Valley garage. An unpolished contraption, the Apple came without case, keyboard, and power supply; this reflected its market of hobbyists, who supplied their own. The Apple had no specific application other than tinkering, which Wozniak invited by sharing the Apple's design specifications.[21]

Within a decade, Apple, now a Fortune 500 corporation, introduced the Macintosh, arguably the most technologically advanced personal computer the world had seen. "The Macintosh has been optimized for the professional or business user; the hobbyist has been firmly shut out," a hobbyist observed. The Macintosh's sophistication hinted at a profound design complexity:

> ...the Mac is much too complex for one person to hold in his head at once. With a simple old machine like the Apple II, if you understand digital circuit logic and assembly language, you can see how the whole thing works...It probably takes a whole team just to understand the Macintosh at that level.[22]

The evolution of Apple products embodies larger trends in the electronics industry. These trends—relentless innovation and increasing product refinement—make electronics development, maintenance, and management an inherently unstable, as well as increasingly complicated, undertaking. Innovation—faster chips, denser memories, and expanding network interfaces—can suddenly change entire programming "environments" or render system "technologies" obsolete. Andy Hertzfeld, the most heralded member of the Macintosh design team, described the mercurial culture of computer development in 1985: "Computers are still in their infancy, and essentially everything gets reinvented every five years. Suddenly you have five times as much memory to work with, if not ten times as much, and the rules start to change."[23]

Apparently, the more costly development component was software, a field that stubbornly resisted the incorporation of automated tools.[24] *Computer Design* magazine observed in 1987 that alongside a declining relative cost of developing hardware for new systems, "software now accounts for about 80 percent of the development expense for new systems...software maintenance costs are even higher."[25]

Corporate management was taking stock of the complexity and instability of bringing new products to life and not liking what it saw. For programmers, long, large, and complex development projects often meant exposure to new technology and more: the possibility of a creative and exhilarating personal experience. These ineluctable aspects of the computer builder's culture were at once manifestly productive and difficult to control for capital. Managers, after all, could not hasten the creativity of program-writing or chip-designing by adjusting the speed of an assembly line. Nor could project progress be measured in lines of code per programmer per day. These dilemmas inspired Babbage-like efforts to reduce the work's complexity without extinguishing its allure. In ways that would be difficult for Babbage to appreciate, computer engineers and programmers have collaborated with efforts to manage their labor—usually without simplifying or routinizing the labor itself. The desire to encourage sophistication yet control complexity is inscribed on the banner of *structured techniques.*

The Computer Blind

Under various names and models, structured programming techniques attempt to introduce capitalist efficiency into the complex process of software engineering. Most firms claim to practice structured techniques ("If you don't do it now, you're a dinosaur," observed a well-traveled UNIX systems programmer of structured techniques in Silicon Valley in 1985.) Both managers and programmers favor structured programming, but typically for very different reasons.

To managers, structured programming is a means of controlling work—of focusing intellectual toil—to improve productivity and product reliability. One critic, for example, concluded that structured programming is "the manager's answer to the assembly line, minus the conveyor belt but with all the other essential features of a mass-production workplace: a standardized product made in a standardized way by people who do the same limited tasks over and over..."[26] It's true that structured techniques are typically implemented from above, especially in military contractor and large civilian firms. And by adopting rigid "programming environments," some managers hope to "enforce" programmer discipline.[27] But the principles of "scientific management" are not easily adapted to the management of scientists.

To programmers, structured programming means a logical method of inquiry and analysis—an approach made necessary by increasingly complicated computer designs. Using structured techniques, programmers can conceive of and attempt to write complex software a little more simply. Systems programmer Victor's response is probably typical; Victor initially opposed structured techniques as a politically-inspired incursion of planning and method into the willy-nilly realm of programmer autonomy.[28] Now he says, "It's the only way you can write a program bigger than you can keep in your head at the same time."

If structured techniques promise to help managers control programmers, programmers adopt the techniques to help them design more complex products. Consultant Philip Metzger suggests the evolution of structured programming has begun to accommodate both objectives. Metzger observes "an increasing tendency...to bind more closely together management and programming techniques." Metzger, a structured programming advocate, continues:

> What strikes me about all these [structured] methodologies is that they are *both technical tools and management tools*. In every case they assist technical people in the execution of their jobs, all the way from analysis through designing, coding, and testing their products. But at the same time these techniques are helping technical leaders and managers to control the development process.[29] (emphasis added)

What does structured programming really mean? With it, can management really "control" the labor process?

In the tradition of Babbage, structured techniques imply breaking up the job of writing a software program into modules, or groups of relatively simple, isolated, step-by-step job tasks. In this way, a program with a projected length of 4,000 lines might be broken up into ten jobs of 400 lines each. Managers and project leaders then assign modules to project team members, who work on them more or less simultaneously.[30] Fewer bugs are said to survive the rigors of structured programming because of its modular construction, its taboo on types of code that entice bugs, and "structured walk-throughs"—often harrowing presentations in which members of a programming team scrutinize and police each other's work for logic or structured "coding irregularities."

Although structured techniques have helped programmers write more complex programs, they have advanced management's agenda toward enhanced productivity very little. Sometimes the "structure" of the design or its specification is flawed, and work on completed modules must be drastically revised, accompanied by budget overruns and project delays.[31] The parcelling out of work also removes overview from those who perform the work and who therefore are well-placed to spot integration-related problems; as a result, the modules may not compile or work well together. Despite structured techniques, coding errors remain an unwanted guest at the table of computer design and development.[32] Reliability has eluded new and many old computer programs, and most managers continue to fight a losing battle to reduce maintenance and upkeep on installed versions of software products.[33]

By the mid-1980s, many of the claims advanced by structured technique consultants were simply insupportable, as the following trade journal feature acknowledged:

> Although structured methods have clearly extended the possibilities of computer programming, they have been less than satisfactory when dealing with large, complex systems, particularly those that are highly interactive and whose specifications are therefore difficult to pin down early in the development cycle. Backlogs continue to grow, bugs proliferate, deadlines are missed, maintenance is as tough as ever.[34]

Just how much structured programming actually affects productivity and reliability (if at all) is hotly debated.[35] In addition to making possible electronics projects of greater complexity, however, structured design and development techniques also accelerated a trend toward subdividing work. Today's programming job titles reflect this occupational fragmentation: a Systems Analyst may design a programming project; a Project Leader and Programmer Analyst may divide it into jobs;

a Systems or Chief Programmer may write the integration software that makes modules compatible with a certain protocol or hardware interface; an assortment of adjectives—Associate, Assistant, Junior, Senior, etc.—identify the programmers who write the modules and perhaps specialize in a certain operating system, or in communications, device, graphics, and other kinds of software. "We're seeing the death of the general purpose guru," observed Michael (the UNIX system utilities programmer).

The fall of the "general-purpose guru" tempts some to conclude that structured programming was a successful management conspiracy to deskill programmers' work. According to computer sociologist Phillip Kraft:

> [P]rogramming is no longer the complex work of creative and perhaps even eccentric people. Instead, divided and routinized, it has become mass-production work parcelled out to interchangeable detail workers.[36]

One might divine such a trajectory if all one read was structured programming texts written to management audiences. But computer programming, unlike so many other occupations, has eluded the broad sweep of deskilling theories. It remains a Babbagian nightmare. Even subdivided among many programmers, computer building requires great skill and grit. As Michael observes: "I'm a utilities guru...I'm not going to stop there. I'm not interested in just that. But you can see how things are becoming large enough so that it's enough for one person to know only that."[37] Tom, who was designing nine microchips using powerful computer-aided-design software tools, defends the irreducible skills he must bring to bear on his highly automated work: "it's like writing; whether you use a typewriter or a wordprocessor, you still have to know how to write."[38]

Although widely implemented, structured techniques promise results that, at best, remain controversial. Programming is hardly any simpler, less harried, or less overtime-consuming than a decade ago, which is comparable almost to an eon in the electronics industry. Structured techniques favor a more disturbing if less apparent trend: a division of labor that discourages product awareness among the computer builders.

By dividing and subdividing the work, structured techniques may make complex programs easier to write, even more possible to conceive—but they also erect barriers between the programmer and the perhaps hostile applications of his or her project. This is so because structured programming dangles before the software worker's busy eyes a carrot that evokes not the project's final form—a tangible commodity—but instead an ambiguous module of code. Programmers are not compelled to acknowledge the program's purpose while they create it, since they typically require even less information about the application as a whole than about the internal requirements of the module fragments.

Look behind the cubicles where computer builders are at work. You will see hardware designers working on one board or one chip at a time, unmindful of the application. You will observe programmers writing modules of code that perform such innocent tasks as counting transactions and storing the total in a table file. You will hear a project leader assign an entire computer program design without explicitly mentioning that, for example, the Pentagon will use the software to refine an experimental missile. You will observe a project team warm to the intellectual challenge of successfully developing a product, ignorant of its use. You are likely to conclude, as most programmers and engineers do, that all applications appear equal, differing only in the amount and kind of work required. There is no need—nor desire in the military contractor's workplace[39]—for more than a handful of project leaders, marketing people, and executives to know about a final application. Structured programming and the intricacy of computer-building encourage the myopia.

The Subversions: Pranks or Politics?

Hacker is a confusing late twentieth century stereotype. For hundreds of years, *hacker* identified an inexperienced or unskilled person.[40] Today, a hacker is a resourceful computer expert, furiously developing high-technology,[41] or a computer prankster who questions authority and breaches security.[42] The hacker is also the graceless *nerd,* a throwback to the "absent-minded" scientist of the 1950s and 1960s.[43] The confusion marks a reputation borne awkwardly by computer programmers and electronics engineers. Most are reluctant to declare themselves hackers, at least to the outside world. Yet hackers and computers enjoy remarkable popularity.

Movies, videos, and television programs depict computer savants wielding exotic tools, committing or solving "computer crimes." Science fiction and suspense novels borrow props, idioms, and plots from the electronics industry workplace.[44] In adventure comics and cartoons, the appeal of the computer-aided hero rivals that of the side-armed cowboy in the pulp genres of a century ago. The hacker, like the cowboy, is a lonely male drifter who stalks an expansive frontier; among hackers and cowboys, outlaw elements provide ready material for popular folklore, and both inspire awe and emulation in the younger generation.

The hacker's popularity stems from the credible belief that he is at the center of a force that is clearly shaping the future. The concrete roles computer technology plays in modern life are less clear. The hacker is at once an exciting and ambiguous figure.

The computer imposes itself at work and play for a multitude of purposes and projects. Apparently, computers can help us predict drought or detonate missiles, give us wristwatch TVs, or detect ozone deterioration. Those who design, develop, or tinker with computers embody these powerful and often conflicting purposes.[45] This ambiguity is too untidy for most journalists and their editors. As a result, the computer builder is often made the subject of unqualified media worship, while the outside hacker is declared an enemy of the people.

In the mid-1980s, male high school and college students—"hackers," "crackers," and "cyberpunks"—broke into nearly every important national and private computer network in the United States. "From the local hobby club's bulletin board to the Defense Department's worldwide Arpanet, nothing seems to escape the hackers' skills," observed an *Electronics Design* editorial in 1983.[46] In 1988, a *Business Week* cover story was still sounding the alarm: "disabling a vital computer and communications system can be as easy as cutting a critical power line or typing a few commands on a keyboard...the consequences of that exposure can be disastrous."[47] On public and underground electronic bulletin boards, hackers continue to advertise the telephone numbers, protocols, and passwords to "secure" computer systems.[48]

The quasi-legal computer probing by alienated U.S. youth is a revealing phenomenon. Sheriffs, deputies, marshals, and federal agents raid their bedrooms and seize their computers in a manner suggesting high crime. Lurid headlines brand them as outlaws or political terrorists and encourage us to reject hacking as a social menace perpetrated by deviant adolescents. Consider the following sample headlines from U.S. newspapers:

Navy, Space Lab Computer Systems Invaded
Reporter Threatened by Hackers
U.S. May Move Against Youths Over Bank Taps
Vengeful Teenagers Hack Away at Reporter's Credit Rating
Prank Calls Go High-Tech
Hacker, 13, Arrested in Credit Card Fraud
A Tale of Hackers, Robbers, and Spies
Teens Got Pentagon Codes: Computer 'Hackers' 'Moved Satellites'

Are teenage hackers political terrorists? They are typically white, upper-middle-class adolescents who have taken over the home computer (bought, subsidized, or tolerated by parents in the hopes of cultivating computer literacy). Few are politically motivated although many express contempt for the "bureaucracies" that hamper their electronic journeys. Nearly all demand unfettered access to intricate and intriguing computer networks. In this, teenage hackers resemble an alienated shopping culture deprived of purchasing opportunities more than a terrorist network. Despite countless opportunities, none so far has intentionally committed any grievous evil against humankind—more than can be said for those with officially sanctioned access. Instead, most are out to explore the world beyond the limited horizons of suburban life. As John Markoff observed in an article about Oryan Quest, a Silicon Valley youth arrested for breaking into Stanford University computers:

> For many teens, the...electronic bulletin boards became a kind of high-tech clubhouse and launching point for exploring a new digital universe. Computers linked by networks created a more compelling world than the most captivating session of Dungeons & Dragons, a role-playing game practiced by teenage science-fiction and fantasy fans. Maybe Mom and Dad wouldn't let their kid out after dark on a school night, but now he was free to travel anywhere in a far-flung cybernetic world, from the safety and comfort of his bedroom.[49]

The political-technical hacker journal *2600* reserves most of its space for protocols and tips on system entry and exploration, regardless of authorization. Access to information and systems, in fact, constitutes the common interest on the cyberpunk and cracker scenes. *2600* occasionally defends this interest in a political voice. When it does, the hacker's concerns often merge with those of the mainstream American consumer. In "Our Wishes for 1986 and Beyond," *2600*, sounding almost like Ralph Nader, calls for

> reasonable prices on 'public' [bulletin board] services. Compuserve, Source, Dow Jones, are you listening? Is it any wonder you're constantly being ripped off [by hackers] with the outrageous prices you charge?[50]

When *2600* had its electronic bulletin board impounded for months by federal agents (despite "no evidence of wrongdoing"), *2600* editors retorted:

> Bulletin boards must be protected! They are a vital means of communication, a resource that can be used by more people every

day. Obviously, this freedom makes some authorities a little nervous...If there is illegal activity occurring, then the people responsible for it should be tracked down. This doesn't mean pulling the
plug on the service that enables them to speak. We have to make
an effort to define the difference.[51]

These are hardly the ultimatums and ravings of terrorists.
Like a rite of passage, the hacker's interest in illegal probing usually
withers with employment.[52] Jobs with computers (in the electronics
industry or elsewhere) provide maturing hackers with what they had to
obtain surreptitiously as pre-employed youths: access to powerful computing devices and networks.

If not a political terrorist, is the teenage hacker a criminal? The
cyberpunk phenomenon, Markoff reminds us, is fraught with criminal
opportunity:

> computers...run our hospitals, our factories, our banking system
> and government, weaving a fine web of electronic information that
> the nation increasingly takes for granted. But that dependence has
> left the most technologically advanced society vulnerable to its
> children.[53]

Increasingly, however, computer crime victims as well as legal
authorities have exonerated the teenage hacker. Asking "Why do hackers invade a data network?" *Electronics Design* editors answered:

> More often than not, their only answer is "because it's there." So
> far, most of the damage done to files and programs appears to be
> more accidental than intentional. In spite of both judicial and
> congressional grilling, greed can rarely be proven as a motive.[54]

In a scolding tone, *Electronics Design* cites network and system
vulnerability and blames the "cavalier attitude of the corporate data
czars" who call for "unenforceable laws against hackers" instead of
addressing "the glaring deficiencies in their systems."

In a similar vein, Levy reminds us that at MIT, the hacking "motive
was exploration, not fraud, and it was considered bad form to profit
illegally from these weird connections."[55] Apple inventor Wozniak, who
parlayed his penchant for (harmless) electronic pranks into a fortune,
defended hacking as late as 1985. A student at his Silicon Valley alma
mater was confronted with expulsion for breaking into the high school's
computer. Wozniak insisted that computer hackers "just want to prove
how far they can get. They're not out to destroy or take data. There's
never been a hacker who ever took $10 out of a computer account."[56]
Wozniak exaggerates a little; with few exceptions, however, young

computerists who run afoul of the law are rarely charged with intentionally damaging anything, but rather with "electronic trespassing," the crime of curiosity. In fact, it is not deviant-savant teenagers that commit computer crimes, but corporate employees.

Apparently in need of cash, or to even a score with management, or just for the hell of it, computer workers—from programmers to entry clerks—wreak havoc with computer systems that far exceeds the damage any teenage hacker has even unwittingly done. According to a National Center for Computer Crime Data project, in 1985, the statistically average computer criminal was 27 years old and "is nothing like the brainy computer science types portrayed by the media." Rather, they were most often "employees who got into disagreements with their employers and either took programs they claimed rights to or did damage to the employer's system."[57] The same year, a special *Wall Street Journal* feature on office technology and sabotage reported:

> a growing number of companies are moving to protect themselves from a nearby threat: their own employees. Much attention has been given to outside hackers who electronically break into sensitive computer files. But 'hackers have done less damage to corporate computer systems than overflowing lavatories,' says Robert Courtney, a Port Ewen, N.Y., security consultant. Dishonest and incompetent employees do the most damage.[58]

Why, then, has the stigma of computer crime descended so exclusively over the teenage hacker? Perhaps for the same reasons that less than 2 percent of computer crime is reported: corporations and federal authorities are not eager to publicize their vulnerability to their computers and those who operate them, including hundreds of thousands of "unskilled" computer operators.[59] *Business Week,* pointing to "the alarming vulnerability of computer systems—and the businesses and government agencies that rely on them," put the implications for upper management squarely into focus:

> The threat is eloquently simple: Computer networks and the information they handle are assets a company can't do without...The potential for trouble is even greater in the service industries that now dominate the economy. Every workday, U.S. computer networks transmit close to $1 trillion among financial institutions, an amount equal to 25 percent of the gross national product...changes in computer technology are making mischief easier. Increasingly, minicomputers and personal computers are being spread through offices and networked together. Such 'distributed processing' multiplies the potential points of access.[60]

This strategic corporate defenselessness is an odd duck in an age that has seen the routinization of work, the turning back of unions, the relocating of industries offshore, and many who proclaimed workers thereby stripped of all power.[61] Under reported and under publicized, employee computer crime quietly suggests something larger than petty electronic sniping and greed: a latent collective power available to millions of computer workers, a power that can press their political interests successfully against their employers everywhere. Sadly, this perspective is lost on journalists who either cry "wolf" at the "outside hacker" or instead advance a vague, elitist politics of technological liberation.

Stewart Brand (*Whole Earth Review*) suggests that computer experts are designing politically appropriate technology so successfully that they have "forced" corporations to market anti-corporate products that encourage freedom of information. Steven Levy (*Hackers*) articulates the *Hacker Ethic,* which embodies the explicitly populist political philosophy of the computer builder. Brand and Levy also credit hackers with saving the American economy. Inspired by his encounters with video game designers, Levy hails

> the arrival of a new kind of hero, one who fought with brains instead of muscle, one who represented America's bold willingness to stay ahead of the rest of the world in the technological battle of supremacy.[62]

Accordingly, the slogan that emerged from the first of several invitation-only "Hackers" conferences organized by Brand, Levy, and others in 1984 was "Keep Designing," also the title of an edited conference transcript published by *Whole Earth Review*. Brand introduces the transcript with what is perhaps his most concise statement of hacker politics:

> I think hackers—dedicated, innovative, irreverent computer programmers—are the most interesting and effective body of intellectuals since the framers of the U.S. Constitution.
>
> No other group that I know of has set out to liberate a technology and succeeded. They not only did so against the active disinterest of corporate America, their success forced corporate America to adopt their style in the end. In reorganizing the Information Age around the individual, via personal computers, the hackers may well have saved the American economy...The quietest of all the '60s sub-subcultures has emerged as the most innovative and most powerful—and most suspicious of power...These supposed lone wolves, proud *artistes,* in fact collaborate with glee.[63]

The evidence of solidarity and oppositional politics among computer builders is wanting. The historical record, as David Noble suggests of engineers generally, is to the contrary.[64] In the 1980s, the computer builders' political sympathies remain out of touch with mainstream populist opinion, officially speaking. According to an *Electronic Engineering Times* survey, computer builders favor "Star Wars" by a two-to-one margin. This, despite growing public opposition to it and widely known doubts about its feasibility. The survey also suggested the computer builder's perceived isolation from society: 87 percent answered no in response to the question, "Does the public understand engineers?"[65]

Unfortunately, the stereotyping of engineers as conservative, isolated people lacking social conscience is credible. They are accustomed to taking risks (such as drinking the water at their Silicon Valley workplaces) and to occasional individual rebellions (such as quitting their jobs). But they and their professional associations are strangers to the traditions of labor solidarity and collective rebellion. As Stephen Solnick observed, "most engineers seem to identify more with their particular industry or discipline than with other engineers." Solnick hoped that "they may finally realize that politics is not an 'improper' activity for their profession."[66]

Like most people, computer engineers and programmers grew up with little, if any, immediate exposure to open, collective rebellion against authority. During the heyday of the anti-Vietnam War movement, many were cloistered in technical institutes or mathematics and engineering departments of universities.[67] Others willingly accepted draft deferments in exchange for classified jobs at Lockheed or Boeing.[68] Today, many of these people are computer professionals who design hostile technology; some of them honestly believe in a strong American defense against a heartless communist evil.

There are also computer professionals who took part in cultural and political rebellions during the ferment of the late 1960s and early 1970s. Many were students in university liberal arts curriculums who have since found a living in the electronics industry. Some read the journals of *professionals for social responsibility* societies; an even smaller number purchase memberships in them; a precious few are politically active or refuse employment in military-related fields. In other words, the computer builders' politics are as muddled and mainstream as you are likely to find among any strata of U.S. workers. On the surface, Levy's *Hacker Ethic* suggests otherwise.

The *Hacker Ethic* was the code Levy gleaned from his study of influential computer entrepreneurs, programmers, and engineers from the 1960s through the 1980s. The code corresponds approximately to the artistic place and emotional stature computer hobbyists assign to their computers in personal life. As a characterization of the mature computer builder's politics, however, the *Hacker Ethic* is wide of the mark. The tenet *All information should be free* reflects the teenage hacker's desire for access to the latest computer technology. If this tenet were taken seriously, Levy and Brand's hacker elite could not draw their royalties and paychecks. *Mistrust Authority, Promote Decentralization* was not an exhortation to social revolt but instead referred to the hacker's preference for distributed, interactive computer systems rather than mainframe-based "batch" systems (the "hulking giants" controlled by a bureaucratic "priesthood" of operators who kept hackers' hands off the consoles).[69]

Here and there, Levy and Brand acknowledge the limitations in practice of the lofty politics they graft onto the computer builder's work culture. Levy writes of the world of the "hardware hacker," a "world where politics and social causes were irrelevant."[70] As interest waned in the once politically feisty Homebrew Computer Club, Levy discerned "not a planner-like contemplation of the social changes [made] possible by mass computing but the white-hot hacker fascination with technology."[71] As Brand observes of Levy's *Hackers*, "Levy portrays a gradual degrading, commercializing of the *Hacker Ethic*."[72]

Every day, an entrepreneur, a general, and a journalist praise programmers and engineers for their inventive accomplishment amid the bewildering detail of their work. On a strictly technical level, it is praise well deserved. But it is dearly paid for. Is it reassuring that, as we become more dependent on increasingly powerful civilian and military computers, we applaud the computer builders' indifference to the implications of our dependency? How can we encourage technological creativity yet protect ourselves against its excesses?

While there is no obvious answer, computer crime reminds us that the electronics establishment is vulnerable to challenges from below. In fact, computer access and technological expertise might someday constitute a check to political power—a force for popular control over hostile technology and its sponsors. Yet this ray of hope is overshadowed by ignorance and controversy. Many are prepared to publicly oppose the countless dark legacies of the computer age: "electronic sweatshops," military technology, employee surveillance, genotoxic water, and ozone depletion. Among those currently leading the opposition, however, it is apparently deemed "irresponsible" to recommend an active computerized resistance as a source of workers' power because it is perceived as a medium of employee crime and "terrorism."

The corporation and the government agency have proven disastrous stewards of the electronics worker's skills and of the social and natural resources the industry devours. Perhaps in a future society the technologists will discover emotional and creative outlets less wasteful and devastating than electronics. But we cannot afford the wager. If our aquifers and atmospheres are to survive the material transgressions of the electronics industry, we must learn to temper our destructive inventiveness with a social sensibility. In fact, electronics technology has become so powerful that its control is now crucial to the outcome of any sweeping social change. This suggests that a real struggle must take place for the political hearts of computer and technical professionals. We will clearly need some of them: who is better qualified to safely dismantle a missile silo, a breeder reactor, a chemical waste dump, or a Pentagon supercomputer than the people who design, build, and maintain such technology?

"Technology control" raises political hackles, and not just those of the technologist and entrepreneur who demand freedom for their enterprise. For decades, a minority of radical critics have advanced the slogan "let the workers run the industries" as a universal antidote to capitalism and to the centralized economies of "socialist" and "communist" regimes that have suppressed workers' organizations as ruthlessly as any capitalist class. But exclusive "workers' control" is too dangerous in an age of powerful and hostile technology. In our lonely era, many of the "workers themselves" have been seduced by their work and will defend it to the last person. We abdicate social responsibility to those who intend to "keep designing" high technology capital at our peril.

The "proud *artistes*," as Stewart Brand depicts the computer-building elite, must realize that their medium materially changes lives and food chains. We must find a way to control and when necessary limit the global resources available to those who propose, intentionally or otherwise, human or environmental degradation. And we must attempt to do so without suffocating our technical curiosities or encroaching too dearly on the independence of workers' organizations.

In the meantime, the computer builder's neurotic romance affirms the fierce passion some of us find in our work, as well as the dangers of blindly doing so.

5

The Cloistered Workplace
From Dungeons Come Dragons

I fall back on the relevance of some of my earlier experiences in government, in national security, where...scientists exchanged ideas on approaches to problems while the actual applications were frequently compartmented.

Former NSA and (Deputy) CIA Director Admiral
Bobby Inman on managing the Microelectronics
and Computer Technology Corporation[1]

The 4th of July Air Show provides a festive interlude during which Silicon Valley shows off its least understood and most silently birthed offspring: high technology, military issue. The jet fighters, assault helicopters, and spy planes attract half a million spectators—by far the largest annual public gathering here and nearly anywhere else in the U.S.[2]

Laden with computers and microchips, the military aircraft return to the Valley like prodigal sons. Estimates of the livelihoods that depend on military spending in the Valley run as high as 50 percent.[3] The Valley's largest employers are prime military contractors.[4] It is the hub for the $80 billion per year military electronics industry,[5] a development site for most missiles,[6] a funnel for military artificial intelligence R&D,[7] and a design center for Star Wars programs and for the avionics aboard most combat aircraft and bombs.[8]

Concerning its military preponderance, Silicon Valley is not so much boastful as resigned; without the military, the U.S. electronics industry might have been stillborn. In fact, there are signs of a timid but widespread resentment toward the military subsidy, which favors large

101

corporations over the fabled entrepreneur, and which has made Silicon Valley an incubator of unwholesome technology.

Many people say they would rather not work for prime military contractors. Some refuse to. Stanford University students attend occasional protests at the Lockheed Space and Missile Company. A distinct minority display bumper stickers that proclaim "A World Beyond War"—the therapeutic message of a Palo Alto-based national organization that advocates peaceful thinking as the path to world peace.[9]

The noisy July 4th Air Show, which ties up traffic and closes down commuting channels, provides a rare focus for these resentments. The rest of the year the military presence is camouflaged. It is unseen, like the $3 million underground bunker that is equipped with computers and two weeks of provisions for 70 Santa Clara officials who hope "to keep the city running" after a nuclear holocaust. Or disguised, like the Lockheed engineers who periodically visit Valley grade schools to treat children to "Mr. Wizard" science shows—but who spend most of their time designing satellites and missiles for use in a nuclear holocaust.

The most enigmatic camouflage is that which keeps knowledge of military products from the producers themselves. It is woven from a decades-old tradition of workplace secrecy. At primary contractors, explicit policies forbid workers from knowing a product's final use. Instead, they are offered project nicknames, a technical language, and a narrow way of looking at work; these obscure military purposes and, in the process, probably undermine product quality. Less formal but comparable policies produce similar results for workers employed by military subcontractors. As a result, a special ignorance structures life in the classified cubicles and shops of military electronics. Those who prepare the battlefields of the future need not dwell on the horrors of war to perform their work. The air show's family entertainment format caters to this sensibility; there are airstrikes without casualties, exploding napalm bombs without burning flesh.

For those prone to troubled consciences, the secrecy is functional. The prohibition of product application knowledge creates a "black box" productive culture in which work's purpose is ignored or forgotten. When programmers write "graphics display software" rather than missile performance reports, when rocket engineers hold back from discussing their work with friends, they shield themselves from responsibility for the horror their work makes possible. When fellow workers carry on like this, it imbues the workplace with an odd loneliness. That which they share—work—creates that which they must avoid talking about—work's products.

The unshared lives of military electronics workers extend beyond their workplaces. During an interview, I asked a Lockheed Space and Missile Company project coordinator what he worked on. He replied that he could not be specific. He paused and then said, "everybody knows that Lockheed makes missiles and spacecraft. It says that on the door. And I am not working on missiles." He then spoke of his wife, who also worked at Lockheed. Because each had a separate security clearance, however, they could not, and did not, talk to each other about their work. Sometime after the interview and work-sponsored therapy sessions, husband and wife separated.[10]

The military electronics worker's silence and isolation are redolent of the medieval monastery, its monks busy transcribing those works of antiquity deemed worthy by the papal censors. By accepting that certain questions are forbidden, even certain phrases unutterable, military electronics workers take vows of ignorance as well as of obedience. In exchange, they can imagine they have relinquished responsibility for their work to a higher authority. In the military electronics cloister, these imaginings are undeterred, and the silence is welcome.

The Forbidden Fruit

Behind a formica reception desk at a large microchip firm, a display case lists the day's special visitors: WELCOME! Litton Guidance, Hughes Aircraft, Lockheed, Raytheon.

Inside, "application engineers" help these and other customers design logic for military and business microchips. In its startup days, the firm did little military work. But a slumping civilian market led first to military subcontracting—designing chips for primary defense contractors—and then to classified work for the National Security Agency. One of the unclassified application engineers is Jeff, a Stanford graduate several months into his first electronics job.

The title "application engineer" is peculiar. For "security reasons," Jeff says, none can know their military customers' chip applications. This stricture does not impede their work. To design microchip logic for a Raytheon or Litton chip, Jeff need not know that it will store microcode for an on-board missile guidance system that may one day claim thousands of lives. "I don't know what it's used for, what system it's part of...usually only the company's name," Jeff says. Yet he is vaguely aware that Litton Guidance, Hughes Aircraft, Lockheed, and Raytheon are major military contractors.[11] He also has informal access to project-specific information at his workplace. Away from work, over pizza and beer, Jeff acknowledges that his company currently has six Lockheed contracts. From gossip among fellow engineers he has gleaned that some of the chips are destined for a radiation-detecting satellite device. I suggest that it may be connected to the Milstar project—Star Wars.[12] "It's just a part to me," says Jeff.

For Jeff, the moral or political implications of his work, its probable contribution to space-based missiles, the question of whether it increases the likelihood of war, are separate issues from the tasks he performs every day. This separation between work and work's product does not create tension for Jeff—nor is his aloofness exceptional. On such issues Jeff stands with most of the other application engineers, steeped in a culture of collective avoidance that is officially encouraged by their employers and Pentagon sponsors.

Fred once worked as an auditor for an oil company but now works for Lockheed as a software programmer with a security clearance. The security "doesn't bother" him: "Maybe I've just gotten used to it." Fred has grown accustomed to other things at Lockheed:

> I'm not thrilled with the application. What I do nicely separates itself from the application though, because what our graphics system produces is nothing different from what you might see in a magazine if they were plotting the gross national product year to year. So where my thinking goes every day, it's got nothing to do with those big nasty missiles.

Fred writes system-level code for a graphics package that displays data in a time-history plot. The software is not classified, but the data it handles will be. The data come from Trident missiles whose warheads are loaded with transducers and sensors that transmit in-flight performance records to Fred's software package. Aided by a work setting that divides programming assignments among fellow workers, his distance from the application is nearly infinite:

> It's very easy not to think about it [i.e., the missiles]...the finished product for me is when they can take data and put it on the screen. I get to see all of that. I don't see where that data came from [i.e., the missiles]....my product is a very small piece of a large thing which includes submarines and all kinds of things [e.g., missiles]. But the thing that I directly work on, I feel like I see the whole thing. That may be kind of unusual.

At Qubix, a startup company, laughter and enthusiastic chatter punctuate a programmers' meeting. Before a white board bearing cryptic

symbols, a presentation of Qubix software unfolds. The talk is sophisticated, specific, but makes no mention of Qubix's first customer—or the
customer's use for Qubix work stations.

When queried later on these topics, most Qubix workers acknowledge that the customer is General Dynamics. Asked if General Dynamics
makes assault jets, cruise missiles, and airborne missile and gun systems,
many plead ignorance. Their ignorance is hard to credit. At the time,
front-page articles were breaking the story of General Dynamics' Pentagon scandal. Many of the articles describe General Dynamics' long line
of military products. Uninformed or not, Qubix people are bothered by
my entreaties. Their responses suggest that military products are unpopular topics of conversation.

The ethics of making war materiel constitute an unspoken dialogue
among electronics workers. A widespread and informal *self-censorship*
complements official boundaries on what workers can know, and this
tends to preempt conversation. Of "big nasty missiles," Fred says he and
his approximately 70 fellow employees "don't talk much about that kind
of thing. I think the people around me tend to feel the same way. Like I
say, I stay away from politics." The social silence sustains a contrived, if
awkward, cognitive gap. For example, Fred let on that he knew surprisingly little about Lockheed's operations. He wasn't sure what went on
inside the Blue Cube (the U.S. military satellite command center adjacent
to Lockheed Sunnyvale),[13] or that Lockheed workers staffed the Blue
Cube, only that "I presumed, just the way people talked, that more highly
classified work went on there."

The Manhattanization of Military Electronics

The censorship, formal and informal, that pervades the contractor's
workplace is a legacy of the military's tutelage of microelectronics. The
rationale is that the less workers know, the less capable they are of
sharing secrets with hostile agents. The centerpiece of this worldview is
the "need-to-know" policy adopted by virtually all primary military
contractors performing classified work since World War II.

The need-to-know policy is adapted from the hallowed tradition
of the military mission. In the military, the concern is not so much that
access to privileged information may result in loss of life, but that it may
compromise the mission. (This is the spirit of the wartime slogan, "loose
lips sink ships," which reminded sailors and civilians to avoid discussing

fleet destinations and embarkation dates that might reach enemy ears.) This policy implies that those who actually carry out the mission, i.e., the subordinates whose lives are at stake, are kept in the dark by their superiors until the last possible moment.

The arms industry's need-to-know policies are thus an intrusion of military convention in the workplace, a tradition already apparent in the *chain of command* and *line* or *staff* models for dividing workplace authority. We are reminded of this lineage by the policy's workplace debut in 1942 during work on the Manhattan Project—the code name for the government's atomic bomb development.

Then, as now, the need-to-know policy created an atmosphere approaching that of the Inquisition. The best possible workplace was one purged of all but the minimum amount of technical detail required to complete a project. Project managers denied workers knowledge of product research and fabrication processes that did not directly bear on their work tasks. Project information—especially regarding the project's destination and use—was strictly and hierarchically controlled. Of the 150,000 persons who worked on the Manhattan Project, perhaps a dozen were allowed a "comprehensive overview of the project's plans and objectives."[14]

Four and one half decades later, a comparable minority of the workers who receive clearances are trusted with "comprehensive knowledge." For the rest, classified status does not, as popularly imagined, confer access to privileged knowledge. Instead, it grants permission to work more or less blindly.

If the public rationale for the need-to-know policy is to minimize espionage, its practical effect on employees' daily lives is to stifle awareness and discourage discussion of the hostile technology they create. This custom dates from the policy's first civilian application. Manhattan Project electrical engineer Robert Odell recalls working on the top secret project in Oak Ridge, Tennessee that developed the radioactive material used in the first atomic bombs dropped on Hiroshima and Nagasaki:

> I was among those who thought we were developing a new kind of fuel. Others thought it must be an explosive. *You didn't ask questions...*We were having a meeting in July of 1945 and one of the supervisors got a phone call in an adjoining room. It was from New Mexico. He came back with a big smile on his face and said, "It went off with a big bang." That was the first time it really hit me. (emphasis added)[15]

Today, the Pentagon continues to insulate the classified workplace with the need-to-know policy. In its *Industrial Security Manual for Safeguarding Classified Information,* the government provides this definition of a worker's need to know:

> ...a determination made by the possessor of classified information that a prospective recipient, in the interest of national security, has a requirement for access to, knowledge of, or possession of the classified information in order to perform tasks or services essential to the fulfillment of a classified contract or program...

The policy is variously implemented. At most primary contractors, including Lockheed (Silicon Valley's largest), the security classifications, in descending order of privilege, are top secret, secret, and confidential. Workers who share a clearance status, e.g., top secret, are also often segregated by project-specific clearances. That means they cannot exchange work-related information or enter each other's project area unescorted. Improprieties are "security breaches" whose implications may transcend the wrath of management, perhaps tripping the alarm of "national security."

What determines the level of clearance? Apparently, the Department of Defense (DOD) deems this question too sensitive to answer unequivocally lest the clearance title reveal the nature of a classified project. According to the *Safeguarding* manual, "top secret" refers to information or material "the unauthorized disclosure of which reasonably could be expected to cause *exceptionally grave damage* to the national security." The disclosure of "secret" material could be expected to cause *serious damage,* while leaks of "confidential" information could be expected to cause mere *damage.* Elaboration, as provided in the *Safeguarding* manual, is vague.[16]

Working to classified military specifications means that workers always have a ready excuse not to discuss the content of their work with their families or friends, or even among themselves. The atmosphere also discourages discussion of the military contractor's product line. For example, classified Lockheed machinists, plumbers, carpenters, and composite workers cannot openly acknowledge, even if they suspect, that they build missile parts. Companies instruct employees that shop talk off the shop floor is forbidden, or worse—grounds for clearance revocation, which may mean job loss (if the firm cannot or will not find unclassified work for the offender). A worker whose record bears the demerit of a clearance revocation is an unlikely job candidate for civilian or military work, since the demerit creates a subversive aura that most employers find troubling.

Of course, there is scarcely a workplace in which work-related gripes and gossip can be stifled. This the classified workplace does not attempt. "You can let off steam," the Lockheed project coordinator observes—as long as the steam has been purged of overt references to the work's military nature. But the military gag rule constricts the boundaries of acceptable, spontaneous discussion among most workers, increasingly as the level of clearance moves from confidential to top secret. Among Lockheed programmers, the social implications of making missiles, not to mention the alternatives to doing so, are topics that fall outside the boundaries. "Like I say," Fred reminds us, "I stay away from politics."

The Forest From the Trees

How is it possible for workers to create classified products without knowing what the products actually do?

One answer, suggested by the Pentagon's perennial acquisition of badly designed and malfunctioning equipment, is that workers cannot produce blindly without compromising quality.[17] The list of faulty materiel has become scandalously long, yet there is virtual silence on the topic, perhaps because there's little the authorities can do; inefficiency stalks the workplace ruled by secrecy.[18] To the extent that classified production can proceed, it does so through a highly evolved division of labor that transcends, and is often at odds with, capitalist efficiency.

Since Charles Dickens and Frederick Engels, the division of labor has been consistently criticized. These authors, and many since, decried the stunting of mind, body, and soul on the assembly lines of capitalism, and later, of socialism. The critiques varied, but not in their essentials: workers feel alienated from their subdivided and boring work tasks and disconnected from products they do not freely choose to create or cannot control. This was the inevitable consequence of organizing the labor process with the maximization of profit as the primary goal.

To meet project deadlines and to reduce notorious cost overruns, military contractors also attempt to "rationalize" their workplaces to maximize efficiency—and profits. But national security introduces a competing principle around which to organize the labor process: secrecy. In practice, the need-to-know policy conspires with the division of labor to perform a special role: *obscuring a worker's contribution to hostile technology.* This highlights a modern category of alienation, the separation of work from its final purpose.

The politically motivated need-to-know policy could not be implemented without a division of labor. As in civilian electronics, numerous job tasks separate military products from the raw materials and concepts they incorporate. Most of the workers performing the in-between tasks needn't know each product's intended use, only its translation into technical specifications. For example, the narrow focus of Jeff's workday is on microchip circuitry—clusters of "on" and "off" switches, several of which would fit across the width of a sheet of paper—and whether they perform to special military specifications simulated in his company's design software. This makes possible Jeff's ignorance of the classified projects he contributes to. It follows that the Pentagon has a political stake in encouraging product ignorance—a stake it is not wasting any time claiming.

For decades, the Pentagon has issued specifications by which contractors classify, test, and deliver work. Now, it is coming much closer to dictating the way in which work itself is organized. The DOD is positioning itself to demand from computer system and software vendors a work environment that will likely deepen the gulf between job task and product use. The vehicle is *Ada,* the Pentagon's official computer language, and is, upon examination, a Trojan Horse bearing a management policy.

As of summer 1984, all new weapons and other "mission critical" systems for the Pentagon must be written in the *Ada* programming language. As of January 1986, all systems built for NATO bear a similar requirement. These decisions affect an estimated 400,000 computer workers in the Pentagon's direct employ, and countless others in military contracting shops—eventually, anyone who sells software to the DOD and NATO. The goal, of course, is to reduce the large number of computer languages that currently run on the Pentagon's computers and those of its allies.

The message conveyed by the DOD and a growing number of boosters is that *Ada* is not just another programming language. *"Ada* was developed to not only allow, but to encourage the use of sound engineering discipline," observe two *Ada* consultants. There may not be much room for choice in this matter. Pentagon-approved *Ada* compilers (the devices that interpret and translate software instructions into a series of actions that computers perform) accept only those programs that can pass a battery of tests for "configuration management," "modularity," and much more. These tests "will force people to use structured techniques," according to a spokesperson whose company makes *Ada* compilers. Army Colonel Dick Stanley of the DOD's *Ada* Joint Program Office asserts that "it's virtually impossible" to write unstructured *Ada* programs.[19] Widely practiced in civilian industry, structured techniques imply breaking up the job of writing a software program into modules, groups of relatively simple, isolated, step-by-step job tasks.[20] Some programmers prefer this because it allows them to write ever more sophisticated and complex programs. Management, however, hopes to use structured techniques to get from computer design to bug-free product faster by assigning the modules to several engineers who then work on and test them simultaneously.

Whether and how structured techniques improve software productivity is a controversial question. Computer engineering is an inherently creative and increasingly complex process. It resists subdivision and routinization, and it suffers immeasurably from efforts to restrict the vision of its creators. An intriguing question is the impact on military product integrity.[21] For example, IBM's Federal Systems Division, an outstanding and longtime supporter of structured techniques, is three years late delivering a military satellite control system to the Air Force. The problem: software glitches.[22]

What is more certain, and probably more central to the decision-makers at the Pentagon, are the advantages that structured methods will offer in the realm of security. By subdividing work into hierarchically organized "compartments," structured techniques erect barriers between the engineer and the project's hostile purpose. Since programmers require less information about the application as a whole than about the internal aspects of the program's modules, managers can use structured techniques to formalize a division of labor that is more conducive to the need-to-know policy. The sinister implication is that workers can—unwittingly—create and refine weapons of deadly sophistication.

The imperative to divide and subdivide military labor has remarkably obscured the connections between firms as well as within them. Aproximately 150,000 subcontractors supply the Pentagon's 20,000 prime contractors. Over 2,000 subcontractors participate in Lockheed's Trident missile program alone. The B-1 bomber is the work of 5,000 subcontractors located in every state except Alaska and Hawaii.

In the Valley, more than 500 firms receive primary military contracts in excess of $10,000. However, hundreds more receive subcontracts from the primary contractors. Subcontractors sell chips, boards, cathode ray tubes, accounting programs, and so forth to other companies which, in turn, may sell to the Pentagon. This ripples the military connection, making it even more difficult to track.

When the subcontracting path to the Pentagon is several corporate layers deep, many employees simply don't know about the connection. For example, at Ramtek, a graphics display hardware company, only marketing, sales, management, and a handful of key employees seemed to know that a frame buffer device sold to another firm was destined ultimately for military service. Several Ramtek employees said they were happy that they didn't work on military projects.

The maze of military subcontracting suggests the futility awaiting electronics workers who leave a military contractor to take "civilian" employment—only to discover there is a subcontracting relationship to a military supplier.

Speak No Evil

Language is the most innocent accomplice to the military worker's ignorance.

Almost every workplace and occupation has its argot—technical language that serves as a shorthand for describing work problems and procedures. The advent of computers and microelectronics, however, envelops the workplace in language several times removed from the outside world. Whether the work involves observing whales or tracking missiles, computers flatten and homogenize it into a colorless world of files, records, fields, reports, updates, and processing. As a workplace tool, technical language has its place. But where hostile technologies are designed and brought to life, the computer vernacular and its legion acronyms have the cumulative effect of putting social conscience to rest.

It's not difficult to imagine what sort of work goes on at a facility such as the Air Force Weapons Laboratory in New Mexico. But you would never know by reading the 138-page government document that lists weapons-lab job descriptions.[23] What is required of the civilian computer workers at the laboratory? "A high degree of specialized computer processing applications." What projects will employees work on? "Computer systems which use CDC's NOS/BE and NOS/VE operating systems and utility programs." But what do the systems really do? "These systems support a wide variety of technical R&D analysis functions and applications." The specializations might as well describe a marine biology lab or the Federal Reserve Bank.

Of course, those who hire on at the weapons lab would know, in varying degrees according to their clearance levels, that their work involves bomb and missile development. But the Air Forces's language suggests that their daily work culture will not remind them of their work's purpose. The job descriptions—"system generation/installation," "system software maintenance," "documentation support task"—suggest nothing so concrete.

Teledyne Microwave workers make avionic subsystems for the HARM missile. A former worker describes how work is divided into project groups with titles such as the Switch/Attenuator Team, the Multiplier Team, the IRM (Integrated Receiver Module) Qual (Quality) Team, and the IRM Production Team. Neither the project titles nor the ambiguous microchips and circuit boards that the teams turn out suggest their ultimate destination. As a result, workers are not confronted every day by the fact that HARM warheads employ 146 pounds of explosives to scatter 25,000 shrapnel fragments, each of which is preformed to inflict maximum damage.

Language need not be technical to mislead. Lockheed employment advertisements in military electronics magazines' and daily newspapers' job classifieds sometimes conceal the military connection in plain language. "Our Palo Alto Research Lab offers you a stimulating environment in a tranquil setting near Stanford University…[Lockheed] invites you to break away from established theories and venture out in new directions—creating new technologies that will take concepts and turn them into reality." "Reality" at the Palo Alto Research Lab is designing post-holocaust technology, such as the Pentagon's Milstar satellite program. But to prospective recruits, the ad language is a cue that work does not unfold in the morbid surrounding that Pentagon projects might otherwise imply.

Some contractors help rehearse their employees' social conversations. When friends and other outsiders casually ask, "What do you work on?" primary contractor Watkins-Johnson, according to an ex-employee, admonishes its workers to utter two words: "electronic defense." Further elaboration is considered—potentially—a security breach. As it is, "electronic defense" is an impoverished characterization of the Watkins-Johnson line, which includes "electronic warfare suites" and radar components for battleship-, land-, and jet-launched missiles, including the HARM missile, whose primary role is offensive.[24]

If a worker is not really making bombs and bombers, but instead constructing "projectiles" or testing "fuselage designs," then responsibility for the products of the worker's labor, too, is obscured. How much easier to motivate military programmers to perform "data path analysis" to time and speed "usage requirements"—especially if the "data path" conveys heat-seeking missile trajectories for "usage" by a jet squadron, none of which military "software engineers" will need to know to complete their work. As the deference to computer terminology emerges in military industry, the need-to-know policy presses its invasion of workplace language. The jargon is a thicket that invites even curious programmers and engineers to lose sight of the implications of their work.

"A tool that can do anything…"

Doris is a production control expediter at the Teledyne Microwave facility that makes HARM missile circuitry and avionics modules. She feels badly about her contribution to the missile project. "I want to be creative, in an artistic sense, instead of destructive." Doris says she would rather solder stained glass windows than expedite the soldering of war components. "But I can't get to it," she laments, in reference to a discouraging labor market.

By contrast, Fred sees his job as creative and challenging. He is vaguely disturbed about the implications of his work, but remains uninspired about brighter prospects and resorts to the private ploys of resignation and fantasy:

> We're making these big nasty missiles, and everybody hopes they'll never be used. It just seems like they could build bridges, help people someplace else…It's not just the U.S., it's not just Russia, it's a whole mental attitude that goes on that—maybe I just ignore it. I've got no interest in taking anything of theirs. I live in comfortable apathy about a lot of that. It would be nicer if it was all gone.

More often, military electronics workers tend to dismiss their responsibility by noting the distance between their job tasks and those that are more directly linked to a hostile product. Michael, a utilities software programmer, worked on a log-in protocol for a computer system his company hoped to sell to the National Security Agency. (His employer also sells computers to the Air Force.) According to Michael:

> I'm at ease a little bit 'cause I do know that I'm not putting the bomb together. My guess is that most people would not work directly for military applications, but would be comfortable working in an environment [in which] they knew part of [their work] wound up in a military application—that they weren't directly fueling it. *That detachment is a sort of protection.* (emphasis added)

Victor, a systems software programmer, finds refuge in the ambiguity of microelectronics technology. He insists that he "wouldn't work for a...company that does military work," but that working on "a tool that can do anything"—i.e., civilian or military tasks—is acceptable. "If you're making a sewing machine to sew parachutes or wedding dresses [or] if...you know you're...sewing parachutes, that's the difference."

"As long as I'm not working on weapons systems, that's fine with me," says Stanford Computer science professor Thomas Binford. But Binford acknowledges that his research on stereo vision has direct relevance to cruise missile guidance systems. "If I chose not to do my favorite project because of that, I'd go to my second favorite project and I'd find the same thing. I'd keep going down the list and then I'd be left saying 'What is there left for me to do?' "[25]

Peter Hochschild, a Stanford computer science graduate student, is more to the point: "A lot of people here don't even think about the issue. They look for a research problem that's technically challenging and intellectually interesting, and *they divorce it from its applications.*" (emphasis added)

The reflections of Victor, Michael, Professor Binford, and Peter Hochschild are no doubt earnest appraisals. Is writing missile-performance analysis software less damnable than using it to perfect the missile's flight? How much less lethal is writing an accounting program that enables the Air Force to operate more efficiently than making chips that will guide bombs to their targets? If there are obvious, unambiguous answers to such questions, they are lost in the everyday culture of the military electronics worker. Perhaps the experience of military electronics work is essentially ambiguous.

Reckoning moral responsibility by measuring the distance between one's labor and the product is a legitimate inquiry, but only if one can hope to measure reliably. The division of labor in military electronics suggests the interdependency and responsibility of all workers but—and this is the paradox—encourages profound distance between worker and product. This psychological distance is protected and extended by the cloistering—the need-to-know policy— that mystifies the military product and censors the product's ghastly purpose from the producer's daily life. As a result, workers can manufacture, in addition to military electronics, a naiveté about the impact of their labors and, at least among obliging and complicit fellow workers, escape ridicule for an ill-gotten innocence.

6

Wayward Professionals

All professions are a conspiracy against the public.

George Bernard Shaw

In 1980, a Silicon Valley electronics firm launched a recruitment campaign with a widely noticed photo-advertisement. It featured a man in a suit and tie on a surfboard riding a wave. The incongruous imagery extended to the young professional's face, which expressed both terror and determination. "Catch the Wave," beckoned Advanced Micro Devices. It was the economic equivalent of a wartime enlistment poster.

With calculated appeal, the iconography marked the transition from the self-centered 1970s to the work-centered 1980s. The ad's premise was that there were people for whom work meant nearly everything; enough at any rate, to make big risks appear personally attractive. The salient implications almost splashed off the page: assume a high-profile, harrowing position from which you might slip in a punishing fall, buried by the wave that only moments ago supported you. The wave's inexorable force—the corporate drive to catch and stay on top of quickly changing electronics markets—offered brief exhilaration. Staying on top of the wave was an individual feat, not a team effort, and one that dictated a keenly aggressive attitude. The firm characterized work's new cachet in stark terms:

> Advanced Micro Devices' unparalleled growth has created unparalleled opportunities for talented and motivated people—*people who want to take advantage of an exceptionally demanding and exceptionally rewarding environment.*[1] (emphasis added)

The metaphors of inspired dedication to potentially self-destructive work in an unpredictable environment were echoed elsewhere. In

115

1985, a United Technologies magazine ad (entitled "Technology's Human Face") challenged:

> Young men and women now planning and starting careers are faced with an environment of unparalleled change. The tiny device we call the integrated circuit...is bringing explosive changes to business and industry.

The personal risks of a professional career were part of the "entrepreneurial spirit." "Technology is advanced by people with ideas—people who can nurture those ideas and take risks to put them into effect." In this context of "unparalleled change," the professional-as-entrepreneur could achieve personal fulfillment—the self-actualization pursued (outside the workplace) during the previous decade: "Technology is created by talented, motivated people working under conditions that allow them to achieve their full potential." This, however, required making work a dominating life interest.[2]

By mid-decade, the electronics industry's widely regarded devotion to work had created unparalleled problems. At some companies, over 80 percent of the employees were non-alcoholic substance abusers.[3] The Valley's unsurpassed divorce rate and notorious romantic malaise, attributed by a Silicon Valley psychotherapist to work-centered values (the "Silicon Syndrome"), meant that couples were separating more often than staying together.[4] "People are choosing to be single because of work," explained another psychotherapist, who estimated that 60 percent of Silicon Valley electronics workers "from the line on up" were seeing therapists.[5] Advanced Micro Devices was paying for up to eighteen visits per family to "outside counselors for help with alcohol, drug, financial and marital problems."[6]

If a raucous celebration of work had made Silicon Valley famous, workers, the therapists now urged, should be wary. Perhaps nowhere was the change as startling as at Apple Computer. In 1982-83, Apple's Macintosh development team wore T-shirts proclaiming "working 90 hours a week and loving every minute of it."[7] By 1988, Apple was soliciting bids for an *onsite* psychotherapy facility.[8] Apple deemed the move cost-effective: therapists counseling Apple employees offsite suggested that at least 65 percent of Apple employees were "in therapy."[9]

The electronics corporations, and a coterie of consultants to management at large, have taken credit for reviving the Work Ethic, just as they now disavow the tragic consequences to personal life.[10] In this, they are both opportunistic and dishonest. Among salaried, occupationally mobile electronics workers, a more organic work-centered ideology took root, one that was independent, even skeptical, of specific corporate "cultures."

The hegemony that work assumed in personal life was genuine. It marked the rise and faltering of a new professionalism whose clients were corporate and whose class interest was borrowed from the old professional entrepreneur.

Corporate Culture

As the 1980s began, the upheavals of the previous decade left many workers psychologically, as well as materially, indigent. A strange new array of social facts was stubbornly insinuating itself into U.S. life. The collapse of Keynesian controls in the mysterious coincidence of inflation amid recession, the failure of tax incentives to reverse manufacturing disinvestment and widespread layoffs, the explosion of real estate prices, the growth of service industries, and ubiquitous speculation were forcing an unpopular retreat from the pretensions to middle-class affluence.[11] The two-income family and a shortfall of public spending were hastening the demise of the nuclear family and basic education.[12] A shift of jobs from the cities and small towns of the east to the habitats of the south and west was uprooting relatively stable communities and humbling the population's expectations.[13] All of this was undermining the credibility and transmission of traditional values, muddying social convention, and steeping what we might call the national character in confusion. The material and ideological fabric that supported the U.S. conception of work as an opportunity for the industrious was unraveling. As a result, morale was sagging badly in the workplace.

The workplace of the 1980s was so sodden with loneliness that management consultants worried openly about employee motivation. A new management perspective, in fact, a tacit rejection of its scientistic calculation and vulgar behaviorist origins, was in the offing. The reign of the efficiency engineers, who had structured alienation and boredom into so many U.S. factories and offices in the name of raising productivity, was now seen as part of the morale problem. With unacknowledged irony, management consultants urged their clients to take seriously a motivation crisis that was largely of their client's making. Corporate managers began to sample the vernacular of popular psychology and a gamut of fashionable motivational theories, and liked what they heard.

A 1979 monograph (prepared by Stanford Research Institute International for the National Office Products Association) reflected management's new concerns as well as the new argot:

> alienation of the [U.S.] office worker is expected to be a growing problem. [The office of the future] may quite possibly become a more impersonal place in which to work—it certainly will be quieter, more secure, and less expensively lighted, and this suggests a potentially far more lonely existence for the individual office worker...We expect to see the office environment beset by a continual set of skirmishes between forces encouraging specialization...and forces encouraging the individual worker to do more of the tasks himself...If our analysis of the large office environment in the 1980s is correct, where the office environment is increasingly made up of a series of individual and very privately operated workstations, then there are considerable implications to management with regard to individual motivation, conveyance of team spirit, and assistance in the individual worker's goal attainment.[14]

The concern with "loneliness," corporate "assistance" in "goal attainment," and suspicion of the "forces encouraging specialization" marked management's foray into the shallow psychology of *corporate culture*. A garden variety of employee participation projects sprouted in larger U.S. workplaces. In Silicon Valley, company fitness centers and employee sabbaticals debuted. Ford spent millions on a series of "Quality" ad campaigns that featured prideful, motivated employees conveying "input" to managers. At Ford and elsewhere, quality-of-work-life circles, labor-management teams, and employee question sessions were initiated, guided, and sometimes abruptly halted by management. Regardless of their erratic courses, the projects were important symbolically as attempts to reach out and "touch" employees in the therapeutic sense. Therapy was at the heart of the new management techniques, which were out to tap the wellspring of self-motivation (and not coincidentally to revitalize corporate profitability).

In *Brave New Workplace,* Robert Howard recounts the rise of the therapeutic management theories.[15] Management consultant Michael Maccoby, director of Harvard's Program on Work, Technology, and Character, stressed the social context in which the motivation gap was occurring. Maccoby drew management's attention to changes that sociologists Christopher Lasch, Robert Bellah, and others were observing in the national character: the stunting of our ability to construct personal meaning and a growing reluctance to identify ourselves with a world beset by bureaucratic and threatening forces that were loosening family ties, redefining friendship, and leaving us with unstable and commercially-derived models for behavior and ethics.[16] Something like an existential crisis of meaning was at hand, Maccoby argued. Within this larger crisis, Maccoby identified a management opportunity: the cultivation of a "self-development ethic" that would encourage workers to view their employers and their work as an oasis of meaning, a vehicle to personal growth. Grounded in the loam of self-development psychologies in vogue during the 1970s, the movement toward a therapeutic workplace culture, what Robert Howard called an attempt to "craft the corporate self," seemed to be an idea whose time had come.[17]

In the United States, books by and about managers and motivation consultants often outsold those about movie and sports celebrities, a phenomenon that surely established the perceived gravity of the crisis. The best-selling non-fiction book of 1983, *In Search of Excellence* by Thomas Peters and Robert Waterman, proselytized for a regime of management motivation-therapists.[18] Based on a survey of "best-run" companies, this book became *de rigueur* in management training seminars.

Although the goals were roughly the same, *Excellence* marked the distance management had traveled from the scientistic time-and-motion methods of yesteryear ("to fit Taylor's old model, or today's organizational charts, man is simply designed wrong..."). Peters and Waterman were in search of the charmed, "driven" employee whose work provides meaning and whose motivation runs deep. Why couldn't productivity and psyche grow to mutual benefit? "We desperately need meaning in our lives and will sacrifice a great deal to institutions that will provide meaning for us," the authors observe. "Excited" and "personally involved" in work, new employees would remain productive even in the face of the new and possibly less interesting assignments that changing workplace technology might bequeath them. It was up to the employer to provide the right environment. With metaphors rich in nostalgia for U.S. stability, the authors describe the corporation as a new "home," a "community center," a "family"—a sanctuary for troubled selves in the '80s and beyond. Likewise, in *Reinventing the Corporation,* John Naisbitt and Patricia Aburdene redefine the workplace as "an environment for personal growth" and managers as happy "facilitators" of "expertise."[19] By mid-decade, corporate culture consulting, including a rapidly growing segment known as "organizational transformation" (OT), had become a multi-billion dollar industry.[20]

The warm corporate promise of "providing a setting conducive to personal growth," parsed into the more effectual language of the scientific manager, was finally about "raising productivity."[21] Without this overriding mission, "excellence" consulting, corporate culture, and OT could never have been taken seriously. Outside of management circles, however, who was taking it seriously? Howard, who had accurately analyzed the movement's underlying objectives ("the systematic manipulation by corporate managers of people's desire for meaningful work"),[22] attributed to it a credibility it never achieved. U.S. workers were not taken with the therapy of excellence. *The Wall Street Journal* reported "mixed reactions" to "attitudinal training" among workers who complained that "the seminars and exercises they attend are the first and last time they hear about improvements on the job; once the training ends, so does management's commitment to change." At "many" firms, the *Journal* continued, the training created "bitter conflicts between employees who embrace the new concepts and those who don't...many older employees say the seminars—and management—are simply paying lip service to serious concerns in the workplace."[23] Observed Harley Shaiken, "Unfortunately, most of the so-called transformation work today is really just a substitute for giving workers real autonomy and responsibility."[24]

As for OT consulting, investigative reporter Mark Dowie noted in 1986:

> [P]ractitioners of OT admit that in the five years since their trade has been recognized as a respectable field of management consulting, *not one single major corporate or government culture has been transformed by their efforts.* "There are departments and divisions of large companies we can hold up as examples of our success," says Linda Ackerman, an OT specialist based in McLean, Virgina, "but I can't think of a single large organization that has transformed itself as a result of our work." (emphasis added)[25]

By 1988, *Newsweek* was acknowledging the limitations of the entire therapeutic workplace project: "Ultimately, stress-management programs, after-work aerobics and late-night back rubs can do only so much to alleviate the morale problems dogging so many U.S. companies." The *Newsweek* post-mortem tolled on:

> Since the publication of books like *In Search of Excellence* in the early '80s, some of the principles of smart decision making have become cliches. The best firms encourage contact with customers and allow employees to run with good ideas. Yet it is remarkable how few companies fit the description...[26]

U.S. executives were apparently sincere in seeking new management approaches. Confused by their declining fortunes and buffeted by the turbulent business climate of the 1980s, management was, as one observer put it, "in the market for magic" or, as another noted perhaps more precisely, in search of "mental technologies."[27] Was management taken in by the motivation consultants? Significantly, one of the most lucrative consulting firms by 1987 was Werner Erhard's TransTech. In a transformation that mirrored much of American culture from the 1970s to the 1980s, Erhard abandoned personal development (est—Erhard Seminar Training) in favor of a management consulting based on "breakthroughs," "possibilities," and promises of quick results.[28] His Marin County-based TransTech packaged its motivational pearls and sold franchises to over 40 consulting affiliates. (At one point, according to Dowie, all but one of the affiliates included est graduates.) Erhard quickly parlayed TransTech into a $25 million consulting empire that, through affiliates, reached an unlikely clientele including the Soviet Communist Party and the U.S. Justice Department as well as NASA and Fortune 500 companies such as Ford, General Electric, McDonald's, Lockheed, RCA and Allstate Insurance.[29] If the popularity of Erhardesque techniques identified the crank fringe of the corporate culture movement, it also fueled growing skepticism.

Under a more stable economic regime, some of the new management approaches might have appeared plausible. From 1979 through 1984, however, roughly 11 million workers fell victim to what U.S. business journalism called "downsizing": mass layoffs, offshore plant relocation, corporate failures, and mergers.[30] The following two years (1984 to 1986), nearly 600,000 mid- and upper-level executives lost their jobs.[31] This was precisely the period during which managers attempted to implement their corporate cultures. In 1988, with no end to the "bloodletting" in sight, *Newsweek* wondered what could be salvaged:

> Few executives, after whacking costs by closing divisions and laying people off, have the energy or the ideas to preside over an era of fertile innovation. Even if they did, the remaining employees may not be in the mood to follow the men who wielded the ax.[32]

Artifice and Artifact

Underneath the teamwork and human potential metaphors, corporate culture in Silicon Valley was an amalgam of entrepreneurial lust, technological fascination, and employee benefits. Against the drab social landscape and flat culture of the surrounding habitats, corporations created a semblance of warmth and friendliness by sponsoring Wednesday morning pastry breaks, Friday afternoon happy hours, weekend river rafting trips, employee trade show junkets, and endless T-shirts and desktop knick-knacks commemorating product releases and market-positioning campaigns. For recent emigres, especially foreign-born computer specialists, corporate culture became a surrogate welcome wagon—a refuge from mainstream U.S. culture that was alternately beguiling and indifferent. But sooner or later, the corporate motivations surfaced. Even among the young, introverted layers of electronics workers—the many engineers, technicians, and programmers for whom the construction of social life in the 1980s presented a grim and unpromising project—corporate culture became something to take advantage of, not to take seriously.

The renowned Silicon Valley work-schedule flexibility issued less from corporate munificence than from necessity. Flexible start times ensured that employees would eventually arrive at work from far-flung bedroom communities and through the growing traffic congestion. To be first in the market with products, electronics firms also demanded the flexibility of sustained overtime from their employees at rates well above the national average.[33] In fact, a manipulative logic imbued almost every artifact of each corporate culture. The firms encouraged a company lifestyle that might stir the allegiance of occupationally mobile technical workers whose scarce skills were indispensable to meet the competition. Accordingly, the "perks" of corporate culture, including flex-time and access to recreational facilities, were rarely extended to manufacturing workers.[34]

In the best of times, the surfeit of overtime and deadline pressure generated by the electronics firms made corporate concern for the individual appear transparent, affected, and self-serving. When prosperity waned, the fictions of corporate nurturing were impossible to support. Silicon Valley electronics firms, including many lauded as model corporate cultures, laid off workers at rates in excess of 1,000 per month in 1985-86.[35] In the process, the "no-layoff" policy disappeared at Convergent Technologies, Intel, and Advanced Micro Devices; at IBM, upwards of 45,000 employees were asked to transfer, quit, or retire early amid plant closings and consolidations.[36]

As it was, the reputations attributed to some Silicon Valley firms by published consultants were misconstrued or misleading. In 1983, Peters and Waterman gave microchip giant Intel an "excellent" performance rating. The following year, Intel was rated one of America's "100 Best" places to work.[37] Intel president Andrew Grove, in his *San Jose Mercury News* column on management, shared the wisdom of the apparently successful "Intel Culture." In one column, Grove consoles a worker maligned by an authoritarian boss at a small firm:

Small (sometimes even large!) owner-run companies often tend to be run in an arbitrary, dictatorial way. That, in fact, tends to be what limits their growth...try to evaluate a new employer carefully, so you don't exchange serfdom in one fiefdom for the same position in another.[38]

According to former employees, however, Grove and Intel management were just as unenlightened.[39] Intel department managers frequently browbeat their people into working more than eight hours a day and informally imposed six-day work weeks. Intel earned a reputation for underpaying and overworking fresh-off-the-campus and emigre engineers.[40] Acknowledgement of Intel's heavy-handedness came from no less a source than *Fortune* magazine. Months before Grove wrote the column excerpted above, *Fortune* awarded him second runner-up for "toughest boss" in The United States. The award was based on a survey in which being "autocratic, ruthless, grueling and intimidating were qualifications for the title."[41]

ROLM corporation was cited by nearly every corporate culture consultant for its prep school ambience, country club facilities, and employee autonomy—including sabbaticals (for those who stayed on long enough to qualify). At ROLM, "where the future is now," you could play racquetball, tennis, basketball and volleyball, swim laps, lift weights, learn self-defense, enjoy a steam bath or sauna, and bank at an automatic teller machine—without ever having to leave work. In exchange, workers had to adopt the "ROLM philosophy":

> The ROLM work environment is predicated on a dual responsibility. ROLM provides opportunity to grow and be promoted, fair treatment for each individual, respect for personal privacy, encouragement to succeed, opportunities for creativity, and evaluation based on job performance...ROLM people are expected to respond by being individually accountable, enhancing teamwork, performing to the best of their abilities and *understanding and implementing the ROLM Philosophy.*[42] (emphasis added)

As ROLM matured it cloaked itself less in the sheep's clothing of paternalism and more in the haberdashery of bureaucracy. In 1988, ROLM awkwardly amended its "philosophy" by implementing IBM's "clean desk" program. Premised on an active distrust of employees, the policy provides for roving squads of security guards who randomly enter offices after hours to scrutinize "unsecured" papers for proprietary material. "Violations will be reported and appropriate action taken by your manager," concluded the ROLM security memo.[43] (Further invading employee privacy, ROLM makes office phone systems with built-in employee monitoring utilities.)

The facades of the ROLM Philosophy, the Intel Culture, and even the H-P Way cracked under the weight of corporate austerity and restructuring that entailed pay-cuts, salary freezes, forced furloughs, widespread layoffs, plant relocations, new limits on departments' "entrepreneurial" autonomy, and more overtime. In and out of unstable work, workers regarded with skepticism management efforts to enshrine the corporation as a fount of "personal growth."

For many, corporate culture was a fig leaf hiding the transience, stress, and loneliness that work created in people's lives. In this austere and uncertain atmosphere, a more serviceable ideology circulated: professionalism. To salaried workers and to ambitious wage workers, professionalism recommended a personal commitment to work that explained—and encouraged—job hopping as the unfolding logic of a career.[44] This view of work, like the career itself, transcended loyalties to specific employers and jobs, and even accommodated cynicism of corporate interests. Self-centered and self-serving, professionalism was in keeping with the spirit of the 1980s.[45] It probably accounted, far more than the corporate-centered ideologies, for the recuperation of work. When career aspirations rose in a vertical trajectory, however, professional self-imagery disguised a corporate servitude that all but suffocated individual autonomy as well as time for interests outside of work.

The Professional Retreat

Professionalism enjoys wide currency despite vague and various meanings. The straightforward connotation it once bore as a code by which licensed entrepreneurs conducted their business has blurred.[46] Today, professionalism is an evolving ideology; its meanings must be gleaned from diffuse sources. An initially confusing source is Silicon Valley, which is popularly identified with the entrepreneur. Here, the self-employed class of the old professional-entrepreneur pales before the ubiquitous corporate employee.[47] Yet among many programmers, engineers, technical writers, marketing analysts, accountants, and their managers, *professionalism* enjoys the presumption of importance and desirability.

In 1984, a best-selling self-help guide for upwardly mobile men and women characterized the operational outlook of the new professional. *The 100 Best Companies to Work for in America* (by Robert Levering, Milton Moskowitz, and Michael Katz) evaluated corporate cultures as so many designer career opportunities, thereby expressing the new professional's apparent independence. The authors's previous work, *Everybody's Business: An Almanac,* was also a self-help guide of sorts. Subtitled *The Irreverent Guide to Corporate America,* the *Almanac* provided unflattering, even muckraking reviews of U.S. corporations; corporate crimes and labor injustices were considered "everybody's business."[48]

In *100 Best,* the authors reviewed some of the same *Almanac* corporations from the narrow perspective of career. Levering, Moskowitz, and Katz ranked each corporation according to pay, benefits, job security, chance to move up, and "ambience." The authors' glance at Silicon Valley corporations was at best superficial, and at worse, misleading; throughout, workplace "ambience" consisted of received impressions of "corporate culture," which the authors, for the most part, took at face value.[49] *100 Best* was more significant as an effort to address and articulate the concerns of the new professional, not those of production workers.

Does a company that infuses dangerous chemicals into local drinking water and exposes employees to lung-searing fumes make a good employer? Silicon Valley's Advanced Micro Devices (AMD) is the fifth largest maker of integrated circuits and one of the *100 Best.* Though the authors forewarn readers of AMD's highly competitive corporate structure, they laud AMD president Jerry Sanders as "a folk hero" and conclude that "AMD employees appreciate the Sanders style." However, former AMD employees Anita Zimmerman and Judy Washington were not interviewed by the authors. Zimmerman, once a high school runner and gymnast, was an AMD chip-mask etcher quickly promoted to mask-etching trainer. That is, until chlorine-based gas leaks at her AMD shop permanently destroyed her lungs and left her jobless. According to Zimmerman, many other AMD workers were chronically exposed to such gases. It seems AMD supervisors, imbued with the competitive AMD-esprit, were consistently reluctant to immediately evacuate the facilities for repairs.

Judy Washington, an AMD process-control technician, often complained to supervisors of gas smells and other signs of chemical exposure, but was told to mind her business. After working at AMD for two years amidst acids, solvents, and gases such as boron and phosphine, Judy developed a chronic cough, sore throat, breathlessness, and towards the end, nausea, dizziness, and memory lapses. When her doctor recommended leaving her job, Judy requested a transfer; AMD told her to go home until a new job could be found.

Even at the level of trivial inquiry pursued by the authors,[50] essential and obvious qualifications are neglected. Commuting is a good example.

ROLM's headquarters and recreation center reside in the heart of what regional authorities identify as the most congested Bay Area rush-hour traffic knot. Furious industrial and office construction in the area surrounding ROLM and nearby chip-maker Intel (also one of the *100 Best*) are making the daily ROLM commute even more unbearable. In fact, the logistics of getting to and from ROLM make a necessity of its "flex-time" (arrive-at work-when-you-can) policy, which the authors characterize as a perk.

100 Best reflects the priorities of people who consider their political principles and the quality of their non-work life to be utterly negotiable in the bargains struck with career. Gone from *100 Best* is the populist political-mindedness with which the *Almanac* bristled, including reviews of workplace dangers, firms' treatment of offshore assembly workers, as well as the hostile social applications of electronics products.[51] On behalf of prospective professional employees, the authors neglected everything beyond the corporate parking lot: the character of surrounding communities, the availability and cost of housing and childcare, educational facilities, the commute, and water quality. By these and other unmentioned but relevant indices (including the preponderance of substance abuse and work-fractured families among employees), the ratings for Silicon Valley corporations highly regarded in *100 Best* tend to plummet catastrophically.[52]

In depicting corporations as eminently desirable workplaces without reference to their impact on workers' personal lives and society at large, the authors presented a twisted view of work and career to their audience. Levering, Moskowitz, and Katz also betrayed the larger irrationality of the times: that work is somehow meaningful outside of its social environment. In light of information technology's immense economic and environmental impact, the computer professional's aloofness from social responsibility is disturbing. It is also something new—an acquired corporate trait—in the evolution of professionalism.

The new professionalism is a hybrid, borrowing from the old and adding new strains. The ethos of the modern professional no longer exclusively embodies the experience of the self-employed class (or collegiate association). Instead, the new professionalism transcends class to include: the self-employed, the salaried (especially technically-skilled) employee, as well as corporate managers. Here it emerges as a shared culture of career—an ideological bridge over which classes might brook mutual antagonism. The theme of professional collaboration is traced throughout *100 Best;* the introduction, entitled "Beyond Technique," refers to the authors' belief that a new, non-manipulative, non-adversarial management-worker relationship is apparent among the "best" corporations.[53]

That an ideology of professional career should thrive in the volatile climate of the 1980s makes historical sense. The old professional arose in response to the historic chaos of emerging capitalism.[54] The culture of the professional in the United States was rooted in the feverish industrialization, corporate mergers, and scientific advances after the Civil War.[55] Seeking stability in a period of economic upheaval, nineteenth-century doctors, lawyers, accountants, and morticians shrewdly turned to a modern protector: bureaucracy. They convinced legislatures to confer upon their associations the status of "experts" and a public power to certify training and research institutes, license new practitioners, and establish standards.[56]

Nineteenth-century professionals could reckon their self-worth not only in remittances for services rendered, but also in the apparent benefits they provided society. Physicians relieved human suffering. Architects designed human dwellings. Even lawyers, accountants, and morticians could imagine that they served larger human enterprises such as justice, honesty, and hygiene. These social concerns and virtues were inscribed in the pre-Civil War era's professional "code of ethics." The archaic *helping professions* also reflects an earlier estimation of the social worth of medical, legal, psychiatric, and related fields among the middle- and upper-classes. Here the new contrasts sharply with the old.

Beyond the lonely project of career, the new professional apparently knows or cares little about service to community. One survey found that, in Silicon Valley, lower paid blue-collar workers contribute far more to charity and community projects than do higher-paid young professionals.[57] In fact, popular culture has assigned an almost childlike selfishness and lack of social conscience to the new professional. (The new professional acronym "yuppie" is uttered as an epithet more frequently than not.) The reputation is often deserved, but just as often misdiagnosed.

In Silicon Valley and elsewhere, it was not wanton greediness but rather passion for work and fascination with innovative technology that transcended interest in practically all else, including the professional's current employer. As a Silicon Valley personnel consultant put it, "These days, there is more allegiance to a product or a technology than to any particular company."[58] He might have added "any particular home": in a 1986 survey, nearly 50 percent of Silicon Valley fathers said that their jobs, not their families, were of primary importance to them. In an unknown but large number of cases, the time devoted to work and technology, enlarged by time spent recovering from it, overwhelmed relationships with friends, spouses, and children.[59]

Apparently, the new professional welcomes work and workplace innovation even when it means a lonelier daily existence. In the following excerpt from a computer magazine column, a technical writer summarizes the impact of new computer publishing technology that has diminished time spent with other workers (whom the author earlier refers to as her "clients"):

> Sure, some days I miss that bristling interaction with a group of other people in a conference room. [Now] I talk more with the terminal about the merits of bold versus italic, a two-column format versus three. Maybe it's just as well, because I'm focused more on the page, and less on personalities. And after all, what I'm really interested in is producing good work.[60]

The emphasis on technical detail and the abstract "good work" is redolent of the old professional's uncompromising standards and detachment from the product. Like their Renaissance and post-Civil War era forebears, computer professionals exercise a high degree of control over the labor process.[61] Ownership of the product of that labor, however, was conceded by the old professional to the client. The lawyer's victory was really the client's; the life or limb the doctor saved was the patient's; the taxes and books the accountant prepared belonged to others; and likewise for old professionals from tenured teachers to morticians to tailors.

The professional's detachment from the client's affairs survives the modern revision. Parasitical and hostile electronics applications are rarely acknowledged by the creators even as they comply with corporate and military sponsors.[62] This separation is favored by the amorphous tools and products of labor: information technology. Microchips, manuals, and software (unlike a doctor's stethoscope, thermometer, and bandages) lack clear or intrinsic human purpose. The computer professional designs database software and microchip logic, not stock exchange programs or missile guidance systems. The abstract and insular nature of computer work invites tool fetishism and interest in "producing good work" rather than responsibility for making a specific product whose social purpose its makers may find unflattering and disagreeable. That responsibility falls, by default, to the corporation.

The Corporate Client

The new professional's corporate client marks a strategic violation of the code of the old professional. During the consolidation of middle-class sensibilities in a shared culture of upward mobility in the nineteenth and early twentieth century, "the professional resisted all corporate encroachments and regulations upon his independence, whether from government bureaucrats, university trustees, business administrators, public laymen, or even his own professional associations."[63] Today, the professional's occupational identity continues to reflect the collective experience of peers, but also becomes vicariously that of the modern business corporation, which saturates that experience. Under the thumb of corporate employment, the substance of the professional's independence is thin.

In his mid-twentieth-century classic, *White Collar,* C. Wright Mills sensed the professional's budding occupational confusion. Mills identified a new "professional ideology" that clung to almost "[a]ny position that is 'responsible and steady' and, above all, that carries prestige." In the restructuring of the post-World War II U.S. economy, Mills described a merger of "skill and money" in which "professions have become more like businesses and businesses have become more like professions."[64]

Mills anticipated a process that was largely complete by the 1980s: the corporate accommodation of the professional's skills and self-imagery. No matter how removed from immediate supervision, the new professional is "responsible" almost everywhere to a corporate etiquette of working life. This dependence on corporate employment, in an era of volatile capital, rarely makes for "steady" work, no matter how skillful the professional is at obtaining it.

The professional's sense of autonomy is supported today by the privileges enjoyed relative to wage workers rather than by independence from the corporate world. By negative comparison, the professionals' freedoms are considerable. Few Silicon Valley salaried workers, for instance, dine in parking lots at the mobile cafeterias frequented by wage workers, and not merely because salaried workers generally feel awkward around wage workers, although that is part of the reason. Professional employees can fill extended lunch breaks with jogging, tennis, walks, aerobic exercise, shopping, personal business. Most wage workers, lacking extended lunch breaks, can't.

The salaried employee can take care of personal business on company time; most make free personal, including long-distance, phone calls; many come and go as they please. Some travel at company expense to conventions or customer sites. When programmers, engineers, and technical writers are bored, they can amuse themselves with computer games and electronic mail—or leave work for a movie, shopping, or errands. Many salaried workers also have at their disposal "support staff" (secretaries and clerks). Work's deadlines and allure prevent many salaried technical workers from taking what others would consider full advantage of the situation; they also are removed from the executive manager's decision-making powers. But the little freedoms accumulate and, no matter how much they are taken for granted, flatter the salaried worker with executive-class courtesies and considerations that encourage the sense of being "master of your own fate."[65]

The wage worker is much more likely to be mired in boring, repetitive work with the additional burden of close and frequent supervision. A minimum of on-the-job autonomy and frequent overtime deplete the wage workers' opportunity for conducting personal business during the day; paychecks may be docked for trips to the bank, the dentist, and childcare conferences. Many are discouraged from making personal phone calls; some, especially clean-room workers, must line up during breaks at pay phones to make outside calls.

Even austerity can bolster the computer professional's sense of autonomy. When a company's products are scorned by the markets, the injustice of hierarchy applies: the assemblers and clerks' jobs often disappear first, even though the salaried engineers, programmers, and marketing and accounting people are more clearly responsible for the firm's hapless products. The salaried professionals have access to rare technical knowledge; they design the commodities that make so many production and clerical workers' jobs an empty, alien process— deciphering blueprints, inspecting solder, copying and formatting memos and budgets. This contributes to a subconscious relationship between production and design workers that takes familiar forms: in the clean room, women's jobs depend upon higher-paid men who design the chips.

The flattering terms of the computer professional's bargain with Silicon Valley firms ride on the high demand for experience, proven skill, and credentials. The marketing culture of permanent innovation often makes the demand for technically specific expertise erratic. Still, in the bleakest of times, phone calls from professional headhunters pester already-employed programmers, engineers, and technical writers with enticing job options. In the best of times, no one calls the electronics wage worker. Despite the many relative freedoms, the notion that a professional career is its own reward masks a vulnerability and isolation that consolidates corporate advantages over the professional.

Nearly everywhere I have worked in Silicon Valley, salaried employees have been unaware of each others' pay levels. They negotiate salaries individually with managers, who are themselves forbidden to reveal other workers' salaries. While management discourages a collective awareness of salaries among its professional employees, it clandestinely shares such information with other divisions, and often, with other corporations. This information is then centrally located in personnel departments, which dispatch it to managers for employee reviews and hiring. Discussing salaries with fellow workers is *unprofessional*—and grounds for dismissal at IBM and elsewhere.[66] The unspoken rationale for this policy is to avoid rivalry, ill will, and other unproductive results among professionals who discover unjustified salary discrepancies. The professional's ignorance, however, allows management to hide pay and workload differentials for women, minorities, dissidents, and those who are generally unaware of how high a salary they can plausibly negotiate. The mystery is celebrated in the professional mythology that likens technical workers to self-employed businesspeople—competing entrepreneurs with secrets to keep.

A firm's salaried workers are exempted from labor codes that regulate the amount of overtime people can be forced to work. Their salaries theoretically reflect unpaid overtime. Electronics corporations, however, demand chronic overtime of their design-and-development workers.[67] Such manipulation—whether of employees' dedication to after-hours work or of their ignorance of salary and general isolation from one another—suggests the corporate service into which the new professionalism has been pressed.

If a corporation was a fickle provider of income, prestige, and vertical mobility, the new professional could assert his or her independence through shrewd career moves. Warns the *San Jose Mercury News'* "Career Progress" column, "Keep in mind that most employers have very short memories. You may work for a firm for 20 years, but one of these days some new owner may come along and decide to do some trimming, and your job will be gone." To avoid "career rut," the author reminds readers that "the most important factor in career success is making moves. And often this will mean moving on—and up—into another firm."[68] Even "moving on" requires professional tact. Another *Mercury News* column entitled "Stay Cool in Heat of Quitting," urges salaried workers to follow the "unwritten etiquette of resigning":

> The take-this-job-and-shove-it style of resigning is something everybody fantasizes about but most professionals know better than to try it...Two objectives should prevail in any job change situation: First keep your bridges intact. You never know when you

may need to retreat. And second, protect your professional image...Call a quick meeting and inform your staff. Then seek out friends and other colleagues and thank them for their support during your employment. If possible, follow up with written notes; hard copy will go a long way toward fixing your professional image in their minds.[69]

A different etiquette prevails when firms fire their professional employees. At a small computer graphics firm in 1983, many of my fellow salaried workers were greeted at their cubicles by grim security guards one morning. In a scene played over and over again in the Valley, the guards announced the employees' "termination," scrutinized the removal of personal property from desks and benches, and escorted astounded workers directly to the door, where final paychecks were waiting. This way, laid-off workers were informally held incommunicado until safely outside the workplace. Before it was all over, 10 percent of the workforce had disappeared. That corporations relieve their highly-paid technical workers and even managers in such a manner suggests the power such workers have to inflict immediate disruption and destruction as well as the professional's essential expendability—like any other worker. The incident was a reminder that the respect corporations pay their professional employees is, along with material rewards, swiftly withdrawn when profits sag or projects lose favor.

The conventional wisdom in Silicon Valley throughout the 1980s was that computer professionals had smugly accepted their corporate lot in occupational life: few could be seen forming combative workplace organizations. There were professional associations, but these were hardly militant.[70] With few exceptions, the Society for Technical Communication (STC), the Association of Scientists and Professional Engineering Personnel (ASPEP), and others assisted the electronics industry by establishing product and work performance standards. The associations promoted the standards and technology innovations through journals and newsletters and at seminars and luncheons. In these forums, the etiquette of corporate servitude often was presented as a parable of professional independence. In the following excerpt, a president of an association of technical writers explores the ethics of conformity with corporate attire:

> What kind of dress, then, is appropriate for a technical communicator?...According to [Dress for Success author John] Molloy, a person can evoke a favorable response to his needs through skillful manipulation of dress. Is this ethical? I believe it is. As technical communicators, our job is to help authors convey their message to their readers. If we, by projecting an image of profes-

sionalism, can more readily convince them to accept our professional judgement, we will be that much more successful in performing our work.[71]

Smitten with a businesslike self-image, professional men and women indeed succumbed to a demanding corporate worklife. Professional employees, privately loyal to careers that provided transcendent meaning and real privilege, could imagine their endeavors worthwhile. A growing number of casualties could do so less convincingly.

The "corporate culture" engineers had identified a crucial trend: that work's capacity to provide meaning in our lives would make a refuge of the workplace in the volatile economy of the 1980s and beyond. This was annointed by the new professionalism. Professional work offered personal achievement and exile from an impersonal world. If it demoted corporate loyalty, it did so without gaining any real control over the content and pace of work. This remained a corporate prerogative (within boundaries established by the erratic electronics labor and product markets). Accordingly, the new professional's career was rootless, harried, and lonely. Among many it entailed masochistic self-denial, a merger of friendships and business contacts, an operational withdrawal from families and social life, and a preemptive deferral of social responsibility.

The professional's corporate retreat invests George Bernard Shaw's quip with fresh meaning. If today's "professions are a conspiracy against the public," the conspiracy has widened to include a senior corporate partner as well as fresh prey. For the seductions of work also could be measured in substance abuse, trips to therapy centers, unhealthful and obsessive diets, a grueling athletic culture, compulsive shopping, and political disarmament. Silicon Valley and its wayward professionals were not well.

7

PsychoTherapeutico

Let me hear you shout: We don't need a psychiatrist! We have aerobics!

Celebrity fitness instructor conducting class at
Aerobics Expo '84 in Silicon Valley[1]

It hardly matters what I buy, I just get a kick out of buying. It's like that first whiff of cocaine. It's euphoric and I just get higher and higher as I buy.

Silicon Valley shopper[2]

Remember, it's not what you do, it's your attitude.

Silicon Valley Beyond War activist[3]

The Therapeutic Allure

When volatile capital makes work less stable and everything less certain, when neighborliness means not bothering people,[4] when individuality gets levelled in the identical bedroom communities[5] and isolated work of Silicon Valley, therapy offers to make life bearable. Political remedies for shared problems elude people whose lives are structured around working too hard and exhaust their free time shopping, jogging, and struggling to counter the stress and discomforts of their over-work. In a lonely era, and especially in Silicon Valley and kindred habitats, therapy is favored because even when it is crass or manipulative, it speaks the language of personal experience. It is an individual response to a community-based, political problem.

No longer the exclusive preserve of upper classes, therapy is transcending the narrow *modus operandi* of a previous era. *Therapy for the masses* is arriving. Strictly speaking, "therapy" still means a weekly trip to a licensed therapist, a trip Silicon Valley inhabitants make as frequently as anyone.[6] However, therapy's consoling vernacular can be heard elsewhere: enlightened corporations extol the personal rewards of work; easily available and virtually unlimited credit make it possible for harried workers to take their unmet personal needs to the shopping mall where marketing specialists labor to maintain the illusion that each product promises not just utility, but renewed self-esteem for its purchaser; fitness and nutrition specialists give the Silicon Valley worker, whose sense of identity or personal power derives from an unstable corporate world, access to feelings of self-control and self-love. Silicon Valley's notorious drug dependencies are another, barely acknowledged, indicator of the urgency with which people seek relief from work and its discontents.

With the compulsiveness—and with many of the symptoms—of a drug habit, Silicon Valley imbues its free time with the fury and excess of work. Work is a port in the storm of life's uncertainties, because no matter how harrowing, work offers meaning (career logic, technical sophistication) and, for some, an escape from loneliness. The price of battening down all of social life to stay afloat at work, however, is both dear and widely unchallenged. The positive and negative poles of work's magnetism are evident in work's resurgent popularity[7] and in the tripling in claims for work-induced stress in the "Work Decade."[8] Self-conscious about leisure's instrumental role in sustaining work, Silicon Valley takes it in concentrated doses—partly because work and traffic jams compress free time, but also because the collective appetite for relief is apparently insatiable. If shopping relieves boredom and exercise eases stress, then the intensity with which Silicon Valley shops and exercises indicates intolerable boredom and debilitating stress. As individuals burden play with the utilitarian mission of relieving anxiety, play crosses the threshold into therapy (and becomes less playful).[9]

It is not unusual that mass therapy encompasses extreme and impulsive behaviors in a society fragmented by abrupt and open-ended flux in capital, housing, and labor markets. Unsteady jobs and changing communities erode continuity between work, neighborhood, family, and play. So people choose trends or lifestyle "enclaves" which help them feel, if only superficially, linked to others. As Robert Bellah explains,

Members of a lifestyle enclave express their identity through shared patterns of appearance, consumption, and leisure activities, which often serve to differentiate them sharply from those with other lifestyles. They are not interdependent, do not act together politically, and do not share a history.[10]

Without an integrated social context, self-worth is reduced to performance within the isolated enclave: hence the overriding influence that fitness and shopping have assumed in modern life, transfixing people in nearly total, if brief, exertion or immersion. Rather than a strategy to shed unhealthful pounds, fitness and nutrition become a way of life, a "total" strategy of combating fat and purifying muscle tissue. Rather than a means of soothing the effects of stressful work, the aerobics class assumes a quasi-sacred aura with fitness instructors regarded as celebrities or gurus.[11] In a grotesque parody of George Romero's *Dawn of the Dead,* compulsive shoppers wander through malls, purchasing on credit nothing in particular.

What happens when we become so desperate and self-conscious about sustaining unhealthful work that we begin to view daily life from a therapeutic standpoint? The answers are both reassuring and disturbing. Reassuring, because in the cauldron of unstable, demanding work, people tend to seek advice and acquire habits that repair frayed nerves, loosen stiff limbs, and release shackled emotions. Disturbing, because in workaholism, shopping, and fitness, people adopt expedients that may support psychic survival but that fail to challenge the logic behind modern life's compulsiveness.

The therapeutic allure confronts us as a collection of troubled individuals, not as a community; as people with highly personal dilemmas subject to therapy, not as citizens with social problems seeking political recourse. In its presumption of the compromised subject ("patient") unable to make his or her way without the intervention of clinical authority or its self-appointed surrogates, therapy intervenes in daily life with quiet hegemony. And it urges relief now with an insistence that can disable other life interests. In extreme cases, love, friendship, marriage, parenthood, and even work suffer demotions because therapy must come first. Finally, the new "mass therapies" are far more vulnerable to abuse than traditional therapies because there is no therapist to guide and adjust the prescription (not that traditional therapists uniformly do this). On the contrary, the new therapists—corporate efficiency experts, market researchers, ad copy writers, health advocates, and the accommodating czars of consumer credit—have immediate interest in prolonging the treatment. This tangible interest and the urgency of the need for relief imparts the crude, impulsive character of a fix to much of what we do with free time.

A therapeutic ethos also infiltrates the sphere of politics. It does not suppress social critiques that encourage collective rebellion. Rather, it tends to appropriate them, recasting social change as a byproduct of the wholesomeness of individual outlooks. For guilt-ridden military electronics workers and alienated professionals, Silicon Valley has become headquarters for a support-group-as-politics that expresses what is most honest and most frightening about "mass therapy."

Can't Eat Gotta Run

Just as its annual $500 million illegal drug bill[12] blackened Silicon Valley's reputation, "exercise abuse" has emerged as a new and ironic social problem. Hailed as a corollary of Silicon Valley's economic vigor, a bracing regime of fitness and nutrition is showing signs of running amok. Science writers and clinical authorities chronicle "exercise addiction."[13] A University of Arizona research team observes that the social psychological profile of the compulsive male runner bears a striking resemblance to that of the female anorexic.[14] Mass circulation fitness-and-diet magazines have inserted disclaimers in their advice columns, warning of "overtraining."[15] The fitness-and-nutrition craze is one example of how a trend or hobby can begin to function as a "mass therapy" for those Silicon Valley workers who have nowhere else to go for a sense of community or feelings of self-worth but their aerobics classes.

Celebrated in national campaigns since the 1960s, serious (daily) adult exercise remained the preserve of screenstars and professional athletes in the post-World War II United States. By the 1970s, coincident with work's recuperation, rigorous adult fitness began to shed its association with crank subculture.[16] Evidence included the preventive health care or "wellness" cultivated in independent and, later, in company- and university-sponsored newsletters.[17] But for an increasingly visible minority, "wellness" was far too staid a description for the aggressive and intimate appropriation of fitness and nutrition. By the early 1980s, professionals and office workers pursued aerobics and running with a discipline and vanity that enormously exceeded those of America's 1950s pastimes (weekend baseball and golf). A 1988 nationwide survey of over 8,000 working women found that 83 percent exercise at least three days a week: nearly 50 percent exercise five times a week or more.[18] The fitness trend was applauded in boardrooms everywhere, but nowhere more loudly than in Silicon Valley.

The list of corporate benefits to the budding health craze was long and apparently unimpeachable: fitness helped the desk-bound professional cope with the stress of work and daily life, boosting morale and productivity. It helped immunize corporations against the plague of absenteeism. Medical insurance actuarials reminded the corporation of the health-care and retraining costs associated with "unfit" workers.[19] These were the therapeutic goals—all converging on improved performance at work—for which fitness was the treatment.

Both year-round clement weather and a frenetic work culture established Silicon Valley (and the San Francisco Bay Area) as the runner's capital of the world.[20] Silicon Valley also boasted the largest concentration of "Parcourses" (jogging paths with "workout" stations) in the world.[21] New condominium and apartment developers catered to high stress lifestyles by featuring private running and cycling paths, tennis courts, and mini-gyms. Enlightened corporations reimbursed their employees for health club memberships. Others designed health spas and swimming pools into college campus-style complexes. Several Silicon Valley churches, leading a national trend, began sponsoring aerobics, dance, and even martial arts classes to establish a foothold in the fitness enclaves.[22] "The Holistic Ministry," a fundamentalist group offered a chaste fitness alternative with "Praisercise" for Christians who wanted "to tone their flesh without tempting it."[23]

As the activist "fitness" supersedes the passive "wellness" in popularity, the endorphin high becomes available on a moment's notice. In Silicon Valley, car trunks fairly burst with running shoes and jogging jerseys, leotard tights and water bottles, hand-held runner's weights and other sports accessories—items that follow many people to their vacations as well as to their workday workouts.

An otherwise fickle world of fashion applauds and encourages the fitness trend, creating new styles of casual dress and "activewear." Sweatsuits, rugby shorts, and weightroom tops have become desirable street attire, emblems of the healthful obsession. Higher up on the fashion chain, Paris designers are "getting hip to the fitness boom" by creating clothes "for a body that has been toned and firmed with exercise rather than for tall whippet-thin models."[24] Workout makeup, in "six sheer-but-concealing" shades, has made its marketplace debut.[25] In the 1980s, entire families don sweatsuits and running shoes for the weekend. Whether they exercise or not, their fashion statement is one of aggressive health.

The new fitness fuses with concerted approaches to nutrition as well as weight-loss strategies. Fat-free entrees and designer-diet dishes ("Scarsdale" specials, "Pritikin" salad dressings) have crept into corporate cafeteria menus. Ad agencies rush to retrofit old products with new healthful jingles.[26] Amateur athletes, some of whom prefer to exercise instead of eat during lunch breaks ("can't eat, gotta run"), pursue weight loss with a dedication that contrasts sharply with the female dieting culture of the 1950s and 1960s. The era of the catastrophic "power" diet has arrived.

Testimonials to the marriage of dieting and exercise appeared in the new "Health and Fitness" page, featuring a "How I Stay Fit" column, in the *San Jose Mercury News*. One such column carried the story of a mid-forties Silicon Valley sales manager for whom "diets never worked...[c]utting down on food just made him more obsessed with it." So, under the care of an internist who had treated nearly 1,000 Silicon Valley "patients," the manager lost 70 pounds in two months on a potentially fatal liquid diet of under 500 calories a day. The manager pleaded wholesome motivations: "I was just over 40, at that time in your life when you start looking at your family and thinking, 'How can I take care of myself so I will always be around these neat people?' " His catastrophic weight loss was one of several extreme measures. To maintain his post-diet trim, the manager swam a mile every lunch hour and rode 20 miles—on a stationary bike—every evening.[27]

The preferred modes of exercise and the quality of sustained exertion they entail don't leave much room for the socializing that was part of earlier American sports cultures such as softball, bowling, and golf. Extreme fitness and dieting are a reaction to and a reflection of the loneliness of the work-skewed "lifestyle." The emphasis at work and play is on discipline and individual control. These accents are echoed in a holistic health movement that arises to service workplace stress. Stress seminars and conflict-resolution workshops, as well as mainstream and alternative therapists and outpatient clinics, offer "stress audits," "perceptual restructuring," biofeedback, self-hypnosis, abdominal breathing, imaging, and deep relaxation techniques to relieve work-related ills.[28] This dovetails with therapy's intrusion into the culture of fitness and nutrition.

A 1987 *Runner's World* feature that freshly explored the compulsive runner's motivation—a delicate topic—reflects the self-consciously therapeutic approach to fitness:

> Periodically examining your motivation [to run] can refresh your memory and your resolve. There's nothing like stopping to consider all the good things that happen as a result of your running to get

you excited again. Then, the next time you face the nagging question—Why am I doing this?—you'll have all the answers at hand. No further questions; time for a workout.[29]

Mindful of the dreary funk a bad workout can trigger in the obsessive runner, the author, citing "sports psychologists," consoles:

> A runner must remember that what matters is the grand scheme of things. One bad training session isn't a disaster, and one day missed isn't a mortal sin. If you're not up to a workout one day, it doesn't mean your willpower has disappeared.

Searching for reasons to run, and finding many, the *Runner's World* feature insists that "a runner's supposed loneliness is a burden of the past," and recounts the case of a discouraged "miler" who resumed running after finding a "support system" in new running mates: "Running provides positive input, no matter how the rest of our life is going." An interviewee agrees emphatically: "If you went out and ran 8 or 9 miles you did a constructive thing that day. That part of your life was under control, even if everything else was a shambles."

While fitness has become an oasis of self-control and concrete purpose in a world of unhealthful work ("I feel like hell and I go out for a run, and before I know it, everything's O.K."), a dark side is apparent in both the symptoms of withdrawal that overwhelm many injured fitness fanatics and the longing for the biochemical "high" that accompanies heavy exertions. Some obsessive athletes were "cheating," spending so many hours in company spas that corporations and spouses began to reevaluate the notion of fitness as a boon to work and a balance in family life.[30] It was the scourge of the fitness habit.[31] And it wasn't long before journalists were convincing mainstream editors of the seriousness of the problem among professionals.

In 1987, the *Wall Street Journal* printed the following profile:

> [She] was an exercise addict, unable to stop running and doing aerobics even when it hurt. Now in therapy for her problem and holding her aerobics classes to three times a week, she ruefully recalls the recent past: 'What kept me going [attending aerobics classes while injured] was the panic of weight gain and facing what [else] I would do with my day.[32]

This woman and others like her were running or "aerobicizing" so frequently and with such commitment that when they injured themselves, personal crises erupted. Unable to cope with the anxiety and depression of withdrawal, some continued to work out, compounding their injuries and sidelining themselves indefinitely. Others began to seek licensed therapists.

New genres of sports therapy—more professionals—emerged to minister to the disconsolate exercise addict. By 1987, some 1,000 doctoral-level psychologists were treating patients for psychodynamic sports-related problems in the United States. The same year, a Sports and Exercise Psychology Division was established by the American Psychological Association.[33] In Silicon Valley, "sports medicine" centers and clinics that treated professional athletes have opened their wards to a flood of amateurs.[34] The *San Jose Mercury News* advises professionals on the delicate matter of picking an aerobics instructor who won't add injury to exhaustion.[35] "Low-impact" aerobics have emerged to accommodate the injury-prone.

The new fitness and nutrition therapists speak frankly about their patients: "When they can't control what else is going on in their lives, they can control what they eat and how much they exercise," asserted a therapist who counsels women with eating and exercise disorders. A colleague warned: "Then they lose control [of fitness because of injuries] and have no options whatsoever." "There's just something they're trying to destroy or run away from," observes a fitness center manager.[36]

The candor of the diagnoses might have marked the beginning of a social enlightenment. When *The Wall Street Journal* identified the "feeling of worthlessness, loneliness" behind fitness compulsions, it pointed a finger at both the work and the lifestyle of the modern worker.[37] When a *Newsweek* cover story on stress suggested that "today's business world has generated corrosive ways to wear down bodies and spirits," and plausibly depicted the uncertainty of contemporary workplace culture ("The buzz around the modern water cooler is full of anxiety and paranoia"),[38] it tacitly indicted the corrosiveness and uncertainty of the system. But in its age of loneliness, Western society prefers therapies of self-maintenance.

Big Shopping

If conspicuous consumption is a distinguishing trait of industrializing societies,[39] compulsive shopping is a still-evolving mutant strain in late twentieth century capitalism. As Christopher Lasch suggests in *The Minimal Self,* our mode of consumption is the flip side of that of mass production. Thus, the compulsive shopper's pursuit of the latest products finds a reflection in the increased rate at which new products are developed and marketed, which, in the electronics (including software) industry, approaches several hundred each year.[40] In Silicon Valley, shopping resembles a mass therapy for the ennui of work-centered lives shorn of spontaneity and saturated with stress. "Shop Till You Drop," the theme of a Silicon Valley service that buses patrons from workplace parking lots to shopping outlets, suggests both the allure and the aimlessness of shopping. With access to a seemingly endless stream of credit and easy, one-stop shopping malls, today's compulsive buyers have no problem feeding their addiction.[41]

Like the imagery advertising so deftly attaches to fashion commodities, the wherewithal for the shopping expedition is borrowed. An explosion of consumer credit has heated up the retail economy and placed it on precarious footing. By 1988, with personal savings at all-time lows, nonmortgage debt approaches $600 billion, up five times from that of 1960.[42] With the force of Pavlovian association, one study observes, people are willing to pay far more for commodities when they see a picture of a credit card near a cash register.[43] Advances in electronic funds transfers, making possible instant credit approval and extension, have taken the governor off the circulation of consumer credit.

The same banks that are overextended in Mexico and South America now court the U.S. consumer. Banks derive upwards of 30 percent of their total profits from their credit card divisions, and at interest rates that our grandparents would have considered usurious. Roughly 60 percent of credit card holders use them as an informal, open-ended, and often spontaneous loan.[44] As shoppers sink into debt, they are rewarded with fresh lines of credit.[45] The least examined and perhaps most profound effect of credit card debt is the tightening of ties to one or more jobs (which secures the isolation, stress, and time "crunch" to which the new shopping caters).

As the widening channels of credit expand venues for consumption, the shopping center adds convenience: one-stop shopping for those on time-starved schedules. Through a delicate web of investments, finance capital has made shopping easy on a scale and in densities that have no parallel in the annals of merchandising. Regional malls, in search of higher shopper densities, add retail outlets exponentially. Silicon Valley malls expand by up to 60 stores at a time.[46] Shopping center proprietors "position" their retail outlet mix in wars of patronage. Mall mergers have occurred. Through this frenzied retail investment, the consumer marketplace articulates itself in complex, often senseless segmentation. Consumers could choose the bargain club shopping of the warehouse outlet, the nostalgic shopping of the flea market, the *haute* shopping[47] of the boutiques, and everything in between—including a hierarchy of special label shops and designer ministores-within-stores. Likewise, shopping diversifies its appeal by privatizing family consumption patterns. In contrast to the practical family shopping of frugal spouses in the 1950s, women and men alike, as well as teenage girls and boys, shop for and by themselves more than ever before.[48] More than any other public place, the closed space of the privately owned mall is where North America congregates. By 1987, over 70 percent of adults were visiting a regional mall weekly, a frequency that was surpassed in Silicon Valley, where the shopping density at some malls is nearly 50 percent higher than the national average.[49]

Since so many of the habitats lack a town center, a village square, or a commons, it is hardly surprising that people regularly visit malls. The shopping center is the new commons.[50] In the grand fashion of nineteenth century political economy, Marx[51] chronicled the enclosures of England's rural commons as capitalism's most decisive early victory because it transformed the very ground that made possible an alternative "mode of production." The enclosures of the commons created a landless people, "freed" to earn wages in urban factories. In the habitats of the 1980s, the last vestiges of the commons of main street and village square as public gathering spots are giving way to malls and the activity peculiar to them: shopping. In older cities, such as Sunnyvale in Santa Clara County and my hometown of Sheboygan, Wisconsin, city centers and streets are torn up to make way for new shopping malls and parking lots.

Shopping's urgency is transposed into a disturbing priority in the condensed schedules of the 1980s. Each week, adults average six hours of shopping, far more than the 40 minutes spent playing with children or the hour spent gardening or reading books. Teens spend more time at malls than anywhere else except school and home and are probably envied for it: what some working women want even more than free time during the day is longer shopping hours.[52] Before, after, or between work, people rush to transact purchases: some shop via catalog and phone in mail orders from their workstations. During work, they chat about, or privately plan, fresh purchases. Returning home, credit-bound shoppers, deep in debt but not yet delinquent in their monthly payments, receive unsolicited, pre-approved credit cards through the mail. In 1988, *The Wall Street Journal* proclaimed, "Shoppers' behavior has been a major driving force for the economy and has made shopping, arguably, the nation's favorite pastime next to television-watching."[53]

Whatever draws people to shopping centers has less and less to do with fulfilling conventional needs. When researchers asked over 34,000 mall shoppers their primary reason for a visit, only 25 percent responded that they had come to shop for a specific item.[54] Other studies suggest that half or more of all hardware and grocery items are purchased on "impulse."[55] Whim and novelty, not replacement of broken appliances, now guide most houseware purchases.[56] University studies have begun to isolate the compulsive shopper's symptoms. One study found that one in three shoppers said they regularly experience an irresistible compulsion to buy.[57] In another, four out of ten shoppers admitted that their closets were filled with unopened items.[58] By the mid-1980s, a Silicon Valley credit counseling agency was flooded with calls from "overspenders" fending off bankruptcy.[59] Alarmed and bewildered, the nation's most influential business journal constructed this national profile of the compulsive shopping crowd:

> They don't really need what they are shopping for. Often they don't even know what they're after. Some buy things they never wear or rarely use; many buy and then return what they bought, then buy again and return that."[60]

The report lists six very private motivations for shopping. Most, including "alleviating loneliness," "dispelling boredom," "shopping as an escape," "fantasy fulfillment," and "relieving depression," are borrowed wholesale from the vocabulary of psychotherapy.[61]

Unavoidably, the experts began to address the compulsive shopper. According to a marketing professor whose research identified the most avid shoppers as the single, the widowed, and the divorced, "Shopping appears to be a substitute for a relationship."[62] Silicon Valley credit counselors suggest that shopping has become a path to instant gratification made irresistible by widespread despair and loneliness.[63] Shopping, according to a psychologist and president of a New York consulting firm, "is a lot more than simply providing for necessary things. It is obviously fulfilling many needs—a lot of people don't like to confess that."[64]

A Berkeley "wellness" newsletter, in an article entitled "Mall Mania," advises "the compulsive shopper" to lock up credit cards, maintain a purchase "diary," and "analyz[e] the motives of compulsive shopping." The doses of therapy prescribed escalate: "If unhappiness is the cause [of compulsive shopping]...a support group may help." But "if self-help doesn't work, the shopper...should consider psychotherapy."[65]

The bill has come in for the homogeneous isolation of the ranchstyle subdivision, the condominium theme park, and the landscaped apartment complex. Hotly pursued for their safety and reclusion, these housing arrangements secure a slight reduction in street crime compared to that of city-block neighborhoods.[66] But drug dependencies, divorces, and time spent alone all rise alarmingly in Silicon Valley, suggesting a lonely and unwholesome collective existence.

The shopping opportunity is not always a cheap or an effective escape, but it is certainly a ready one. Shopping is a fling from the discipline of daily time-management strategies that rule work, commuting, and most other activities. For many, shopping makes the discipline endurable. "Just the thought of shopping makes me feel better," proclaims the modern working mother.[67] America now looks to it (more frequently than to vacation travel) for new and flirtatious experience beyond the stunted sociality and sameness of its sprawling habitats. But compulsive consumption caters to fleeting urges that no commodity can satisfy for long. In this, shopping is assigned a mission from which it cannot help but return empty-handed.

Shopping had in fact become an impulsive journey into a new *mondo bizarro* of marketing fantasy that plays upon an inner realm of modern desires. A marketing paradigm—"psychographics"—emerged to identify and help cultivate new consumer vulnerabilities. Its mission was to resupply the marketing intellect with modern channels.

The New Channels

In the 1980s, Silicon Valley's own Stanford Research Institute (SRI) International pioneered the most prominent and probably widely used psychographics system, the Values and Lifestyles program (VALS). Silicon Valley was a likely breeding ground for psychographics theory. Without stable families or workplaces, consumption "patterns" for its many social groups lacked demographic consistency, became less reliable and hence—for advertising campaigns—less predictable. This, and the chaos of overdevelopment that defied residential zoning coherence, upset marketing's traditional demographic tools.[68] But psychographics, and VALS in particular, isn't bound by demographics.

VALS attempts to characterize and order social values, beliefs, fantasies and dreams to better attach these to commodities through the medium of advertising. This, however, requires coming to terms with the identity crisis that contemporary culture poses for consumers. To marketing, the new alienation appears as an array of daily emotional problems caused by the collapse of widely shared values and an accompanying instability in every realm of life.

SRI International was on intimate terms with the new alienation. A modern, multipurpose consultant to the Pentagon, the medical industry, and industrial management as well as advertising agencies, SRI published some of the first monographs on habitat lifestyles. These included remarkably candid accounts of the new alienation, such as the following, published in 1979:

> alienation of the [U.S.] office worker is expected to be a growing problem. [The office of the future] may quite possibly become a more impersonal place in which to work...this suggests a potentially far more lonely existence for the individual office worker.[69]

The SRI reports and surveys chronicled the fantasies and fears as well as "higher needs" stirred and left unfulfilled by society. A profound new consumer wantonness was in the offing. VALS articulated a paradigmatic shift within the marketing community in order to better explore the possibilities for profit.

In the 1983 paperback introduction to VALS, SRI's Arnold Mitchell renders a composite snapshot of the compartments of modern American culture. *The Nine American Lifestyles* traverses the spectrum of the fragmented American character: Survivors, Belongers, Achievers, Experientials, etc. Atop a hierarchical topology is the totally integrated individual who overcomes fragmentation by balancing "inner-directed" and "outer-directed" traits and needs.[70] The fastest growing inner-directed group constituted 20 percent of the national population in 1980 and a much higher proportion in Silicon Valley and the San Francisco area. Equating "integration" with "psychological maturity," Mitchell and VALS set forth a marketing sociology that treats consumers as an amalgam of lifestyle constructs. SRI's VALS program and psychographics have evolved into a strategy to confront consumers with emotional and "experiential" material that is longed for but lacking in modern life.

For marketing, the VALS topology has been both practical and insightful. Since disintegration is the chief sociological fact of modern life in the habitats, it follows that commodities should adopt the iconography of what is missing in consumers' lives, offering a path (consumption) to balanced psychological life. VALS-based psychographics also implicitly reject a popular sociological fraud of the era: the much maligned "materialism" of the cynical upscale professionals. Strictly speaking, it is not *materialism* that drives people to shop beyond their means and needs.[71] Shoppers aren't pausing to rationally select useful goods nor are they "price-shopping." On the contrary, they pursue the fantastic symbols offered by commodities, and by consumption itself. From the technical sophistication of a "dress watch," to the durability of ballistics-grade travel luggage, to the purity of the organically grown tomato, people are shopping for qualities that make them feel secure in an unstable world.

SRI was among the most persistent of marketing researchers in evoking the stuff of psychotherapy: experience and emotion. By 1985, SRI researcher James Ogilvy announced, "Advertisers are recognizing that to consumers, emotions are stronger than ideas"; and that "in the information economy, one's higher needs are satisfied through experiences." Betraying a preference for black-box behaviorism, Ogilvy articulated a chilling construct: "The line between a product and its image is blurring. People look at products as if they were mood-altering substances." In other words, marketing could take advantage of and encourage a growing separation between product and primitively derived needs in favor of a higher consumerism defined as: "anything you can do to your mind with a product or service."[72] "Psychographics," as one observer succinctly put it, "help businesses position their products in the minds of consumers."[73]

"Positioning" commonly involves explicit attempts to mollify social loneliness. New modalities of ad copy speak to outsiders, urging them to look into the warmth and intimate society of casual and carnal acquaintance. "Who are we?" asks Esprit, the West Coast fashion house, in a brochure pushing designer denim for teenagers. "It doesn't matter where you're from, what kind of job you have, or what you believe in. There is a common bond. You recognize it [your bond, their denim] when you see it." Among the outwardly bonded, however, there is plenty of room for inner, individual statement. Esprit features "three different washes and two kinds of fabric, yielding a wide variety" of denim that includes six separate bleach washes made according to discrete "industrial processes." The Esprit brochure itself offers a distinct "feel" with a corrugated soft brown cover.[74] A competing design house features a thoroughly jean-clad teenage couple sitting in a tire on a street, gazing unassuredly in different directions. The spare, "integrating" jingle: "Jordache Basics...because the world—isn't."[75] Also frequently invoked are the lifestyle icons and dramas that evoke whatever is missing from the consumer's real life but imagined desirable by marketing research: open roads for high-performance cars, loving children who don't drop out, contented and cared-for elderly citizens.[76]

A potent historical period that influenced the thinking and values of the largest milieu of "inner-directed" consumers was that of 1960s political and cultural rebelliousness. Lacking fresh oppositional movements that could define daily problems in broader political perspectives, there was a retreat to the ambit of individual control.[77] VALS-based product marketing helped advertising update the origins of alienation, locating them in the real world of stressful work and the anonymity of the habitats. Thus, VALS provided the "creative environment" for the alternative value and lifestyle advertising that came of age in the 1980s.

From the high ground of psychographic perspective, less and less restrained by prurient sexual mores, the marketing mind sees in contemporary American culture a wide spectrum of longings and values that advertising might reaffirm: from family love and domestic stability to fat-free gluttony and casual sex. Thus, a semblance of sociological *verité*—a silhouette of the new alienation—often emanates from ad copy. A journalist discerns facets of that alienation in "the new Madison Avenue sexuality":

> Its central characteristics are its introspection and separation from social context. Fathers, sons, and businessmen have not disappeared from contemporary advertising imagery, but they have been supplemented by someone else: the single male figure, existing in a sexually charged social void with perfect, Nautilus-chiseled contours. He exists alone, his body a work of obvious labor in the gym, his lifestyle apparently affluent, but beyond that, unspecified.[78]

Utterly banal as popular culture,[79] shopping elicits private motivations that run deep. If the fulfillment of "higher needs," the prized "integration," is impossible to achieve in daily life, then at least the emotional and experiential semblance could be borrowed from advertising's prefabricated self-imagery. All that is required are new and frequent purchases.

VALS marks a more explicit and certainly more forthright incorporation of therapeutic technique into mass advertising. The new advertising helps propel shopping into a dominant and, for some, dominating, pastime; a crossover into a world of fantasy that is more voraciously consumed than the commodities themselves. The human relief spelled by shopping is profound but brief.

Political Disarmament

At work, scientist Don Homan studies air samples from nuclear explosion test sites for the Lawrence Livermore National Laboratory.[80] For six months in 1984, Homan worked evenings in his garage on a civic project: sculpting a 1,800-pound peace monument for the city of Livermore. Homan defended the apparent rupture between his work and home life: "Just because I work at the lab doesn't mean that I don't want peace."[81]

For decades, the U.S. workplace has deflected politics. Its products presumed desirable, its methods tolerated or defended as trade secrets, the workplace and its corporate sponsors instead imposed a social contract: a continuous stream of affordable commodities in exchange for a free hand to develop technology and exploit resources. Employers have endured savage *economic* battles with labor over the terms of the contract. Even when unions forced improvements in conditions and wages, or when consumers demanded safer goods, the corporate prerogative to produce how, what, and for whom it will remained intact. Unions and most workers have refused to avow, much less challenge, the political choices represented in and by their workplaces. The exception has been during wartime.

The ideological merger of patriotism and anti-fascism during World War II created a figleaf for cold war politics within the U.S. workplace, especially within the nascent military electronics industry. Former electronics countermeasures engineer and World War II Navy radarman Bob Kincholoe recalled the period in Silicon Valley: "after World War II there was this feeling that it was important to maintain a defense capability because it seemed like we had gotten so close to having a real breakdown of the whole world order. The Nazi's came very close to winning."[82] By the 1960s, some continued to fulfill draft obligations by working in the electronics industry. The "defense capability" rationale, along with national support for the Indochinese War, however, wore thin. For reasons of conscience, Kincholoe dropped out of military electronics: then and now, a path followed by few.

Silicon Valley has reaffirmed with a vengeance the tradition of the workplace as sanctuary from politics and, at military contractors, from much of the outside world. Ostensibly, the electronics industry's political contests have been with trade and military officials to secure favor and subsidy, or with local elites to accommodate growth and absorb social costs by bending statutes and stretching public protections. These campaigns encourage the widespread repugnance for politics among electronics workers. "Politics" is, at best, an awkward topic of conversation. When I asked Lockheed missile ballistics programmer Fred about the political implications of his job, he responded, "I enjoy what I do very much. When you get into the political aspects of the thing, well, that sort of bogs me down." Fred confides, "I really feel that there's a lot of money being spent on things that could be better spent elsewhere. Like we're making these big nasty missiles, and everybody hopes they'll never be used. It just seems like that they could build bridges, help people someplace else." At the same time, Fred acknowledges that at work, "We don't talk much about that kind of thing. I think the people around me feel the same way."[83]

If contempt for politics in the workplace remains pervasive, technology's increasingly visible political complexion confronts us more persistently and perhaps more immediately today than ever before. Certainly electronics technologies now pose political questions. So much of it was ordered, and continues to be funded, specified, policed, or managed by military specification. How long can we sustain—and survive—the misfeasance and malfeasance of "defense" electronics, of which "Star Wars" is but one grim project? The manufacture of electronics technology is among the most unhealthful and profoundly toxic human enterprises ever undertaken. How long can we continue to ignore the dire ecological implications of the industry's dependence on toxic chemicals, its insistence on using solvents that shred the ozone? These questions threaten to *force* politics into the electronics workers' life. They also remind us that a political confrontation with the electronics workplace may be a project with a deadline.

For at least two reasons efforts to impose social control of technology are likely to depend on the allegiance of electronics industry workers, especially those with skills in scarce supply. First of all, technical expertise will be crucial to defuse the toxic artifacts and excesses of decades of unrestrained hostile technology that litter our environment. Secondly, electronics workers will necessarily figure prominently in political battles with industry and military elites over technology selection and design. These may strike us as far-off, if not idle, questions and concerns, but they soon may be thrust into daily conversation by social and environmental problems that are more and more difficult to ignore. Like the war scientist/peace sculptor, many who actually create hostile technologies must now contrive a peace with their political consciences.

In the 1980s, a visible minority of physicians, engineers, scientists, and other "professionals" formed a variety of groups for "social responsibility." Their activities include producing newsletters, distributing slide shows, circulating petitions, lobbying politicians, as well as appealing across borders through forums, tours, and award ceremonies that link technology workers throughout the world. Some have focused, perhaps too narrowly, on the vulnerable *technical* premises of Star Wars projects; others on nuclear winter.[84]

Like Physicians for Social Responsibility (PSR), Computer Professionals for Social Responsibility (CPSR) too often retreats to the gloom of unfolding weapons and surveillance technology. As Christopher Lasch observes of social critics in the 1980s: "In the nuclear age, survival has become an issue of overriding importance; but the attempt to awaken the public to its collective implications often tends to strengthen the inertia it seeks to overcome...By dramatizing the dangers ahead, opposition movements inadvertently strengthen the siege mentality."[85] On the fringe of this milieu is perhaps the largest organization of this kind, based in Silicon Valley.

Beyond War, which by 1986 had grown to 30,000 members in just four years under the stewardship of nearly 300 full-time volunteer leaders, is a study in contrasts.[86] Beyond War focuses on "the inevitability of nuclear war" under present circumstances. Its message prominently features the wisdom of converted military and scientific elites who helped create or refine nuclear weapons but who later recanted. Beyond War's seminal message is in fact lifted from a remark by Albert Einstein in 1946: "The unleashed power of the atom has changed everything save our modes of thinking and we thus drift toward unparalleled catastrophe." Beyond War staff includes people whose incomes derive from careers in nuclear and conventional arms design, traffic, and deployment—CIA personnel, military electronics executives, nuclear weapons engineers—as well as lawyers, accountants, real estate developers, and technology entrepreneurs.[87]

Beyond War urges us to "change our way of thinking," to acknowledge that "nuclear weapons have made all war obsolete." When it comes to proposing, however, Beyond War recedes from the political into the realm and vernacular of encounter groups.[88] Some members harbor roughshod notions about "social engineering"[89] and appropriate capitalism,[90] but what holds them together is an emphasis on psychological "conversion" to a "unity principle."[91] In short, Beyond War is interested in transcending war, not stopping it.

As Beyond War (and ROLM corporation) co-founder and former CIA engineer Dean Richeson explains, "Once people change their mode of thinking, [there is] no limit to the forms or outcomes it can take."[92] But worldly forms and political outcomes elude Beyond War. "Beyond War is not a specific program of political or military actions," according to member Martin Hellman, Stanford professor and world renowned encryption specialist.[93] It is against unilateral disarmament, civil disobedience, strikes, or sabotage and disapproves of groups that endorse them.[94] These strategies are "negative." Former Silicon Valley executive and White House Fellow William McGlashan, speaking before the World Affairs Council, rejected armed struggle against South Africa's apartheid regime and opposed peaceful demonstrations against U.S. intervention in Central America. These tactics "set up enemies" and "alienate" most Americans.[95] So, apparently, did a nuclear-weapons-free zone referendum that appeared on the ballot in Palo Alto, Beyond War's national headquarters. The referendum proposed to give weapons makers Lockheed, Hewlett-Packard, Watkins-Johnson, Varian Associates, and others four years to convert or leave town. With a record war chest as well as "thousands of dollars more in computer and employee time," and with the unanimous backing of the Palo Alto City Council, the weapons makers defeated the referendum.[96] Loudly abstaining was Beyond War, which refused to enter the fray or to urge its many Palo Alto members to vote or organize support for the initiative.[97]

When pressed, Beyond War leaders point to the United Nations and international treaties as the shape of the political outcomes they seek. Staffperson Ed Kyser on the UN: "The mechanisms are there, the structures are there, the countries are there, everything is there, except the attitude."[98] In its haste to approach the world with the right attitude, however, Beyond War revises history. For example, Beyond War literature suggests that the abolition of American slavery and extension of civil rights to blacks was a peaceful process of "building agreement" and then "implementation," obscuring references to the illegal activities of abolitionists, the Civil War, and decades of racial violence, history which Beyond War disavows.[99] Another instance: Beyond War staff cited the 1963 U.S.-USSR Test Ban Treaty as a model "agreement."[100] The treaty, which banned atmospheric nuclear testing, allowed underground and underwater testing, methods by which the United States was then conducting most of its bomb tests. President Kennedy prevailed over test-ban treaty opponents by pledging more weapons, and many concluded that the treaty, backed by the Joint Chiefs of Staff, was a ruse.

So what does Beyond War do? With a multi-million dollar budget and a modern multi-media marketing approach to communications, Beyond War transmits its message of transcendental peace in newspaper ads that quote Generals Eisenhower and MacArthur, in literature that often resembles *est* (Erhard Seminar Training) tracts, during retreats to estates in the Santa Cruz mountains, and through its logo—a view of planet Earth from outer space. The most frequent venue for prospective and current members of Beyond War, however, is the small group. For the uninitiated there are "Beyond War Interest Events." For the interested, there are then three "orientation sessions." For the oriented, there are "enrichment days," "personal implication seminars," "clarification days," and "tough issues nights." As one member told a journalist, "Sometimes I go to four meetings a day!"[101] Inevitably, prospective members are asked to take—and live by—the Beyond War pledge:

- I will resolve conflict.
- I will maintain a spirit of good will. I will not preoccupy myself with an enemy.
- I will work together with others to build a world beyond war.[102]

While the pledge and frequent meetings reflect Beyond War's origins in California encounter groups,[103] it's rarely clear what the "implications" to members are. For example, Dean Richeson acknowledges that he was "more responsible than any other [ROLM Corporation co-] founder for the decision to build ROLM's first product...a military computer."[104] Richeson saw "no conflict, no dilemma" hawking war materiel at work and declaring for a world without war as a Beyond War member off the job. It is likewise with other Beyond War leaders.[105] As a staff member explained, "the issue is not to stop working for Lockheed, but to change attitudes about how we resolve conflict."[106] It is no small irony that Richeson and other Beyond War members often sound and act a lot like the military and political leaders whose attitudes they seek to improve. The nonchalance with which leaders balance public support for arms reduction and professional contributions to arms escalation is disturbing.

Still, few could fault Beyond War's stated goals: nonviolence and a world without war. Noting the shrewdness of Beyond War's "nonpolitical" pitch, Hillel Zeitlin, a psychotherapist, observed that by presenting ideas as a "new way of thinking" that transcends a political point of view, Beyond War "bypasses the pigeonholing that comes with most political discussions." Regarding the social context for Beyond War's "nonpolitical" approach, Zeitlin observed, "In the U.S. today, it's not popular to be political because politics are not viewed as having possibilities of really changing the world."[107]

Zeitlin, who reviewed Beyond War literature, also noted Beyond War's tendency to cloak its views in "global truisms" that preclude refutation. For example, Beyond War finds evidence for its "unity principle," which girds its "new mode of thinking," in evolutionary biology, ecology, physics, psychology, economics, and in the structure of thought itself. Zeitlin notes that by "universalizing the idea" and by avoiding fallible, public stands on concrete issues, Beyond War takes positions "that defy critical understanding."

Zeitlin suggests that Beyond War's "highly affective appeal" for "total commitment, total absorption" from members may "numb our capacity to engage in critical processes by equating critical capacity with 'the negative.' This can lend itself to a really vicious exploitation like the

Peoples' Temple of Reverend Jim Jones, who preached the need for a combination of religion and politics. This ultimately became 'follow the leader.' Defying the leader became a sign of bad faith." Considerations of social class severely limit this comparison. The concerns and expectations of the affluent, white Beyond War staff compare poorly with the disadvantaged, minority worshippers of the Peoples' Temple. Beyond War's roots, language, group dynamics, and audience make the analogy to *est's* "Hunger Project" a better fit. Zeitlin agrees "the Hunger Project seems not essentially a program for feeding people, but for selling an idea—that hunger can be ended. It's short on specific ways and means." Both the Hunger Project and Beyond War use "highly abstract, emotionally evocative language, as if to say, 'This is not an idea to be understood, as much as a truth to be absorbed,' " comments Zeitlin.

The analogy between Beyond War and the Hunger Project suggests a profound connection between modern social movements and self-help therapy. This connection was suggested inadvertently in a thoughtful article on Beyond War by *San Jose Mercury News* Sunday features writer Susan Faludi. Faludi attended several Beyond War group sessions, noting throughout her assignment the meticulous detail and punctuality with which Beyond War organized and conducted its events. Faludi concluded that perhaps:

> Beyond War is not so much an effort to eliminate the threat of nuclear war as a struggle to live under its shadow. Whether, buried in the preoccupation with efficiency and agendas and timing, there is an attempt to restore control on the most personal level, to somehow make it all, in [BW patron and founding father] Harry Rathbun's words, 'make tremendous sense.' A kind of order is gained by name tags and rules, by starting and ending an interest event on time.

The author's conclusion is remarkable for its eloquence, honesty, and affirmation of support-groups-as-politics: "And if going to meetings every night provides a method for relieving the pressure of mushroom-shaped clouds on the brain, well, why not? We all must find ways to live in madness."[108]

In psychotherapy, as in real life, it is easier to talk about problems than to solve them. It is often a breakthrough just to identify problems. For those who don't examine it too closely, Beyond War identifies the folly and warns of the danger of status quo politics in a nuclear age. Many nice people join Beyond War. As part of a broader social movement, however, Beyond War's inward focus rewards complacency, providing a political umbrella for a milieu of socially concerned people who value *acknowledging the need* for change more than change itself. In this, the "nonpolitical" Beyond War shares much with ideologies and therapies that appeal to our hearts more than our intellects.

This recalls George Orwell. A "change of heart," Orwell observed in an essay on Charles Dickens, "is in fact the alibi of people who do not wish to endanger the status quo." Orwell applauded Dickens' popular indictments of the Industrial Revolution but found fault with a recurring theme in Dickens novels—the tendency for well-heeled British capitalists like Scrooge to develop guilty consciences and human hearts, from which issued improvements in the lot of impoverished characters such as Bob Cratchett. In this thematic device—the "change of heart"— Orwell saw an unlikely and impractical remedy for what ailed nineteenth (and, for that matter, twentieth) century England.[109]

Perhaps Beyond War members, whose language, wealth, and idiosyncracies could provide character sketches for a twentieth century Dickens, have had a "change of heart." Perhaps Beyond War people really believe it possible to effect social change without confrontation, without argument, without politics. Apparently, people find Beyond War more attractive than countless political groups concerned with the same issues. This raises a fear, explored in dystopias such as *Brave New World* and *1984,* that the iron cage of a technological state suffocates human spirituality and resourcefulness with such cunning that our political imagination atrophies, that civil society is rendered frail and, by default, receptive to the allure of ideologies and therapies beneficial to corporations and the state.

Legacy

> Rootless men and women take no more interest in the future than they take in the past.
>
>   Christopher Lasch[110]

Essential to the therapeutic allure is a culture that makes captivating distractions available, indeed, cultivates the public and private appetites peculiar to them. In *The Minimal Self,* Christopher Lasch suggests that "a culture organized around mass consumption encourages narcissism...not because it makes people grasping and self-assertive but because it makes them weak and dependent." Such a culture, according to Lasch, writing in the early 1980s, "undermines their confidence in their capacity to understand and shape the world and to provide for their own needs."[111] Can the "grasping and self-assertive" traits that electronics entrepreneurs made famous be reinterpreted as the expressions of a culture that "makes them weak and dependent" and thus vulnerable to the therapeutic allure? If "bread and circuses" reflect the spirit of deca-dent Rome, perhaps "work and therapies" capture the spirit of Silicon Valley.

If Lasch's insight applies, then a shock that brings down the credit basis of mass consumption may be required to disabuse us of our borrowed smugness and our social waywardness. Certainly capitalism relies more and more on credit and on the consumption credit fuels to sustain itself, thereby making the system more vulnerable. But the political economy of credit has survived apparently intractable crises. It is arguably the most innovative field of U.S., if not global, capitalism.

The therapeutic allure suggests another corrective: the mass therapy of a subversive social movement. If Paris 1968 or Gdansk 1981 are any indication, social movements can quickly put years of intricately fabricated survival strategies into historical perspective, showing how vulnerable they always were. As the upheavals in Phnom Penh 1975 and Tehran 1979 remind us, however, collective rebellions are no elixir, just as they are neither preordained nor utterly spontaneous.

Having noted the possibilities, we also must consider the context. In Silicon Valley, the pool of political alternatives seems to offer a narrow selection from the absurd to the dismal.

In *River's Edge,* a late-1980s film *noir* based on an incident in Silicon Valley that drew worldwide attention, a high school youth rapes and strangles to death a young girl outside of a habitat.[112] When friends of both victim and killer confront the corpse and discover the senseless motive, they form a pact to protect the killer, "the survivor" of the crime. The pact is subverted, but not before depicting a disturbing, youthful alienation.

Parts of the script for *River's Edge* could have been taken from the crime ledger. "They showed no emotion or conscience, it was like they had ice water flowing in their veins," complained the police inspector at the time. "I have never seen a group of people act so callous[ly] about death in my 15 years of police work," observed a sheriff's officer.[113] Coming from troubled or broken families, undisciplined at school, the sexually experienced, drug-addled teens of Silicon Valley are portrayed in *River's Edge* as cynical, mainstream young adults, not as outsider deviants.[114] They are not rebels as much as victims. Around them, a subculture of rebellion thrives but is not cohesive enough to steer itself as a collective project. The young adults simply have not been provisioned by their families or communities to convey or reflect a shared morality. When tragedy strikes, they are vulnerable. They react with a criminal lack of concern; in fact, they react very little at all. The legacy of the real case that the film, despite many distortions, captured, was the chilling vision of a generation adrift in the nihilism of the times, cut off from the stability earlier generations could find, however elusive, in a variety of social institutions.

The context for the events depicted in *River's Edge* was the small town-turned-habitat Milpitas. In less than a decade, Milpitas lost a Ford assembly plant and then attracted electronics firms to its outskirts so successfully that, by 1988, the Milpitas environs had become the site of the highest per capita income in California.[115]

Can we imagine a more ironic situation than one in which rising conventional indices of economic progress—per capita income, industry startups, new jobs, technology innovation rates—now measure, in personal life, something alien to progress, something almost pathological? When progress is in such thorough discord with human happiness, it is time for profound change.

Perhaps the most engaging potential spring for profound change is the rekindling of public concern over ecological devastation. For the first time since the end of the Vietnam War, the United States is beset by a crisis that can be neither ignored nor managed effectively behind closed doors. In 1988, amid one of the hottest summers on record, the news dailies warned of the vast biospheric changes likely to occur within many of our lifetimes. The electronics industry is a central culprit in both the accelerated shredding of the ozone and the despoiling of air and water.[116] The ecological crises threaten to assign new and unflattering political identities to the once invincible electronics entrepreneur and computer builder: cheerful innovators and absent-minded wizards—or grim reapers?

The intriguing questions remain. Will Silicon Valley residents who ignored previous environmental tragedies respond to more frequent and threatening water and air quality advisories? Will they quietly endure forecasts of a scorching transformation of their clement weather and of rising tides along the Valley's wetlands? Will they take in stride, as they have before, the workplace evacuations and toxic industrial explosions?[117] Or will they finally demand to know which convenience, what compelling new computer design, what uncanny gadgetry, how many trade secrets, and which national security mandate justify their industry's devastation of the biosphere and degradation of their daily lives?

The Information Age has stripped us of our social sensibilities, but it has not yet consigned us to a new dark age. For all the ennui it has brought us, our infatuation with electronics technology has also placed the levers of social change within reach of those previously declared powerless or marginal. An indomitable power to subvert economic and political policy now resides in the consoles of over 30 million computer workers who process the fiscal, economic, and social alchemy that is late capitalism. It is a lever contemporary social critiques largely ignore; perhaps rightly so. For without the political will, or at least a glimmer of collective self-consciousness, the lever cannot be pulled on behalf of meaningful and popular change.

Notes

Chapter One

1. The book titles listed below suggest the honorific treatments of Silicon Valley phenomena: Thomas Mahon, *Charged Bodies* (New York: New American Library, 1985); Michael Malone, *The Big Score: The Billion Dollar Story of Silicon Valley* (New York: Doubleday, 1985); Paul Freiberger & Michael Swaine, *Fire in the Valley* (Berkeley: Osborne/McGraw Hill, 1984); Carolyn Caddes, *Portraits of Success* (Palo Alto, California: Tioga, 1986); Steven Levy, *Hackers: Heroes of the Computer Revolution* (New York: Anchor Press/Double Day, 1984); and Everett Rogers & Judith Larsen, *Silicon Valley Fever* (New York: Basic Books, 1984). Somewhat less effusive, with illustrative vignettes of the movers behind the electronics industry's war room-to-boardroom history, is Dirk Hanson's *The New Alchemists* (New York: Avon Books, 1982). The exceptions include Theodore Roszak's *The Cult of Information: The Folklore of Computers and the True Art of Thinking* (New York: Pantheon, 1986), a social/philosophical critique of the triumph of information over ideas, and *The High Cost of High Tech—The Dark Side of the Chip* by Lenny Siegal and John Markoff (New York: Harper & Row, 1985), which the *Nation* (1 March 1986) reviewer characterized as a "price-of-progress primer."

2. David Talbot, "Fast Times for High Tech," *Mother Jones,* December 1983; Malone, *op cit.* p. 7.

3. Thomas Peters & Robert Waterman, *In Search of Excellence* (New York: Warner Books, 1982).

4. According to a *San Jose Mercury News* "Santa Clara County Work Values Survey," (conducted August-September 1984) over 59 percent of those polled said they were "very satisfied" with their job, compared to less than 47 percent nationally; 30 percent of Valley employees worked more than 40 hours weekly compared to 19 percent nationally. Curiously, 72 percent of those working 51 hours or more per week said they were "very satisfied" with their jobs. The *News* commissioned Survey Sampling, Inc. of Westport, Connecticut to generate the random sample of over 1,500 Silicon Valley workers. Alan Gathright and Pete Carey, "For Workaholics, A Never-Ending Labor of Love," *San Jose Mercury News,* 19 February 1985.

5. See chapter 4 for more on the computer populism of Stewart Brand and Steven Levy's "Hackers"; also Langdon Winner, *The Whale and the Reactor: A Search for Limits in an Age of High Technology* (Chicago: University of Chicago Press, 1986). For glimpses of the hobbyists behind personal computer populism, see Freiberger & Swaine, *op. cit.,* and Levy, *op. cit.*

6. Alvin Toffler, *The Third Wave* (New York: Morrow, 1980); John Naisbitt, *Megatrends* (New York: Warner Books, 1982).

7. M.J. Piore & C.F. Sabel, *The Second Industrial Divide: Possibilities for Prosperity* (New York: Basic Books, 1984).

8. In the 1950s and 1960s, computers were widely viewed as part of a broader machine culture that would eliminate and de-skill manufacturing jobs, no matter how much gadgetry and "convenience" would result. The most eloquent summary of this view remains Harry Braverman's *Labor and Monopoly Capital: The Degradation of Work in the Twentieth Century* (New York: Monthly Review Press, 1974).

9. Among the list of many: Silicon Glen (Scotland), Silicon Forest (Portland/Beaverton, Oregon) Silicon Gulch (Phoenix, Arizona), Bionic Valley (Salt Lake City), Silicon Valley East (Troy-Albany-Schenectady, New York), Silicon Prairie (north Dallas/Austin), Silicon Mountain (Colorado Springs), not to mention Route 128 (Boston) and Research Triangle (North Carolina).

10. Los Altos resident Zschau, after losing the Senate race to Alan Cranston, returned to the data storage media firm he co-founded.

11. The notoriety of Christmas corporate merrymaking in Silicon Valley was reflected in a 1984 *Wall Street Journal* feature that described an Advanced Micro Devices (AMD) extravaganza. AMD, also notorious for firing and denying damages to its chemically injured workers, staged a "six-hour, $700,000 black-tie extravaganza...[with] performances by a 40-member boys' choir, a 50-piece orchestra and the popular rock group Chicago. Fifty pastry chefs have spent the week baking enough tarts, cakes and cookies for 10,000 guests." Patricia A. Bellew, "The Office Party is One Thing at Which Silicon Valley Excels," *The Wall Street Journal,* 21 December 1984.

12. Estimates are from California Employment Development Department statistics for Santa Clara Valley cited in John Eckhouse, "High-Tech's Risky Exodus," *San Francisco Chronicle,* 3 July 1986; Gary Richards, "Call it Service Valley," *San Jose Mercury News,* 25 March 1987. According to Don Clark, Intel, in 1986, cut "7,200 people from its workforce as part of its efforts to rebound from a two-year slump." Don Clark, "History of a Chip Maker," *San Francisco Chronicle,* 15 July 1988.

13. By June 1987, potted plant leasing companies, such as Tiffanies, were advertising sales of plants returned from electronics firms, such as LSI Logic.

14. For volatility and permanent innovation, the electronics industry simply has no parallel in the history of American manufacturing. A unique combination of circumstances—including short product cycles, rapid product and tool obsolescence, the high cost of equipment, cutthroat competition, high firm failure and merger rates, government restrictions on purchases by military electronics firms, the density of cash-short startups, the reduction of federal fixed-asset tax incentives (the 10 percent investment tax credit and the curtailment of accelerated depreciation), the growing influence of speculative finance capital, and the subsequent evolution of property, equipment, and labor leasing business services—all favored leasing in Silicon Valley and the electronics industry. A Silicon Valley building architect explained: "Product life-cycle in Silicon Valley averages only two years. The shortened cycle of concept/R&D/producing/marketing demands continual changes in managing, manufacturing, warehousing, etc....The shortened time periods create explosive needs for change. These seldom allow the lengthy traditional acquire property/design/build/occupy/shake down process. Often the only option is to stay

within the confines of existing leased and/or owned facilities." Tim Nobriga and Carl Swenson, "Hidden Development in Silicon Valley," *Silicon Valley Magazine,* January/February 1985. Chapter 2 examines the impact on workers, as well as how electronics products impart instability to large portions of the economy.

15. Christopher Schmitt, "The Designer's Dilemma," *San Jose Mercury News,* 18 August 1986.

16. "In fact, Santa Clara County has the highest concentration of temporary workers in its labor force of any area in the country." Karen Southwick, "High-Tech Industry Relies on Temporary Work Force," *San Jose Mercury News,* 7 December 1984. The reporter was summarizing a U.S. government study by Palo Alto labor market analyst Donald Mayall.

17. According to Rogers and Larsen, "The most common incentive for job-hopping is money; a move to a new job usually represents a raise of 15%." Writing in 1983, the authors probably were generalizing about the salaried technical workers they interviewed; it was hardly true of wage workers in the industry, whose pay rarely rose and whose job-hopping was most often involuntary, the result of layoffs or plant relocation (see Rogers & Larsen, p. 88, *op. cit.*).

18. Mary A.C. Fallon & Ray Alvarez-Torres, "Out of Work—Overnight," *San Jose Mercury News,* 16 June 1986.

19. Hewlett-Packard, IBM, and CDC run their own temporary agencies. IBM refuses to disclose how many contractors it hires, although a worker estimates up to one in four of IBM's Valley production workers are temporary; many of its salaried staff are contractors. Hewlett-Packard spent $1.6 million on temps in 1981; by 1983, the figure had risen to $5 million. According to an H-P spokesperson, temps help H-P maintain its record of "never having a layoff anywhere." See Karen Southwick, "High-Tech Industry Relies on Temporary Work Force."

20. The industrial vacancy rates for tenant-occupied buildings derived from a nationwide Grubb & Ellis survey. The survey measured empty space relative to local market. Houston was third with 4.2 million square feet and a 27.7 percent vacancy rate; Boston, at 14.9 million square feet, was fifth at 21.1 percent. "County Tops in Industrial Vacancies," *San Jose Mercury News,* 18 September 1986. By 1987, Silicon Valley remained "among the most overbuilt [office markets] in the nation," and downtown San Jose, "home of one of the nation's most expensive redevelopment efforts, may soon become the most overbuilt office market in the country," observed local reporters. In May, 1988, the vacancy rate in downtown San Jose was nearly twice the national average and second only to that of Austin, Texas. Stephen Maita, "Bay Area's Office Glut," *San Francisco Chronicle,* 30 April 1987; Kirstin Downy and Bert Robinson, "S.J. Becoming Capital of Empty Offices," *San Jose Mercury News,* 19 October 1987; "San Jose in Second Place for Vacant Office Space," *San Francisco Chronicle,* 3 May 1988.

21. "We are a victim of the oversupply condition caused by insurance companies, pension funds, savings and loans and out-of-town developers who came into this market all at the same time," whined a Silicon Valley industrial

developer in 1987. George Avalos, "Developer Woes Heat Up in the Valley," *San Jose Business Journal*, 2 March 1987.

22. "Manga: Nihom Keizai Nyumon," ("Comics: Introduction to the Japanese Economy") According to Chalmers Johnson, writing in the *Far Eastern Economic Review* (and reprinted in the *San Francisco Examiner*, 6 April 1987), "Japan's leading economic newspaper, the *Nihon Keizai*, commissioned one of the nation's most famous comic-strip artists, Shotaro Ishinomori, to do a hardbound companion to its deadly serious "Zeminaru Nihon Keizai Nyumon" ("Seminar: Introduction to the Japanese Economy").

23. In many regards, U.S. electronics was never really a U.S.-based industry, if by "base" we mean manufacturing. Since the early 1970s, the U.S. semiconductor and electronics firms have been among the largest employers of Third World labor in the United States and abroad. By the mid-1970s, for example, the five largest chip makers collectively had over 60 production facilities abroad—more than these firms maintained in the United States. See John Keller, "The Division of Labor in Electronics" in June Nash and Maria Patricia Fernandez-Kelly, *Women and the International Division of Labor* (Albany: State University of New York Press, 1983).

24. Much of the wafer fabrication had moved to Texas and New Mexico. Christopher Schmitt, "Chip Firms Moving Manufacturing Out of Silicon Valley," *San Jose Mercury News*, 1 February 1987.

25. John Keller, Thane Peterson, Mark Maremont, Katherine Hafner, Mat Rothman, Russel Mitchell, and Kevin Kelly, "Special Report: A Scramble for Global Networks: Companies are Spending Big on Worldwide Communications Systems" (and companion articles), *Business Week*, 21 March 1988; for the political economy of computer integrated manufacturing (CIM), see *Information WEEK's* cover story and spread: Lee Green and Thomas Derr, "Gearing Up for CIM," *Information WEEK*, 13 April 1987.

26. U.S. technical schools and post-graduate engineering programs are filled mainly with foreign nationals, muddying further the notion of a "U.S.-based" electronics industry. "Taiwan has sent nearly 100,000 of its brightest students to the United Sates for graduate degrees, mostly in science and technology.... [T]he Science Division of Taiwan's Coordination Council for North American Affairs....is in the midst of compiling a data bank on the estimated 10,000 Chinese engineers and technicians employed in the Silicon Valley." (Frank Viviano, "Transplanting the Silicon Valley, *Image*, 21 June 1987.) Other estimates include those by an AP reporter: "At least 7,000 of approximately 20,000 engineers in the Silicon Valley are foreign-born, according to a variety of sources. That figure is reflected nationwide, where 30 percent of the electronics industry's engineers are immigrants, according to the National Academy of Engineering...By comparison, foreign-born engineers comprise only 6 percent of the general U.S. population. They come mainly from India, Hong Kong, the Republic of China (Taiwan), France and Ireland." ("Silicon Valley Reliance on Foreigners Stressed," *San Francisco Chronicle*, 16 May 1988.)

27. The foreign ownership of the "U.S." electronics industry became briefly newsworthy in 1987 with Fujitsu's $200 million bid to purchase controlling interest in the quintessential Silicon Valley chipmaking firm, Fairchild

Semiconductor. Under pressure from the Pentagon, the CIA, and the Commerce Department "to assure the independence of the American electronics industry," Fujitsu dropped its offer (and National Semiconductor subsequently acquired Fairchild, lopping off hundreds of employees in the process). (Peter Kilborn, "Key Officials Oppose Fairchild Deal" *New York Times*, in *San Francisco Chronicle*, 12 March 1987.) Few noted at the time that Fairchild was already owned by the French conglomerate, Schlumberger, Ltd. As Robert Reich wrote in 1987, "Most American high-tech companies are well along in the process of losing their uniquely American identities. Faced with Japanese competitors that have more money to spend on research and development, and better-trained employees, even the largest and most well-endowed American firms have concluded that joining them is a wiser strategy than trying to beat them." (Robert Reich, "The Rise of Techno-Nationalism," *The Atlantic*, May 1987; see also my letter on same, *The Atlantic*, September 1987.) The top 25 foreign-owned or controlled U.S. electronics firms had over $35 billion in U.S. sales in 1987, up sharply from the previous year. See "Top Foreign Electronics Firms in the United Sates," *San Francisco Chronicle*, 10 March 1988. Not appearing on this chart are the U.S. portfolios of many foreign firms. See the following note on Teknowledge.

28. On the strength of exhortations such as this one, from Intel Corp chief executive Andrew Grove, the Defense Science Board, working closely with the Semiconductor Industry Association, proposed that the federal government provide $1 billion and "special antitrust exemptions" to launch a consortium ("Sematech") of computer and instrument/equipment companies and chip makers. An additional $1 billion would be allotted for semiconductor research. (Sematech was approved in December 1987 with $100 million; by May, 1988, agreement on Sematech's relationship to the Pentagon was reached. A Sematech research center, staffed by engineers from over 100 Sematech members including Texas Instruments, IBM, and AT&T, is under construction in Austin, Texas; see Reuters, "$100 Million OKd for Sematech," *San Francisco Chronicle*, 13 May 1988.) But a co-author of the Defense Science Board report was skeptical: "The consortium proposal isn't a long-term solution. *It doesn't address the fundamental structural issues at the heart of the industry's problems* [emphasis added]." (P. Waldman and B.R. Schlender, "Falling Chips, Is a Big Federal Role the Way to Revitalize Semiconductor Firms?" *The Wall Street Journal*, 17 February 1987.) It remains to be seen if Sematech will prove anything more than a new venue for porkbarrelling. In the meantime, however, the Justice Department has proven sympathetic to a wave of electronics industry mergers and takeovers. In Silicon Valley boardrooms, it was called "strategic partnership." A *San Jose Mercury News* journalist quipped, "Silicon Valley 1985 could be dubbed 'partner's paradise,' considering the dozens of deals consummated and the hundreds of small technology-based companies contemplating marriage." For example, by 1986, ownership of expert systems maker Teknowledge was approximately evenly distributed between the following: General Motors, Procter & Gamble, military contractor FMC, French oil giant Societé Nationale Elf Aquitaine, French nuclear engineering firm Framatome SA, and Nynex Corp., a U.S. phone com-

pany. Michael Miller, "Art of 'Strategic Partnerships' is Refined by California Firm," *The Wall Street Journal*, 6 December 1985.

29. Reich estimates that "40 percent, by value, of the advanced electronics finding their way into American weapons systems are now coming from Japan. If the present trend continues, the proportion will rise to 55 percent within five years. A substantial portion of the advanced electronics for Star Wars will be produced in Japan." Reich, "The Rise of Techno-Nationalism."

30. "The growth of high-technology industry in the United States is directly linked to World War II," writes Brookings associate Kenneth Flamm. In his history of the U.S. electronics industry, he calls the development of the computer a "wartime success." Flamm concludes: "The natural question—whether, in the absence of government support, private, commercial interests would have stepped in over the near term with efforts of approximately the same intensity— may be answered with a fairly clear 'no.' " See Kenneth Flamm, *Targeting the Computer: Government Support and International Competition* (Washington: The Brookings Institution, 1987, pp. 6-7, 18). In the 1950s, the Air Force virtually sustained the semiconductor industry; in the late 1950s, the Minuteman II project, which required much smaller and more reliable circuitry than the germanium-based transistors aboard Minuteman I, gave Fairchild Semiconductor the impetus to develop silicon-based integrated circuitry. From Fairchild issued every major and most minor players in the U.S. semiconductor industry through the 1980s. "The Minuteman program," recalls a 1950s-era Fairchild employee, "gave Fairchild the liftoff." Dirk Hanson, *The New Alchemists*, p. 99.

31. "All 50 states and at least two dozen foreign countries now have programs in place to grow economies similar to Silicon Valley's. But if the real Silicon Valley is any model, their efforts may provide mixed blessings indeed." (Michael Rogers with Richard Sandza, "Trouble in the Valley—What Price Prosperity in the High-Tech Wonderland?" *Newsweek*, 25 February 1985.) "Ominous developments are becoming commonplace in California's Silicon Valley and other U.S. high-tech enclaves. America's vaunted leadership in high technology, the wellspring of innovation for the entire industrial sector, is eroding rapidly in every major electronics market. The trend reflects nothing less than a crisis in U.S. high technology." (John Wilson, "America's High-Tech Crisis—Why Silicon Valley is Losing its Edge," *Business Week*, 11 March 1985.)

32. See note 3, Chapter 6.

33. "Divorces outnumber marriages in Santa Clara County today. The divorce rate in Silicon Valley is even higher than the rate for California as a whole, and California's rate is 20 percent above the U.S. average." (Everett Rogers and Judith Larsen, *op. cit.* p. 157.)

34. Rose Ragsdale, "Valley Slump puts a Generation Out of Work," *San Francisco Examiner*, 1 December 1985.

35. "[R]etirement plans are virtually unknown in Silicon Valley. Most companies have no retirement plans at all; youthful employees do not consider retirement benefits when making a job change. Nobody expects to be with the same company long enough to retire. Silicon Valley employees perceive their current job in terms of months or years, but certainly not in terms of lifetime employment." Everett Rogers and Judith Larsen, *op. cit.*, p. 147.

36. "Electronics industry employment in Santa Clara County has plunged by 15,800 jobs in the last 20 months. Low-paid manufacturing jobs have been hit the hardest." (John Eckhouse, "High-Tech's Risk Exodus," *San Francisco Chronicle,* 3 July 1986.) "Since 1984, Santa Clara County, the heart of Silicon Valley, has lost more than 20,000 electronics jobs." (Steve Massey, "Silicon Valley Study Optimistic," *San Francisco Chronicle,* 1 October 1987.)

37. See notes 43, 44 and 45 for chapter 2.

38. "Pat Wheeler qualified for federally subsidized housing and daycare last year even though she worked full time fabricating chips for Signetics Corp. of Sunnyvale...A single parent, the Santa Clara resident says she never could have survived on the $6.77 an hour she earned at Signetics without governmental assistance. 'There's no way I would have made it.' " Wheeler, a 38-year old mother of two, in the electronics industry for over 10 years, had to quit her assembly job when her shift changed and she couldn't arrange childcare. "The new shift ended at 1:30 (am) and the daycare center closed at 12:30." Today Wheeler helps elderly people in their homes for $4.63 an hour, trying to find another job in a wafer fabrication plant. (D. Hauser, "Surviving at the Bottom of the Ladder," *San Jose Mercury News,* 5 November 1984.) Six months after this report was filed, layoffs and plant closings had pushed wages for assemblers and wafer fabrication operators even lower. A California state employment placement supervisor in San Jose observed, "Before, wafer fab operators were earning $9 to $10 an hour. Now they're lucky to get $4 to $5." Kathleen Pender, "High-Tech Job Market Reaches a Low Point," *San Francisco Chronicle,* 10 June 1985.

39. Preliminary results of the Digital Equipment Corporation (DEC) study of several hundred Hudson, Massachusetts plant workers attracted national attention in December 1986. The focus was on workers who process microchips. Summaries of the study were released to DEC and *The Boston Globe.* The study, according to *Globe* reporter Bruce Butterfield, found "double and higher the incidences of worker-reported rashes, headaches, and arthritis" and, among male workers, "significantly higher incidences of nausea." The most publicized finding, however, was of a twice-normal miscarriage rate—39 percent—among workers in wafer-etching areas. An alarming 29 percent miscarriage rate was found among wafer photolithography workers. For more on the study and the industry's response to it, see my "Chips 'n' Dips," *Processed World* 17, Spring 1987.

40. See the following note.

41. IBM and Fairchild use a variety of solvents dangerous at the level of parts per billion: DCE, an acknowledged carcinogen, and TCA, a suspected carcinogen whose correlation with fetal disorders became notorious in 1982. That year saw an alarming increase in birth defects in a south San Jose neighborhood near leaking Fairchild and IBM TCA tanks. Denying the correlation, despite animal research and the special state study that corroborated it, Fairchild, IBM, and other culpables finally settled the neighborhood's class action suit out of court and *in camera* in 1986. (But not before IBM's policy of disavowal visited IBM employees. According to an IBM-San Jose production worker, IBM reacted to news of the 1982 miscarriages by *removing bottled water dispensers from some*

facilities in the contaminated zone, leaving employees no choice but to "back IBM" by drinking tap water, or bring in their own bottled water.) Finding widespread human damage in both the 1983-84 and the 1985-88 studies, California and Silicon Valley health officials balked. In the earlier study, despite overwhelming evidence, officials refused to establish a causal link between the IBM and Fairchild leaks and the fetal disorders and miscarriages. When the later study indicated that not isolated neighborhoods but entire regions were at risk, the officials concluded "We have enough evidence to warrant further study but not enough to warrant a health advisory." For more see my "To Save the Aquifer, We Had to Spoil the Water," *Processed World* 22, Spring 1988.

42. Mitchel Benson, "Santa Clara County's Killing Air," *San Jose Mercury News,* 29 May 1987; Susan Yoachum, "PCB's Found in Mercury News Ink," *San Jose Mercury News,* 17 March 1984.

43. Jim Dickey, "Bigotry Against Asians," *San Jose Mercury News,* 2 February 1984; "Anti-Asian Bigotry Surging," *San Jose Mercury News,* 3 February 1984.

44. Frank Rose, "In the Grip," *Esquire,* February 1985.

45. Andrew Grove, "The Uncertain Future of Silicon Valley," *San Francisco Chronicle,* 26 May 1987.

46. For more on the unions and the electronics industry, see chapter 2.

47. *Harper's Index,* September 1986.

48. James Fallows, "The Changing Economic Landscape," *The Atlantic,* March 1985.

49. Thomas Murray, "Silicon Valley Faces Up to the 'People' Crunch," *Dun's Review,* July 1981.

50. See chapter 2.

51. See the Employment Data and Research Division of the California Employment Development Department's *Annual Planning Information for the San Jose Metropolitan Statistical Area 1986-1987,* p. 3. In 1986, according to a labor statistician (QED Research Inc.'s Richard Carlson) speaking at "Silicon Valley The Future" at the University of California Santa Cruz (sponsored by the Silicon Valley Research Group, 24-25 October 1986), computer-based business services was the fastest growing "sector" in the U.S. economy, growing 9 percent in the first nine months of 1986; the rate was over 20 percent in Silicon Valley, according to Carlson. According to Commerce Department figures, computer professional services grew by 20 percent and data processing services grew by 13 percent in 1987 and both were within the top five fastest growing service industries. ("Fastest/Slowest Growing Industries," *San Francisco Chronicle,* 1 January 1988.)

52. "One of the most striking characteristics of Silicon Valley is an amazingly high rate of job mobility. Some estimate that job-changing may be 50 percent each year. This turnover rate is highest among line-operators, board-stuffers, and assemblers; and somewhat lower among engineers and managers, who may turn over 'only' about 30 percent per year." Rogers and Larsen, *op. cit.* p. 87.

53. Many part-time employees attend De Anza College in Cupertino, the largest junior college in the United States.

54. See chapter 2, as well as Barry Bluestone and Bennett Harrison, *Report to the Joint Economic Committee of Congress,* released 19 December 1986.

55. Thomas Peters & Robert Waterman, *In Search of Excellence.*

56. Robert Howard, *Brave New Workplace: America's Corporate Utopias— How They Create New Inequalities and Social Conflict in our Working Lives,* (New York: Viking, 1985); see chapter 6 of this book.

57. Alan Gathright and Pete Carey, "9 to 5: Rewriting the Rules," *San Jose Mercury News,* 17 February 1985.

58. Richard Gordon and Linda Kimball, "High Technology, Employment & The Challenges to Education," Silicon Valley Research Group Working Paper No. 1, 1985, p. 25.

59. Working Vacation spread, *California,* August 1987.

60. Stanley Cohen and Laurie Taylor, *Escape Attempts: The Theory and Practice of Resistance to Everyday Life* (Great Britain: Pelican, 1978); Robert Bellah et al., *Habits of the Heart: Individualism and Commitment in American Life* (Berkeley: University of California Press, 1985).

61. See especially Paul Freiberger and Michael Swaine, *Fire In The Valley.*

62. By 1985, Apple exclusively embraced the office as the market for its hardware, software, and "personal" computer products; accordingly Apple advertising featured business workplace applications. "In their first 10 years, personal computers have had their greatest impact on the business world," concludes John Eckhouse in the last article of a series on the personal computer. (John Eckhouse, "PC's Revolutionized Business," *San Francisco Chronicle,* 13 January 1988.) What became of the "home computers" and the social agendas of small computer enthusiasts? Reviewing a special 1984 U.S. Census Bureau survey (published in April 1988), reporter Ramon McLeod writes "personal computers were most commonly used in the real estate, finance and insurance industries," that "nearly half the adults who owned personal computers never used them...that [the] 53 percent who actually used their home computers spent most of their time 'learning to use' them and playing video games." Underscoring the personal computer's limited appeal, the study found that "the highest proportion of home computer owners were 35 to 44 years old, college graduates, people with incomes over $50,000 and those employed in managerial or professional fields." (Ramon McLeod, "First Big Study of Home Computer Use," *San Francisco Chronicle,* 7 April 1988; see U.S. Bureau of the Census, Robert Kominski, Current Population Reports, Series P-23, No. 155, *Computer Use in the United States: 1984,* Washington, D.C.: U.S. Government Printing Office, 1988.)

63. See note 8, chapter 2.

64. An alarming case in point is the computerized, nonstop global trading in U.S. Treasury debt, which by late 1986 reached a *$100 billion daily average.* "While traditional exchanges vie to expand hours and form overseas trading links...traders in U.S. government debt are...ceaselessly relaying around the globe the responsibility for executing market orders and managing securities holdings, for their own firms and their firms' customers. Using sophisticated communications and computer technology, plus a lot of physical endurance, such traders are setting future growth patterns in other debt-securities markets

and, eventually, for stocks. These traders, in short are redesigning the financial markets." (Scott McMurray, Matthew Winkler, and Masayoshi Kanabayashi, "Endless Dealing: U.S. Treasury Debt is Increasingly Traded Globally and Nonstop," *The Wall Street Journal,* 10 September 1986.) The authors add, "Of course, big banks, multinational corporations and trading firms already deal in currencies and commodities around the clock, largely by telephone. But the boom in U.S. government securities [is] one of the newest, fastest-growing and most treacherous of international markets."

65. I do not infer that electronics technology is the exclusive or even chief cause of global or U.S. financial instability, although some are beginning to wonder. Citing over $50 billion in delinquent or overdue consumer credit card debt, and warning that "much heavier losses loom," Charles McCoy wrote in 1985 that "after three years of wild growth, consumer debt is fast becoming another sinkhole in lenders' credit swamp. Beyond the jolt that threatens for an already-shaky banking industry, a growing number of economists cite such evidence as October's record monthly drop in retail sales as signals that a deterioration in consumer debt has spilled over into the general economy, menacing the recovery and possibly presaging another recession." (Charles McCoy, "Loan Morass: Losses on Credit Cards, Other Consumer Debt Are Climbing Rapidly," *The Wall Street Journal,* 2 December 1985.) Few doubt that computerized trading has heightened market instability in stocks, securities, and interest-bearing notes, through the infamous "program" trading as well as by allowing an accelerated pace of transactions (approaching 300 per second on the fastest transaction-processing computer systems in 1988). For a survey of growing U.S. bank failures, see Donna Smith, "Many More Bank Failures Expected, Officials Say," *San Francisco Chronicle,* 15 September 1986. The acclaimed (presumed) benefits of computerized banking and credit (convenience, cost of service, etc.) are neither widespread nor obvious. For example, a survey by the Consumer Federation of America found that monthly fees and per-check charges for interest bearing checking accounts rose 10 percent each year from 1984 through 1988. Those with "small balances and moderate activity in their accounts pay fees that are 56 percent higher for non-interest-bearing checking accounts than they did in 1984. The survey found that so-called "basic accounts" (for low-income people) were not available widely. Why? The *Los Angeles Times* reporter summarizing the survey noted that "checking accounts with small balances are often money-losers for institutions because of the costs of processing the accounts, so banks and thrifts frequently pass on the costs to consumers through monthly service fees and charges for writing checks or for using automated teller machines." (*Los Angeles Times,* "Banking Services Costing More, Consumer Coalition Says," *San Francisco Chronicle,* 8 June 1988.)

66. Curt Suplee, "The Electronic Sweatshop: How Computers and Cupidity are Turning Your Office into a High-Tech Nightmare," *The Washington Post,* 3 January 1988; also "Our Friend The VDT," *Processed World* 22, Summer 1988; also note 4, chapter 4.

67. While consolidating a policy to announce only successful military launches and experiments, the Pentagon has released phony "Star Wars" test results and moved to classify and censor publication of a wide range of scientific

research. "Administration Officials Release Phony Star Wars Test Results," *The San Francisco Bay Guardian*, 11 June 1986; Ken Garcia, " 'Star Wars' Flap—Research Censorship Threatens Academic Freedom, Project Foes Say," *San Jose Mercury News*, 29 June 1986.

68. Jean Hollands, *The Silicon Syndrome: How To Survive A High-Tech Relationship* (New York: Bantam Books, 1985).

69. Christopher Leinberger and Charles Lockwood, "How Business is Reshaping America," *The Atlantic*, October 1986.

70. Betsy Morris, "Shallow Roots—New Suburbs Tackle City Ills While Lacking a Sense of Community," *The Wall Street Journal*, 26 March 1987.

71. William Gibson, *Neuromancer* (New York: Ace, 1984); *Count Zero* (New York: Ace 1986).

72. Thomas Pynchon, *The Crying of Lot 49* (New York: Bantam, 1966), p. 13.

73. The surprise $60 million shortfall in San Jose's 1984 budget, as well as unreported high-volume trading in the city's portfolio on the bond market, prompted a grand jury investigation. David Kutzmann and Maline Hazle, "San Jose Short $25 Million—City Forced to Seek Loan to Stay Afloat," *San Jose Mercury News*, 31 May 1984; "Plunging Toward Financial Crisis," *San Jose Mercury News*, 16 September 1984; Mike Tharp, "San Jose Officials Criticized by Panel for 1984 Bond Loss," *The Wall Street Journal*, 28 May 1985.

74. Aleta Watson, "S.J. Unified Bankruptcy Case Ends," *San Jose Mercury News*, 19 June 1984; Teresa Watanabe, "'Enrollment Crisis,'" *San Jose Mercury News*, 17 May 1984. Santa Clara County Human Relations Commission Director James McEntee noted in 1987 that "more than half of the Hispanic students in San Jose's East Side High School District drop out." Gary Richards, "Call It 'Service Valley,' " *San Jose Mercury News*, 25 March 1987.

75. See my "Chips of Our Lives," *Processed World* 10, 1984.

76. John Flinn, "Santa Clara Rowdies Ruin Fun at Park," *San Francisco Examiner*, 31 March 1986.

77. Steven De Salvo, "The 'New Poor,' " *San Jose Mercury News*, 18 October 1985.

78. For a history of the jail overcrowding, see Rebecca Aalner, "Judge Quits Jail Overcrowding Case," *San Jose Mercury News*, 24 June 1987.

79. "For the average Santa Clara County family, the expense of child care—about $2,500 a year—is second only to housing." Michalene Busico, "Corporate Care for Kids—Employer Support for Day Care Slow to Come of Age in Silicon Valley," *San Jose Mercury News*, 17 August 1984.

80. Police narcotics units organized "community meetings" among inhabitants of apartment buildings that housed drug dealers and indiscreet users. A few citizens mobilized support for the five supervisors, tacitly defending their neglect of the Valley's jails and convicts. With fresh discoveries of polluted wells, handfuls of locals came out for meetings that heard their testimony and called for reforms.

81. Betsy Morris, "Shallow Roots—New Suburbs Tackle City Ills While Lacking a Sense of Community."

82. Bradley Inman, "Bay Area's Own Not-In-My-Back-Yard Activists," *San Francisco Examiner,* 9 August 1987.

83. Notable exceptions are the public meetings organized by the Silicon Valley Toxics Coalition.

84. KRON-TV "Town Meeting," aired 11 July 1987.

85. Lewis Lapham, "Landscape with Trolls," *Harper's,* September 1987.

86. Betsy Morris, "As a Favored Pastime Shopping Ranks High with Most Americans," *The Wall Street Journal,* 30 July 1987.

87. See the 1980 U.S. Supreme Court decision *Pruneyard Shopping Mall vs. Robbin.*

88. Betsy Morris, "As a Favored Pastime Shopping Ranks High with Most Americans."

89. John Eckhouse, "Living Costs Threaten Silicon Valley Producers," *San Francisco Chronicle,* 18 July 1988.

90. *Ibid.*

91. "In fact, the electronics industry demand for CFC113, which in 1984 accounted for 37 percent of total U.S. production (55.5 million pounds) is growing rapidly throughout the world, particularly in the Third World where electronics manufacturing is booming." Joe Mannina, "Ozone Depletion: Study points to Silicon Valley," *Silicon Valley Toxics News,* Spring 1988.

Chapter Two

1. Author's Lockheed interviews, 1986.

2. How volatile is the U.S. electronics industry? Citing the exodus of manufacturing jobs from Silicon Valley, a Stanford Research Institute International report to the California Senate's Committee on Long Range Policy Planning concluded that innovation is crucial to the U.S. electronics industry's survival: "California could become the 'electronic rustbelt' of the 1990's unless its electronic, computer, and communications industries are able to remain at the forefront of new product and process innovation and development." John Eckhouse, "High Tech's Risky Exodus," *San Francisco Chronicle,* 3 July 1986.

3. See books listed in Chapter One, note 1.

4. Stephen Maitu, "Silicon Valley Outposts Hum Along," *San Francisco Chronicle,* 2 December 1985.

5. In 1986, the electronics industry entered the second year of its worst depression and startled itself by becoming the largest manufacturing employer in the United States (according to an American Electronics Association report, approximately 2.5 million people work in the electronics industry. "U.S. Electronics Sales Fell 2.8% in Quarter, Trade Group Reports," *The Wall Street Journal,* 3 September 1986). The new rank was misleading, since the industry was actively shedding, not adding, tens of thousands of production workers and their managers. In fact, an even worse decline in steel, auto, and other U.S. manufacturing employment boosted the electronics industry's standing.

6. In the quickly evolving U.S. electronics industry, General Electric (GE) reflects the trend away from domestic manufacturing (especially away from consumer products) to retail sales, financial services, and other service-based industries. In 1983, GE sold its housewares division. In 1984, GE purchased Employers Reinsurance Corporation. In 1985, GE agreed to buy RCA Corporation in the largest non-oil company acquisition in U.S. history. As it was, RCA was not only in the (offshore) TV manufacture and TV network business, but also and increasingly a military electronics business and a service company. In 1987, GE agreed to sell its entire consumer electronics business, including the RCA component, to French electronics giant Thomson S.A. In return, GE received cash and Thomson S.A.'s medical equipment unit. GE announced the sale of its consumer electronics business less than two months after telling affected workers they would have two to three years to reverse their division's losses. Janet Guyon, "GE Gives Consumer Electronics a Chance to Change," *The Wall Street Journal*, 3 June 1987. Laura Landro and Douglas Sease, "General Electric to Sell Consumer Electronics Lines to Thomson SA for Its Medical Gear Business, Cash," *The Wall Street Journal*, 23 July 1987.

7. " 'Plain and simple, there's been a switch from the goods-producing sector to the services sector,' observes Cheryl Abbot, an economist with the U.S. Bureau of Labor Statistics. Retail trade, finance, insurance, real estate and consumer services have grown the fastest in recent years and they are all industries that use computers extensively." *Dallas Times Herald*, "Temporary Agencies Adjust to the High-Tech-Office," *San Jose Mercury News*, 29 September 1985.

8. U.S. Bureau of the Census, Robert Kominski, Current Population Reports, Series P-23, No. 155, *Computer Use in the United States: 1984* (Washington, D.C.: U.S. Government Printing Office, 1988).

9. Richard Gordon and Linda Kimball, "High Technology Employment and the Challenges to Education," Conference on Job Creation, Innovation and New Technologies, Brussels, 2-5 September 1985, p. 19.

10. "Semiconductors: Comeback for the U.S.," *Dun's Business Month*, February 1987. According to reports in 1986 from Dataquest, the market research arm of A.C. Nielsen, banking, financial and business services had an installed base of "business systems" ($5.6 billion) that rivaled that of U.S. manufacturing ($5.9 billion). However, banking, financial, and business services (as well as retail sales) were growing faster than any manufacturing. See the following note.

11. "The service sector (including trade, finance, insurance, real estate, services and government) accounted for 56.7 percent of total U.S. employment in 1940. By 1960, the figure had jumped to 62.3 percent and then to 71.5 percent in 1980. In contrast, goods-producing employment (including mining, manufacturing, and construction) shrank from 43.3 percent in 1940, to 37.7 percent in 1960, and then to 28.5 percent in 1980." Elaine McCrate, "Is it Trickling Down?" *Economic Report of the People* (Boston: South End Press, 1986). Also see note 6 above.

12. Fred Zieber, Vice-President of Dataquest, presentation at Silicon Valley Research Group Conference, University of California at Santa Cruz, 24-25 October 1986.

13. "The production labor force, which comprised 60 percent of all electronics jobs in 1965, had declined to under one-half of all electronics employment by 1984." Richard Gordon and Linda Kimball, "High Technology, Employment & The Challenges to Education."

14. C.H. Schmitt, "Chip Firms Flight," *San Jose Mercury News*, 1 February 1987.

15. Steve Kaufman, "County's Economy Mired in Misery," *San Jose Mercury News*, 7 July 1986.

16. Richard Gordon and Linda Kimball, "High Technology, Employment & The Challenges to Education," p. 25.

17. "Tendencies towards concentration are evident in all sectors of the industry, even to some degree in software development. The industry's ownership structure is increasingly internationalized while the explosion of U.S.-Japanese (and U.S.-European) joint ventures in the past few years presage the emergence of a new strategy whereby giant transnational combines attempt to surmount crisis tendencies by establishing permanent hegemony over the technical standards for future systems development and installation. Industrial concentration and globalization has made existence difficult for the truly independent entrepreneurial firms characteristic of the immediately preceding epoch, for *the conditions of technical innovation and industrial advance in electronics are increasingly dominated by global corporations.*" *Ibid.*, pp.15-16 (emphasis added).

18. Frank Rose, "In the Grip," *Esquire*, February 1985.

19. Bruno, A., J. Leidecker, and J. Harder, "Why Firms Fail: Patterns of Discontinuance Among Silicon Valley High-Technology Firms," University of Santa Clara, October 1985.

20. Teledyne Microwave, Eaton Corporation, Applied Technology, Ampex, Memorex, and Varian Associates.

21. The production wages are 30 to 40 percent lower than the national average for manufacturing workers; some of them hover at the officially reckoned poverty line, or are so low as to qualify fully-employed workers for federal and state assistance programs. The cost of living in Silicon Valley, however, is among the highest in the world, with median housing prices soaring near 70 percent above national figures and car ownership and maintenance a must. This economic vise is tightened by the global electronics labor market that pits Silicon Valley production workers against Singapore workers earning $1.10 per hour or Mexican *maquilladoras* workers averaging 80 cents per hour. John Eckhouse, "High Tech's Big Link to the East," *San Francisco Chronicle*, 30 June 1986; Coimbra Sirica, "Maquilladoras in Mexico: How Plants Benefit U.S.," *San Francisco Chronicle*, 24 May 1988.

22. *Annual Planning Information, San Jose Metropolitan Statistical Area, 1986-87*, State of California Employment Development Department.

23. AEA Press Release, 1981.

24. Bureau of National Affairs, Washington D.C.

25. Thomas Murray, "Silicon Valley Faces Up to the 'People' Crunch," *Dun's Review*, July 1981.

26. Author's AEA phone interview, 1987. The national turnover rate, as compiled by the Bureau of National Affairs, was 13.2 percent in 1985.

27. The impact of layoffs is obscured further by the simultaneous creation of new electronics jobs. For example, a Silicon Valley newspaper survey found that between January 1983 and March 1985, 48 high-tech firms laid off 10,000 workers. For the same period, employment—including military electronics work—grew by 36,000.

28. Author's IBM interviews, 1985. At least four dissident groups inside IBM separately charge that IBM's "no layoff" policy is a sham, that IBM cuts its payrolls through firings and forced transfers. For a surprisingly sympathetic account of these groups see Hank Gilman, "IBM Dissidents Hope for Increased Support as Work Force is Cut," *The Wall Street Journal*, 13 January 1987. Also, for IBM-San Jose dissidents, see *Workers Voice*, 453 W. San Carlos, San Jose, CA 95110; and for the oldest IBM dissident group, *IBM Workers United*, P.O. Box 634, Johnson City, NY 13790.

29. *Annual Planning Information, San Jose Metropolitan Statistical Area 1986-87*, California Employment Development Department.

30. Rand Wilson et al., "Do Unions Have a Future in High Technology?" *Technology Review*, October 1986.

31. The statistics were gathered from the following sources: Ray Alvarez Torres, "More Companies Rent Workers to Fill Gaps," *San Jose Mercury News*, 28 September 1986; Karen Southwick, "Permanent 'Temps' High-Tech Industry Relies on Temporary Work Force," *San Jose Mercury News*, 7 December 1984. According to Manpower's Silicon Valley branch—one of the largest—45 percent of its temps are office workers, 23 percent are production workers, and 29 percent are "specialized" technical workers such as engineers and technicians. Author's Manpower interview, 1986.

32. This anecdote was recounted at a National Writers Union, Local 3, meeting in Silicon Valley, 1986. A Corvus spokesperson would neither deny nor confirm the story.

33. Emily Post-it, "Working to Live or Living to Work?" *Processed World* 19, Spring 1987.

34. Author's IBM interviews, 1985.

35. Karen Southwick, "Permanent Temps."

36. Ibid.

37. June Lapidus, "Just to Make Ends Meet," *Dollars and Sense*, November 1986.

38. By 1986, Manpower, the largest temp agency in the world, offered medical benefits, paid holidays, and vacation pay. But, according to a Silicon Valley Manpower spokesperson, "the vast majority of temporaries never use benefits because they don't stay with us long enough." For example, to qualify for one week's vacation pay, a Manpower temp must "have worked 1,500 hours during the preceding 12-month period," i.e., nearly full time. Manpower correspondence, 1986.

39. Alvin Toffler, *The Third Wave* (New York: Morrow 1980).

40. "We are running [sic] with fewer permanent jobs," according to Audrey Freedman, a labor economist for the Conference Board in New York. "We have

less security... To some extent these (temporary) workers are out in the cold. But *the jobs they are doing might not exist otherwise"* (emphasis added). Ray Alvareztorres, "More Companies Rent Workers to Fill Gaps." According to Alvareztorres, "By some accounts, the number of workers without the traditional job ties of permanent employees easily tops 20 million. Temporary workers are expected to increase their share of jobs. Over the next decade, for instance, the temporary help industry should grow by about 5% a year nationally compared with 1.3% annual growth for all jobs, according to estimates the Labor Department calls 'conservative'."

41. Michael McCarthy, "On Their Own: In Increasing Numbers, White-Collar Workers Leave Steady Positions," *The Wall Street Journal,* 13 October 1987.

42. At a conference held by Silicon Valley Research Group of University of California, Santa Cruz, 24-25 October 1986, panels presented empirical workforce sociology, but not a smidgen of research on the traffic in underground immigrant labor.

43. Santa Clara County 1980 figures based on U.S. Census reports. David Kutzmann, "How Santa Clara Valley is Changing," *San Jose Mercury News,* 22 December 1985. The figures include an official estimate of undocumented immigrants, which, nationwide, total 2 million. Everyone, except the Census Bureau, thinks this grossly understates the presence of undocumented workers. Responding to criticism of its methods, the Census Bureau in 1984 revised its estimate of undocumented workers in California upward by over 170,000. Eugene Carlson, "New Illegal-Alien Count Adds to Some States' Populations," *The Wall Street Journal,* 18 February 1986.

44. Jim Dickey, "Illegals '25% of Workers'," *San Jose Mercury News,* 17 April 1984.

45. Thomas Petzinger et al., "Vital Resources: Illegal Immigrants Are Backbone of Economy in States of Southwest," *The Wall Street Journal,* 7 May 1985. Other estimates put the total Bay Area undocumented figure "between 150,000 and 300,000." Rick DelVecchio and D. Garcia, "Immigration Law is Changing U.S." *San Francisco Chronicle,* 26 January 1987.

46. With penalties for employers who hire "illegal aliens," the Immigration Reform and Control Act (a.k.a. Simpson-Mazzoli) of 1986 appears even-handed. Under its provisions, undocumented immigrant workers must 1) provide, to the INS's satisfaction, proof that they have lived in the United States continuously since January 1, 1982 and 2) furnish photographs, fingerprints, and medical information, all of which, the INS states explicitly, can be used against them. For this, plus application fees ranging from $185 to $420, the undocumented worker receives temporary residency and the promise of consideration for permanent residency. The amnesty program, its sponsors hoped, would accomplish in one stroke the task that has eluded the INS for years: documenting the undocumented. In this it failed. "Nationwide, officials originally projected that up to 4 million undocumented aliens would apply. That estimate later was revised to 2 million. So far, the INS has received 1.2 million...applications." As an embarrassed Congress in 1988 debated extending the amnesty deadline (it wasn't), the law's co-sponsor, Mazzoli, conceded that the turnout "falls short of the numbers

anticipated." Those who did apply, however, are now fully registered with *La Migra*, the very agency that they sought for years to avoid. Casting their lot with the INS, which is eminently corruptible as well as subject to the vagaries of regional and national politics, the newly documented workers and their families must wonder what lies ahead for them. During the amnesty application period, studies showed that undocumented immigration actually *increased.* The studies prompted Senator Phil Gramm to remark that "after an initial period when the law was taken seriously, the level of illegal immigration has risen by 60 percent over the last year. When people are asked why they are coming, they say the don't believe the law is going to be enforced;" Associated Press, "Senate Vote Dooms Extension of INS Amnesty Program," *San Francisco Chronicle,* 29 April 1988. Alfredo Corchado and Dianna Solis, "Politics and Policy," *The Wall Street Journal,* 2 September 1987.

47. A.S. Ross, "New Law Fails to Stem Flow of Aliens," *San Francisco Examiner,* 1 May 1988.

48. J.F. Keller, "The Division of Labor in Electronics," (1981) June Nash and Maria Patricia Fernandez-Kelly, *Women and the International Division of Labor,* (Albany: State University of New York Press, 1983).

49. Thomas Petzinger et al., "Vital Resources: Illegal Immigrants Are Backbone of Economy in States of Southwest."

50. *Ibid.*

51. *Ibid.*

52. Rand Wilson et al., "Do Unions Have a Future in High Technology?"

53. Firms that employ undocumented workers do not always employ temps, the former being an even cheaper substitute for the latter. Companies that "lease" temps for 30 percent of their workforce are likely to issue fewer permanent employee layoffs.

54. "The concept of total employment has been replaced by one of floating, uncertain work. In the past few years new and atypical forms of employment have flourished: temporary jobs, substitutions, piecework, subcontracting, shared workplaces, short workdays, tailored hours..." *Le Monde,* 16 September 1985; cited in *World Press Review,* January 1985. Also see note 6.

55. Barry Bluestone and Bennett Harrison, *Report to the Joint Economic Committee of Congress,* released 19 December 1986.

56. Union representation of U.S. workplaces in 1988 was 18 percent, the lowest proportion in nearly 50 years. U.S. Department of Labor, *Handbook of Labor Statistics 1975: Reference Edition,* Bulletin 1865, Bureau of Labor Statistics, 1975.

57. Steve Early and Rand Wilson, "Organizing High Tech: Unions and Their Future," *Labor Research Review,* Spring 1986.

58. In 1986, the independent Endicott-based IBM Workers United, still keeping its distance, signed a "letter of understanding" under which the CWA promised financial and legal aid. Hank Gilman, "IBM Dissidents Hope for Increased Support as Work Force is Cut."

59. Author's IBM interviews, 1985.

60. The most infamous paternalistic anti-union employer, after IBM, is Hewlett-Packard. "We like to believe the enlightened management style in

Silicon Valley precludes the need for third-party representation," according to a Hewlett-Packard compensation manager. At the time, H-P hadn't increased its entry level wage for assemblers in two years. Wilson and Early recount the blacklisting by National Semiconductor during a UE agitation campaign in 1980. Steve Early and Rand Wilson, "Organizing High Tech: Unions & Their Future."

61. James Mitchell, "Silicon Valley's Work Culture Gives Unions the Cold Shoulder," *San Jose Mercury News,* 4 December 1983.

62. Hank Gilman, "IBM Dissidents Hope for Increased Support as Work Force is Cut."

63. For background to the CWA's capitulation to AT&T, see Lucius Cabins, "Interpreting the Phone Strike: The Line You Have Reached...Disconnect It!" *Processed World,* 9 Winter 1983.

64. Tim Shorrock and Kathy Selvaggio, "Which Side are You on, AAFLI?" *The Nation,* 15 February 1986.

65. "The AEA surveyed almost 1,200 firms about union activity in their plants between 1971 and 1982. They reported fewer than 100 NLRB representation elections during that period, with unions winning only 21. *These figures understate labor's problem"* (emphasis added). Steve Early and Rand Wilson, "Organizing High Tech: Unions & Their Future."

66. Richard Halstead, "Unions Collect Cobwebs While Robots Replace Local Workers," *Business Journal,* 9 January 1984.

67. The IAM executive board in Washington, D.C., over the course of two years, could not be reached for comment; apparently it doesn't return calls either.

68. Michael Eisenscher, "Prospect for Organizing High Tech Industry."

69. Steve Early and Rand Wilson, "Organizing High Tech: Unions & Their Future."

70. In *The Changing Situation of Workers and Their Unions,* the AFL-CIO recommends "associate membership" as a means of reaching workers uninterested in unions but in need of legal and financial assistance in workplace battles. The logic, it seems, is that workers can receive help (including AFL-CIO sponsored credit cards) without the stigma of union membership. With the associate membership program, the AFL-CIO unions capitulate to and traffic in their own tarnished image.

Chapter Three

1. The electronics industry's most basic components—integrated circuits—are etched in silicon or (increasingly) gallium arsenide wafers in a dust-free, controlled environment euphemistically called "the clean room." In this environment at least 100,000 U.S. workers (and hundreds of thousands more throughout the world) spend most of their waking hours. The 100,000 figure is a conservative estimate. In Silicon Valley alone, "nearly 400 electronics firms...employ more than 85,000" assembly workers (Eleanor Smith, "Silicon Valley—Chipping Away at Workers' Health," *Not Man Apart,* October 1981). According to a 1986 Associated Press reporter, "the computer chip industry employs more than 55,000 U.S. production workers, with most believed to be

women." ("Miscarriages Up in Women Exposed In Computer Chip Process," *Associated Press*, 24 December 1986.) But this last figure excludes the thousands of U.S. disk drive assembly and magnetic media fabrication workers as well as assemblers in slightly less controlled but often as toxic environments. By 1986, Amanda Spake counted many more: "Nearly one million women currently work in electronics production in the United States; and hundreds of thousands more work for U.S. companies in places like Mexico, Taiwan, and the Philippines." (Amanda Spake, "A New American Nightmare?" *Ms.*, March 1986).

2. See LaDou's observation on the medical industry's avoidance of electronics industry illnesses and injuries, note 9, below.

3. Author's clean room interviews, 1984.

4. I am grateful to PHASE (see note 3 above) and Injured Workers United for the chemical information that appears in this chapter. I have always found the PHASE fact sheets to be reliable.

5. Don Keller, "Spill Forces Evacuation of Workers," *San Jose Mercury News*, 20 November 1984.

6. The occupational illness rate for Silicon Valley semiconductor workers was 1.3 illnesses per 100 workers, well above the rate for manufacturing workers at 0.4 illnesses per 100. Nearly one out of every two occupational illnesses among semiconductor workers resulted from "systemic poisoning"—exposure to toxic chemicals—more than twice the incidence for other workers. These statistics, compiled from a 1980 California Department of Industrial Relations (CDIR) survey, counted managers and employees and thus diluted the danger to workers. Another factor understated the illness rate: due to automation and "offshore sourcing" of wafer processing facilities, production workers comprise a smaller proportion of the electronics workforce than in most other industries. And it is the production worker who labors in harm's way. Finally, the statistics also discount latent disorders, miscarriages, and birth defects, as well as the special wear and tear exacted by this stressful work. For the CDIR survey, see Joseph LaDou, "The Not-So-Clean Business of Making Chips," *Technology Review*, May/June 1984.

7. What caused the industry's statistical modification? By 1979-80, the industry's high illness rates prompted reviews and planned studies by California OSHA (Occupational Safety and Health Administration) and, on a federal level, by NIOSH (National Institute for Occupational Safety and Health). In response, the Semiconductor Industry Association (SIA) "decided to re-evaluate" (as one of their lawyers put it) the way it recorded chemical "incidents." Suddenly claiming it was "overrecording" workplace illnesses, the SIA, in a stroke of the pen, redefined all "one-time" or "instantaneous" chemical exposures as injuries instead of illnesses. Initially concerned, the CDIR questioned the SIA's loose interpretations of "injury" and "illness." According to a CDIR official who asked to remain anonymous, the industry was under-recording "incidents," including the illnesses the SIA now claimed as injuries. Apparently after prompting by OSHA and the SIA, the CDIR dropped an investigation of the SIA's statistical retouching.

8. For more, see Alison Bass, "Defining Toxic Exposure: A Battle of Semantics," *Technology Review*, May/June 1984 and Doug Millison, "Chip

Makers: Doctoring the Books?" *Metro*, 6-13 June 1985. For the PHASE story, see Amanda Spake, "A New American Nightmare?" *Ms.*, March 1986.

9. "An article written by [Joseph] LaDou on the dangers to workers in the electronics industry was published in a prestigious Scandinavian medical journal in 1983. 'There were *no* other articles in the medical literature,' he says. 'My only reference was a textbook on integrated circuits. Over 50 physicians work for IBM, and not one has published on this subject. Outside of IBM, there aren't half a dozen physicians employed in high technology electronics. Doesn't that amaze you? This will be the second largest industry in the United States by the turn of the century, and there is not *one* study of the health of the workers.' " (Emphasis attributed by Spake) Amanda Spake, "A New American Nightmare?" A 1985 study in Great Britain found a higher than normal rate of malignant melanoma in semiconductor workers. Jane Kay, "Perils of Working in Silicon Valley," *San Francisco Examiner,* 10 April 1987.

10. See my "Chips 'n' Dips" in *Processed World* 19, Spring 1987. Nearly two years after the DEC study, the SIA is still promising, but not conducting, an industrywide study of electronics workers.

11. "Even after DEC informed workers of the [1986] study [finding twice-normal miscarriages among clean room workers], there's been 'no perceptible movement' among women of childbearing age to seek transfers from semiconductor assembly, a spokesman says. And the reaction has been the same at Intel Corp. and National Semiconductor Corp., which also have told their workers of the research." ("Profile of a Warning," in "Labor Letter," a weekly column appearing in *The Wall Street Journal,* 13 January 1987.)

12. See note 74 below.

13. For more on chemical hypersensitivity, see Eleanor Smith, "Chipping Away at Workers' Health"; Amanda Spake, "A New American Nightmare?"; Lynne Olson, "The Silkwoods of Silicon Valley," *Working Woman,* July 1984; Ken Geiser, "The Chips are Falling," *Science for the People,* March/April 1985; Edward Welles, "Dirty Business in the Clean Room?" *West,* a Sunday supplement to the *San Jose Mercury News,* 26 August 1984.

14. Dr. Alan P. Levin, in author's 1985 interview. Levin is cited in most of the articles listed in note 21 above. Not all doctors, including Joe La Dou, agree that this condition bears comparison with virally-induced AIDS.

15. Abba Terr, "Environmental Illness: A Clinical Review of 50 Cases," *Archives of Internal Medicine,* a journal of the American Medical Association, January 1986.

16. Edward Welles, "Dirty Business in the Clean Room?"

17. Amanda Spake, "A New American Nightmare?"

18. California Employment Development Department and American Electronics Association figures for Santa Clara Valley and the U.S. electronics industry corroborate the following observations by Eleanor Smith: "Seventy to 80 percent of the [Silicon Valley electronics] assembly workers are women, many of them single mothers and the majority Mexican, Chicana, Korean, Filipino, and Vietnamese"; and by Amanda Spake: "Electronics is the largest employer of all manufacturing industries in the United States, and nearly the largest employer of women (second by a few thousand workers to the apparel manufacturing

and clothing industry)." Eleanor Smith, "Chipping Away at Workers' Health"; Amanda Spake, "A New American Nightmare?"

19. Author's clean room interviews, 1984.

20. According to the Employment Development Department of California's *Annual Planning Information San Jose Metropolitan Statistical Area 1986-87,* a "semiconductor assembler" can expect an "entry" range hourly wage of $4.50 to $5.50, and an "experienced" range of $6.00 to $8.00. For a "wafer fabrication operator," the entry hourly wage ranged from $4.50 to $6.00 and the experienced wage from $6.00 to $9.00.

21. Author's clean room interviews, 1984.

22. *Ibid.*

23. Passage of a controversial California "right-to-know" referendum makes it illegal for employers not to warn workers of a small subset of toxic substances.

24. It is on the docket at injured workers' compensation hearings that the callousness of the semiconductor corporations seems most calculated—probably because such hearings and the precedents they may set are perceived as liability floodgates, i.e., direct attacks on the corporate treasury. The corporation's best pre-hearing defense often is the confusion surrounding workers' compensation insurance.

25. Author's clean room interviews, 1985.

26. *Toxicity Testing,* Steering Committee on Identification of Toxic and Potentially Toxic Chemicals for Consideration by the National Toxicology Program, Washington, D.C.: National Academy Press, 1984.

27. Gregory Northcraft, "Manager's Guide to Clean Room Operators," *Microcontamination,* May 1986. *Author's note:* The study was sponsored by an employer consortium, the Center for Microcontamination.

28. The articles are listed in note 13 above.

29. By 1987, a controversial new building and fire code, the result of long negotiations between local fire officials and industry representatives, was taking effect. The code mandates air detection systems to monitor for leaks in clean rooms. The proposed building code was so full of loopholes that otherwise obliging officials in several Silicon Valley municipalities initially refused to adopt it. Mountain View fire official Frank Moe called the new code "a boon to the industry, a buy-off for them...our version got dumped for the present version which is more weighted toward industry's favor." National Semiconductor spokesperson David Vossbrink characterized his relationship with fire officials during the drafting of the new building code as "a negotiated process...[Fire officials] say, 'This is what we'd like,' and we say, 'This is what we can do,' and we go from there."

30. There is nothing resembling frequent or rigorous inspection for compliance with such standards as do exist. In 1986, a clean room facility in Silicon Valley could anticipate a fire department inspection annually, a Cal-OSHA inspection even less frequently (now not at all: Cal-OSHA was disbanded by fiat of California Governor Deukmejian), and an OSHA inspection once every six years. The San Jose Fire Department scheduled a year to make its first round of inspections for compliance with the air detection ordinance (see note 29

above). What if Valley corporations are "caught" violating safety regulations? As of 1985, the average proposed penalty for serious health or safety violations was less than $200 for OSHA, and, as of 1986, $2,000 for Cal-OSHA. These are hardly dissuading sums for a firm that may spend several hundreds per week on the business luncheons its sales force consumes.

Chapter Four

1. Attributed to David Sharon, a "software design environments marketing manager" for Tektronix. William Suydam, "CASE Makes Strides Toward Automated Software Development," *Computer Design,* 1 January 1987.

2. George Orwell, *The Road to Wigan Pier* (New York: Harcourt Brace Jovanich, 1958), p. 207.

3. Steven Levy, *Hackers: Heroes of the Computer Revolution* (New York: Anchor Press/Doubleday, 1984), p. 71.

4. "Labor Department figures show that productivity in the service sector—where electronic equipment should have maximum impact and which employs nearly three-quarters of all American workers—is scarcely above levels of the mid-1970s, chiefly because of problems [of] understanding and adapting to new technology." Curt Suplee, "The Electronic Sweatshop: How Computers and Cupidity are Turning Your Office into a High-Tech Nightmare," *The Washington Post,* 3 January 1988. While productivity at computerized firms typically languishes, it plummets drastically when "incidents" destroy entire data bases or prompt management to modify or redesign application programs. For reasons explained later in this chapter, the "incidents" are not always reported. For a sampling of "incidents," see Katherine Hafner, Geoff Lewis, Keven Kelly, Maria Shao, Chuck Hawkins, and Paul Angiolillo, "Is Your Computer Secure?" *Business Week,* 1 August 1988. The list of casualties to computer workers is long and varied. A Kaiser Permanent study found "a significantly elevated risk of miscarriage for working women who reported using VDTs for more than twenty hours per week during the first trimester of pregnancy compared to other working women who reported not using VDTs." (Marilyn Goldhaber (MPH), Michael Polen (MA), and Robert Hiatt (MD, PhD), "The Risk of Miscarriage and Birth Defects Among Women Who Use Visual Display Terminals During Pregnancy," *American Journal of Industrial Medicine* 13, 1988.) In another, four-year study of 871 female computer operators, 45 percent reported pregnancies ending in miscarriage, stillbirth, early infant death, premature delivery, or major birth defects. European studies suggest that computers' low level radiation, which has been linked to genetic damage in chick embryos, is a likely cause. See *Processed World* 15, 1985; 17, 1986; and 22, 1988.

5. "Capital spending by large businesses," according to *The Wall Street Journal,* "accounts for the bulk of personal-computer purchases." Surveying those who own, but do not use, home computers, a *Journal* reporter observes "what's striking about these people is that when asked about what computers

can do, they are hard-pressed to think of much that's useful. But ask those without if they will buy computers, or those with computers whether they would buy them again, and the answers are almost always affirmative. They are afraid of being left behind in a computerized world." Kathryn Christensen, "Home PC: People Don't Need It, But They Fear Life Without It," *The Wall Street Journal,* 13 August 1985. For an analysis of our data fetish, see also Theodore Roszak, *The Cult of Information: The Folklore of Computers and the True Art of Thinking* (New York: Pantheon Books, 1986). According to a special U.S. Commerce Department-Census Bureau report (based on 1984 census data), 47 percent of people eighteen years old and over who have computers at home never use them. Of the 53 percent who do use home computers, most of the time is spent learning how to use them or playing games. U.S. Department of Commerce, Bureau of the Census, *Computer Use in the United States: 1984,* March 1988.

6. Kathryn Christensen, "Home PC: People Don't Need It, But They Fear Life Without It."

7. George Orwell, *The Road to Wigan Pier,* p. 205.

8. An example is *Programmers at Work* which consistently flatters accomplished programmers by asking them if their skills are scientific or artistic. Illustrations feature doodles and code. The focus ignores most of the computer's corporate and military social implications. Susan Lammers, *Programmers at Work* (Redmond, Washington: Microsoft Press, 1986).

9. William Gibson, *Neuromancer* (New York: Ace, 1984), p.11.

10. William Gibson, *Count Zero* (New York: Ace, 1986).

11. Craig Brod, *Techno Stress* (Menlo Park: Addison-Wesley, 1984).

12. Steven Levy, *Hackers: Heroes of the Computer Revolution,* pp. 47, 61.

13. According to a survey of American Electronics Association (AEA) employers, turnover among engineers was 17 percent in 1984, compared to a 12 percent general turnover rate. In the Silicon Valley area, however, one out of five engineers, or 20 percent, switched jobs; the rate rose to 25 percent for some hardware specialists. Turnover for "software engineers" nationally was 22 percent and rose to at least 25 percent in Silicon Valley. "Silicon Valley, New York lead in Job Turnover," AEA press releases, March 1985; Leonard Apcar, "The Labor Letter," *The Wall Street Journal,* 9 April 1985.

14. William Broad, *Star Warriors* (New York: Simon and Schuster, 1985), p. 49.

15. Tracy Kidder, *The Soul of a New Machine* (New York: Avon, 1981), p. 66.

16. Michael continues, "Most everyone is working very hard all the time. And there's just a lot of men in the department. There are no women to speak of, so that [testosterone] chemistry gets set up." According to one study, the number of female computer programmers (33 percent) and systems analysts (25 percent) is rising, but these are concentrated in the lower paying, non-computer-building industries such as banks and insurance companies. ("Women in the Computer Industry," Arnold, presentation at June 1985 University of California, Santa Cruz conference, "Women, High-Tech, and Society.") Very few women have pursued the sorts of college and postgraduate credentials that would allow entry into electronics engineering occupations ("High Technology, Employment

& The Challenges to Education," Richard Gordon and Linda Kimball, Silicon Valley Research Group Working Paper No. 1, July 1985). According to an *Electronic Engineering Times* Salary & Opinion Survey, the "average engineer" is likely to be male 98 out of 100 times. (Denise Caruso, "Meet the (Statistical) 'Average Engineer' " from the "Inside Silicon Valley" column, *San Francisco Examiner,* 18 October 1987.) The women entering the formerly all-male culture of programming are often recent emigres—Taiwanese, Japanese, East Indian, Middle Eastern. Some women adapt to the prevailing culture of competitive isolation, but it is not for everyone—male or female.

17. Jean Hollands, *The Silicon Syndrome: How to Survive a High-Tech Relationship* (New York: Bantam, 1985).

18. Harry Braverman, *Labor and Monopoly Capital* (New York: Monthly Review Press, 1974).

19. With automated cash registers and food processing equipment, mathematical and food-preparation skills for sales clerks and fast food workers have declined as job prerequisites. This has kept competition for these jobs high, and wages between the official poverty line ($9,800) and the Bureau of Labor Statistics' (BLS) "low Budget" ($17,000) (1982 BLS figures from "The Perils of a Dual Economy," Michael Harrington and Mark Levinson, *Dissent,* Fall 1985). Likewise, automated clean-room equipment, as well as emigré labor pools, keep engineering skills low and job competition high among production workers in the electronics industry, which employs 2.5 million workers and is now the largest employer in the U.S. manufacturing sector, according to the American Electronics Association (September 1986). Hourly wages start low ($5.22) and stay low ($8.82) (Radford Associates Inc. Survey of 100+ San Francisco Bay Area Electronics Production Workers, July, 1984).

20. "The addition of one intriguing mystery is nearly as good (and often more interesting) as the solution to another." The original context for this observation is marine biology, but it applies to any complex field of inquiry and invention. Stephen Jay Gould, "Reducing Riddles," *The Flamingo's Smile* (New York: Norton & Co, 1985).

21. Paul Freiberger and Michael Swaine, *Fire in the Valley: The Making of the Personal Computer* (Berkeley: Osborne/McGraw-Hill, 1984).

22. "What Have We Lost?" *St. Mac,* August 1984.

23. Susan Lammers, *Programmers at Work,* p. 261.

24. "When developing software, engineers still have the tendency to design and code custom software for each project," notes *Computer Design* editor William Suydam. Suydam contrasts hardware and software development: "Memory chips are designed to maximize the design regularities, rendering as much of the circuitry as possible in identical, repeatable structures. This results in both design and manufacturing efficiency. But the repeatable patterns in software are fewer and less obvious, or at least software is not represented in a way that manifests such highly regular structures." David Parnas, professor of computer science at Queens University (Kingston, Ontario) agrees: "Software development is hard because there are so few exploitable design regularities." There is more "regularity" to some, but not all, hardware design and development. One example is the trend toward semi-custom or application specific

microchips and the use of virtual compilers. William Suydam, "CASE Makes Strides Toward Automated Software Development," *Computer Design,* 1 January 1987.

25. *Ibid.*

26. Philip Kraft, *Programmers and Managers: The Routinization of Computer Programming in the United States* (New York: Springer-Verlag, 1977).

27. The quotes are from Edward Berard and Ralph Crafts, "Ada Wars II Management is Key to Winning," *Defense Science and Electronics,* March 1985; and from interviews with Grady Booch of Rational, an *Ada* compiler maker. (See chapter 5 for more on *Ada* and structured programming in the military workplace.) The programmer's creativity and allegiance are frequent casualties of campaigns to convert the development environment into a "software factory."

28. "At first I thought it was just communist filth," Victor recalls of his first response to structured programming techniques. Author's programmer interviews, 1985.

29. Philip W. Metzger, *Managing a Programming Project* (New Jersey: Prentice-Hall, 1981), p. 130.

30. This is a text book example; the division and assignment reflects the size and nature of the job and of the department, as well as specialties of each programmer.

31. "More than any other single development factor, a specification that inadequately defines system requirements can jeopardize a project's success." William Suydam, "CASE Makes Strides Toward Automated Software Development."

32. "Experience shows that even the most carefully designed systems may have serious flaws," according to SRI International's Peter Neumann. "The typical large computer program is considerably more likely to have a major, crash-resulting flaw than is the typical car, airplane, or elevator. The computer may be the ultimate machine, but today it's less trustworthy than many of its predecessors." Ivars Peterson, "Warning: This Software may be Unsafe," *Science News,* 13 September 1986.

33. "The estimated development cost for the software in a U.S. Air Force F-16 jet fighter is $85 million. Yet the Air Force expects to spend $250 million maintaining that software over the jet's operational lifetime." William Suydam, "CASE Makes Strides Toward Automated Software Development."

34. John Verity, "The OOPS Revolution," *Datamation,* 1 May 1987.

35. In 1986, an advocate suggested that "structured programming was only a small help. It provided only a 10% to 15% improvement in productivity when people were really looking for improvements of 10 to 15 *times.*" John Verity, "The OOPS Revolution."

36. Philip Kraft, *Programmers and Managers.*

37. "...being a UNIX [operating system] guru meant that you knew UNIX top to bottom. Now there are so many subtopics within that UNIX bailiwick that it's almost impossible to...know everything. I see that at work all the time. We have people who, all they're concerned with, are the communications features of the operating system. ...[I]t's too hard to know all the things. There are too many little special things that you can be doing. And so we've started to have

the diversification [for example] where someone['s]…whole expertise is the way that UNIX talks to the disks and to the device drivers…It hasn't developed completely yet, but I think that it's going to happen." Author's programmer interviews, 1985.

38. *Ibid.*

39. See chapter 5.

40. *Webster's* cites 1620 as the first reference to *hacker* ("one that hacks"): "a person who is inexperienced or unskilled at a particular activity." But *hack* precedes the twelfth century, evolving from "cut or reshape by…crude and ruthless strokes" to "manage successfully" and "tolerate." The adjective *hack* (1749 as a truncation of *hackney*) became "working for hire especially with loose or easy professional standards." *Webster's Ninth New Collegiate Dictionary* (New York: Merriam-Webster Inc., 1987), p. 545.

41. Stewart Brand and Stephen Levy define hackers as the superstars of the computer worker occupation, a conception that informs the "invitation only" status of the annual Hacker's Conference, which Brand and Levy helped organize. In the introduction to an edited transcript of the 1984 Hacker's Conference, Brand suggests that "the hackers may well have saved the American economy…In 1983 America had 70 percent of the $18 billion world software market, and growing." Stewart Brand, "Keep Designing: How the Information Economy is Being Created and Shaped by the Hacker Ethic," *Whole Earth Review,* May 1985; Steven Levy, *Hackers: Heroes of the Computer Revolution.*

42. "Starting about 1981 or 1982, the personal-computer market burst open. Software and hardware were designed to allow freer communication than ever before between large and small computers. This brought about the most recent change in the definition of a hacker: A person who often attempts to gain unauthorized access to large systems by using his personal computer equipment…I think [this] definition is probably here to stay." Bill Landreth with Howard Rheingold, *Out of the Inner Circle: A Hacker's Guide to Computer Security* (Bellevue, Washington: Microsoft Press, 1985), p. 26. See also "Unauthorized Access: The Problem of Hackers," in Steven P. Steinhour's quarterly newsletter *Computer & Law,* Summer 1984; Laurie Cohen, "Internal Security," in the "Office Technology" supplement of *The Wall Street Journal,* 16 September 1985; Dennis Kneale, "It Takes a Hacker to Catch a Hacker as Well as a Thief," *The Wall Street Journal,* 3 November 1987.

43. In the 1950s, Jerry Lewis frequently played the girl-shy scientist and in the 1960s, "Gilligan's Island" featured a bashful "absent-minded professor." The square, adolescent technical genius is a stock character in comic and suspense scriptwriting. In the imaginations of formulaic TV and movie scriptwriters, the hacker often develops a romantic interest beyond that in his computer. Of Silicon Valley, Melanie Branon writes: "A 1982 *California* magazine cover portrayed two gorgeous and scantily-clad females fawning over a bewildered nerd clutching his computer. The accompanying article on inventor Steve Wozniak, 'Revenge of the Nerds,' and a later movie with the same title, helped transform the nerd into a star. But he was an odd candidate for stardom…The nerd wasn't very charming, either." Melanie Branon, "The Taming

of the Nerd: Can Eccentrics Survive the Corporate Takeover of Silicon Valley?,"
San Jose Metro, 7-13 November 1985.

44. Fletcher Knebel, *Poker Game* (New York: Doubleday, 1983); Roger Simon, *California Roll* (New York: Warner Books, 1985); and the entire "cyberpunk" genre of science fiction.

45. Computers help us detect and measure ozone deterioration, a technical feat that in 1988 led to the shocking revelation of an accelerated rate of ozone depletion. The electronics industry contributes (as toxic waste) nearly 40 percent of (U.S.) ozone-shredding CFC 113. Joe Mannina, "Ozone Depletion Study Points to Silicon Valley," *Silicon Valley Toxics News,* Spring 1988. Furthermore, infra-red-to-digital imaging helps us identify droughts, such as the current East African drought, before they spread. (Political elites in possession of this information ignored the message.) The electronics industry taints water supplies—often from geologically old aquifers—wherever it deposits its manufacturing facilities. See my "Save the Aquifer, Spoil the Water" in *Processed World* 22, 1988.

46. "Swan Song for the Happy Hacker," *Electronic Design,* 22 December 1983.

47. Katherine Hafner et. al., "Is Your Computer Secure?" *Business Week,* 1 August 1988.

48. The following excerpt (from an editorial appearing in the hacker/computer security periodical *2600*) reflected the widespread and almost casual circulation of passwords and numbers within the cracker community through their electronic bulletin boards: "Nothing is more boring and useless than a board that lists credit card numbers and Sprint codes. What is the point? They either go bad within a day or are monitored closely." "Our Wishes for 1986 and Beyond," *2600,* December 1986.

49. John Markoff, "Rebel With A Modem," *Image,* a Sunday supplement of the *San Francisco Examiner,* 27 March 1988.

50. "Our Wishes for 1986 and Beyond," *2600,* December 1986.

51. *Ibid.*

52. When I asked programmers Michael and Victor about unauthorized exploration of computer systems, Michael replied, "Yeah, we went through that phase...I didn't have a system that I really owned. I was always on the outside."

53. John Markoff, "Rebel With A Modem."

54. "Swan Song for the Happy Hacker."

55. Steven Levy, *Hackers: Heroes of the Computer Revolution,* p. 38.

56. Associated Press, "Nothing Wrong with 'Hacking' Wozniak Says," *San Jose Mercury News,* 14 February 1985.

57. UPI, "The Myth of the Hacker," *San Jose Mercury News,* 16 May 1985.

58. Laurie Cohen, "Internal Security: it Is A Company's Own Workers—Not Hackers—Who Pose the Greatest Computer Security Risks," *The Wall Street Journal,* 16 September 1985. *Business Week* observed, "experts agree that the No. 1 threat, which accounts for at least 80 percent of security breaches, is internal." Katherine Hafner et al., "Is Your Computer Secure?"

59. "Nobody knows for sure how big a problem computer abuse is. Fewer than 2% of the incidents last year were reported to authorities, according to a

recent survey by the Data Processing Management Association." *Ibid.* Nearly one-third of the defendants included in the National Center for Computer Crime Data survey "demonstrated no knowledge of computer science," according to center director Jay Bloombecker. UPI, "The Myth of the Hacker."

60. Katherine Hafner et al., "Is Your Computer Secure?"

61. "It only takes one disgruntled employee to leave and take a company's entire customer base with him," according to Robert Campbell of Advanced Information Management, Inc., a computer security firm. Campbell was cited in Laurie Cohen, "Internal Security."

62. Steven Levy, *Hackers: Heroes of the Computer Revolution,* p. 398.

63. Stewart Brand, "Keep Designing: How the Information Economy is Being Created and Shaped by the Hacker Ethic."

64. David Noble, *America by Design: Science, Technology and the Rise of Corporate Capitalism* (New York: Alfred Knopf, Inc., 1977).

65. *Electronic Engineering Times,* Salary & Opinion Survey cited in Denise Caruso, "Meet the (Statistical) 'Average Engineer' " from her "Inside Silicon Valley" column, *San Francisco Examiner,* 18 October 1987. In 1986, a Gallup poll found 40 percent of American voters in opposition to Strategic Defense Initiative development; by July 1988, Gallup found 50 percent voter opposition to SDI. Jerry Roberts, "Majority of Voters Oppose Star Wars," *San Francisco Chronicle,* 6 July 1988.

66. Steven Solnick, "The Politics of Apathy," *Technology Review,* July 1983.

67. The hackers Levy documents were in tacit, and often explicit, opposition to Vietnam War era politics. As anti-war protests threatened to intrude into the MIT Tech Square hacker lab, Levy recreates the scene with appropriate irony: "While they [MIT hackers] had created a lock-less, democratic system within the lab, the hackers were so alienated from the outside world that they had to use those same hated locks, barricades and bureaucrat-compiled lists to control access to this idealistic environment." According to Levy, the genesis of hacker culture depended on funding from the most widely feared and repressive power in the world: "one charge leveled at the [MIT] AI lab by the anti-war movement was entirely accurate: all the lab's activities, even the most zany or anarchistic manifestations of the Hacker Ethic, had been funded by the Department of Defense. Everything…was paid for by the same Department of Defense that was killing Vietnamese and drafting American boys to die overseas." Steven Levy, *Hackers: Heroes of the Computer Revolution,* p. 124.

68. Levy quotes a Vietnam era programmer from Silicon Valley's Homebrew Computer Club who fulfilled his draft obligation in a DOD lab helping on a game simulation that gauged the radiation effect from hypothetical nuclear explosions: "Being basically insensitive to political issues, I never even noticed…I was willing [to serve] but not willing to shoot people. I worked there at the laboratory to serve my country. I had a lot of fun." *Ibid.,* p.229.

69. *Ibid.,* pp. 5, 12.

70. *Ibid.,* p. 191.

71. *Ibid.,* p. 196.

72. Stewart Brand, "Keep Designing: How the Information Economy is Being Created and Shaped by the Hacker Ethic."

Chapter Five

1. Rosalie, Steier, "Cooperation Is the Key: An Interview with B.R. Inman," *Communications of the ACM,* 26(9) September 1983, p. 643.

2. Attendance over two days at Moffett Field, the Navy's Western Air Base. See cover stories in *San Jose Mercury News,* 5, 6, 7 July 1985.

3. Up to 30 percent of the workforce may be *directly* employed by military or military contractors. In addition, corporations subcontract work at firms that make both military and civilian products. According to Harry Lewnstein, statistician for the 2,600-member American Electronic Association, 200,000 to 250,000 electronics workers are involved in $13 billion worth of prime defense contracts in the Valley's largest county. (*San Jose Mercury News,* 6 June 1986. *San Jose Mercury News* staff writer Pete Carey writes "about 56,000 civilian defense industry workers hold security clearances in the valley according to the Pentagon's Defense Investigative Service (DIS)...[b]ut the total is probably larger." ("Security Clearance: Workers' Ticket to a Hidden Society," *San Jose Mercury News,* 10 April 1988.) The 50 percent figure includes those who derive direct and indirect income from military money and is attributed to the head of a Santa Clara Valley community college business department in 1984. An example of the indirect income effect: FMC, which made Pershing Missile launch and combat vehicles, employs 6,000 people, or less than 1 percent of the Valley's workforce, but, "in just payroll and benefits alone," according to Dick Jacquet, personnel director for FMC's defense systems group in San Jose, "we're talking about $200 million a year that stays in this area."

4. Lockheed Missile and Space Co. (Sunnyvale) employed 24,000 and FMC (San Jose) over 6,000 in 1986.

5. The proportion of electronics in the Pentagon's budget is rising from 34 percent in 1980 to a projected 41 percent in 1997, according to the Electronic Industries Association (EIA). Curiously, that projection assumes no real growth in funding for the Strategic Defense Initiative. The DOD spent $55.9 billion on electronics in 1985 (*Electronics,* 21 April 1986) and nearly $57 billion in 1986 (*Microwaves & RF,* December 1987); by 1988, the industry boasted over $81 billion in military electronics (*Electronics,* November 1988). On the upward trend, *Microwaves & RF* observed, "While US military spending will experience its third straight year of net decreases with little improvement likely over the next few years, the Pentagon's electronics budget continues to grow."

6. Lockheed has produced the Polaris, Poseidon, Trident (I & II), and Tomohawk Sea-Launched Cruise Missiles.

7. Silicon Valley—Palo Alto and Menlo Park in particular—has the densest concentration of Military Artificial Intelligence (AI) research and development, attracting over $500 million by mid-decade. David Beers, "The Divided Mind of Artificial Intelligence," *Image,* a Sunday magazine of the *San Francisco Examiner,* 15 February 1987.

8. Lockheed is designing the military satellites that will guide, sight, and convey launch signals to space-based weapons. Watkins-Johnson, DalmoVictor, Raytheon, and many other Valley firms design warfare avionics.

9. The Beyond War organization is examined in Chapter 7: Psycho-Therapeutico.

10. So notorious is the military electronics worker's estrangement from family life that in 1988, shortly after a multiple workplace murder by a former employee, ESL president Robert J. Kohler spoke frankly on the topic: "That's a problem, a very real problem when you cannot tell your wife or family what you do. They know where you work but not what you do. And then people get so involved that they tend to work more than 40 hours a week and a lot of Saturdays. The wife begins to wonder where's he spending all this time—what's really going on? Your kids [ask], 'What's daddy do, really?' You cannot answer their questions. You have got to say, 'Trust me.'" (Pete Carey, "Security Clearance: Workers' Ticket to a Hidden Society.")

11. Litton makes a variety of radar, electronic countermeasures, cruise missile tracking and guidance components; Hughes Helicopter (once a subsidiary of McDonnell Douglas, now a division of General Motors) makes combat helicopters; Raytheon builds missiles and a variety of custom avionics products. Lockheed Sunnyvale is a strategic military asset: a custom industrial shop for a variety of military products and projects including space-based missile command and control satellites (see note 12) as well as missiles and aircraft for nearly every branch of the military. Not all projects are known.

12. Lockheed landed a multibillion dollar contract to build Milstar, eight jam-resistant and radiation-hardened military communications and surveillance satellites that, the Pentagon hopes, can withstand a nuclear war. It is said Milstar would provide Lockheed with $700 million in yearly revenue by 1988.

13. The Blue Cube, also known as the Sunnyvale or Onizuka Air Force Station, is a four story structure on the outer hem of the concrete skirt surrounding Moffett Field and Lockheed. Employing 3,000 Lockheed technicians, the windowless, paneled Blue Cube commands over 45 military satellites and routes encoded reconnaissance to the National Security Agency on everything from troop movements in Mindinao to construction sites in Minsk.

14. Warren Davis, "The Pentagon and the Scientist" in *The Militarization of High Technology,* edited by John Tirman (Cambridge: Ballinger, 1984).

15. John Kole, "A-Bomb Worker Joins Peace Effort," *The Milwaukee Journal,* 5 August 1985.

16. The *serious damage* accompanying disclosure of "secret" information includes "disruption of foreign relations significantly affecting the national security...compromise of significant scientific or technological developments relating to national security." The *exceptionally grave damage* corresponding to the "top secret" clearance includes "disruption of foreign relations vitally affecting the national security...the disclosure of scientific or technological developments vital to national security." All quotes from *Industrial Security Manual for Safeguarding Classified Information* (Washington, D.C.: Department of Defense, March, 1984), pp. 5, 12, 13.

17. Citing lack of production oversight ("quality control"), the General Accounting Office in 1988 disclosed that for three years $500 million worth of air-to-air Phoenix missiles—the Navy's most sophisticated—came out of production inoperable and remained stacked by the hundreds in bunkers. The GAO also cited problems with three other missile systems, including the antiship Harpoon missile, the air-to-air Sparrow missile, and a HARM component. (An undisclosed number of HARMs missed their targets in the 1986 U.S. attack on Tripoli.) Months later the GAO reported that due to software glitches, a $600 million renovation and back-up system for the "Blue Cube" (see note 13) satellite control system would be at least three years overdue and cost more than $1.4 billion. The infamous B-1 Bomber project (according to House Armed Services Committee findings in summer 1988) exhibits "persistent flaws" in its electronic warfare and radar systems. Longtime B-1 Bomber critic Representative Les Aspin claimed the Air Force had disclosed to him deficiencies that "will prevent the B-1's electronic countermeasures from ever achieving full operational capability." See the following note for sources.

18. UPI, "Defects Make New Missiles Unusable," *San Francisco Chronicle,* 25 April 1988; John Schneidawind, "New Pentagon Satellite System Having Troubles," *San Francisco Chronicle,* 12 August 1988; *Baltimore Sun,* "Bombers' Flaws Cited: Threat to Cut Funds for B-1B," *San Francisco Chronicle,* 11 August 1988.

19. With bootcamp finesse, the *Ada* environment, according to an advocate, attempts to "enforce" structured techniques by changing the "programming environment." The quotes are from Edward Berard and Ralph Crafts, "Ada Wars II Management is Key to Winning," *Defense Science and Electronics,* March 1985; and from interviews with Grady Booch of Rational, an *Ada* compiler maker. The Army, Air Force, and eventually other Pentagon branches approve or "validate" *Ada* compilers. Pentagon validation means that an *Ada* compiler must pass over 2,300 tests. Once validated, the compilers accept only programs that work on it. Rigid standardization is the goal.

20. Chapter 4 examines the rise and refinement of structured techniques in the computer workplace.

21. Is the U.S. arsenal becoming an expansive museum of inoperable and baroque items kept at great cost by an aging empire? What role do structured techniques play in this process? As structured techniques colonize the military electronics design and development process, project delays and product glitches, far from disappearing, have grown in scope and number. Conceivably, structured techniques contribute in unexamined ways to the misdesign-malfunction syndrome that has compromised virtually every big ticket military (including aerospace) item in the 1980s. Military incompetence, in turn, may inform cold war policy. For example, while the NASA space shuttle program was down in the post-Challenger period, a backlog of military payloads grew. But the (military spy satellite) Titan rocket program was nothing short of an embarrassing disaster. As a result, the U.S. remained without a demonstrated capability to launch and place in orbit either spy or "Star Wars" satellites. This might have been an understated force in bringing the Reagan administration to the nuclear weapons table. (In 1988, the space shuttle launches have resumed.)

22. John Schneidawind, "New Pentagon Satellite System Having Troubles," *San Francisco Chronicle*, 12 August 1988.

23. The procurement document is attributed to the Kirtland Air Force Base Contracting Center and is entitled *Computer Systems Engineering Support for Primary and On-Call Hours on Computer Systems: Information to Offerers or Quoters*, 24 September 1985.

24. "HARM's primary purpose is to suppress or destroy surface-to-air missile radar, early-warning radar, and radar-directed air defense artillery systems..." from "H.A.R.M., A Look At The People Behind This Successful Program," in *TeleTimes* (Teledyne Microwave Newsletter), August/September 1986.

25. The Binford interview and the following quote from Hochschild are from Kathy Holub, "Stanford Resists U.S. Attempts to Censor Research," *San Jose Mercury News*, 29 April 1984.

Chapter Six

1. Advanced Micro Devices *Annual Report*, 1984.

2. "Technology's Human Face," United Technologies advertisement, *The Atlantic*, July 1988.

3. San Jose's Sheriff estimated that 85 percent of the 400 employees at one electronics firm were using drugs in a 1987 Michael Malone documentary on Silicon Valley, "Hometown," Part III.

4. Jean Hollands, *The Silicon Syndrome* (New York: Bantam Books, 1985). By 1985, nearly 60 percent of all Santa Clara County marriages could be expected to fail.

5. Author's Growth & Leadership Consultants interviews, 1988. GLC (formerly "Good Life Consultants") psychotherapists derived the 60 percent estimate from a variety of evidence; to my knowledge, no one keeps aggregate statistics on the number of people in therapy in Silicon Valley. It is an inherently difficult query. According to San Jose Stress Institute psychotherapist Sharon Cameron, the incidence of people seeking or seeing a therapist is hidden by workers who elude the stigma of being "in therapy" by disclaiming it.

6. Robert Reinhold, "Life in High-Stress Silicon Valley Takes a Toll," *New York Times*, 13 January 1984.

7. Lenny Siegal and John Markoff, *The High Cost of High Tech: The Dark Side of the Chip* (New York: Harper & Row, 1985).

8. Author's interview with Apple's Human Resource Director, 1988.

9. Apple's Human Resource Director would neither confirm nor deny the estimate. Apple employees and psychotherapists treating them provided the 65 percent figure, which they understood to be based on employee medical insurance claims; Apple's Human Resource Director corroborated this source.

10. Apple's Human Resource Director was sympathetic to the personal costs of Apple employees' long and hard work weeks. Her characterization,

however, implied that the Apple "workaholic" had a personal problem since Apple doesn't formally require overtime.

11. In a *Wall Street Journal*/NBC News poll which asked "Compared with five years ago, do you think it is now more or less difficult for middle-class people to maintain their standard of living?" 65 percent of the respondents answered "more difficult." John Koten, "Steady Progress Disrupted by Turbulence in Economy," *The Wall Street Journal,* 3 November 1987.

12. In a 1984 report on household and family characteristics, the U.S. Census Bureau found the proportion of single parent families with children had risen to over 25 percent, up from 21.5 percent in 1980 and from 12.9 percent in 1970. Silicon Valley, which by the late 1970s had some of the highest abortion and divorce rates, had, according to researcher Judith Larsen, one of the highest proportions of working women: nearly 70 percent of Silicon Valley women were employed outside of the home compared to a national average of 52 percent. "The Career Usually Wins in Job-Family Tug of War, Researcher Says," *San Jose Mercury News,* 8 April 1986.

13. After studying the (Bolingbrook, Illinois) Ottawa Drive neighborhood, where neighbors once "were the best of friends" and shared in "wine-tasting parties, spaghetti dinners and block dances," a *Wall Street Journal* reporter noticed profound changes: "Today, however, neighbors hardly know one another, and progress—when it comes—benefits the individuals, not the community...Ottawa Drive and its families reflect some of the changes that have splintered the middle class. Where upward mobility was once a given, middle-class households here and elsewhere now find themselves heading both up and *down* the economic ladder." Alex Kotlowitz, "Changes Among Families Prompt A Vanishing Sense of Community," *The Wall Street Journal,* 3 November 1987.

14. Joel Makower, *Office Hazards* (Washington D.C.: Tilden Press, 1981) pp. 102-3.

15. Robert Howard, *Brave New Workplace: America's Corporate Utopias— How They Create New Inequalities and Social Conflict in Our Working Lives* (New York: Viking, 1985). For the economic realities behind the new corporate psychologism see: Mike Parker, *Inside the Circle* (Boston: South End Press, 1988) and Mike Parker and Jane Slaughter, *Choosing Sides* (Boston: South End Press, 1988).

16. Michael Maccoby, *The Leader, A New Face for American Management?* (New York: Ballantine, 1983); Christopher Lasch, *The Culture of Narcissism* (New York: Norton, 1979); *The Minimal Self* (New York: Norton, 1984); Robert Bellah et al., *Habits of the Heart* (Berkeley: University of California Press, 1985).

17. In *The Minimal Self,* Christopher Lasch touches briefly on the topic of work and therapy. He refers to "the shift from an authoritative to a therapeutic mode of social control—a shift that has transformed not only industry but politics, the school, and the family." (Lasch, *op.cit.,* p. 47.)

18. Thomas Peters and Robert Waterman, *In Search of Excellence: Lessons from America's Best-Run Companies* (New York: Warner Books, 1982).

19. John Naisbitt and Patricia Aburdene, *Reinventing the Corporation* (New York: Warner Books, 1985).

20. An MIT business professor influential in corporate organizational development observed, "Corporations are so hard up for answers these days that...there's a $3 billion or $4 billion market for transformational consulting out there." Peter Waldman, "Companies Seeking Advice Spawn Host of Consultants," *The Wall Street Journal,* 24 July 1987.

21. "The excellent companies require and demand extraordinary performance from the average man. We labeled it 'productivity through people.' " Thomas Peters and Robert Waterman, *In Search of Excellence: Lessons from America's Best-Run Companies,* pp. xx.

22. Robert Howard, *Brave New Workplace,* p. 123.

23. Peter Waldman, "Motivate or Alienate? Firms Hire Gurus to Change Their 'Cultures,' " *The Wall Street Journal,* 24 July 1987.

24. *Ibid.*

25. Mark Dowie, "The Transformation Game," *Image,* a Sunday magazine of the *San Francisco Examiner,* 12 October 1986.

26. John McCormick and Bill Powell, "Management for the 1990s," *Newsweek,* 25 April 1988.

27. The "magic" quote is Mark Dowie, the "mental technologies" quip is by Michael Doyle of Interaction Associates, whom Dowie cites. Mark Dowie, "The Transformation Game."

28. Apparently, Erhard's management consulting borrows some of est's infamous psychic browbeating techniques. Consider the following sample filed by a *Wall Street Journal* reporter who observed a video of Erhard lecturing Soviet bureaucrats: "Standing in a Moscow auditorium beneath a picture of Lenin, Mr. Erhard turns to Alex, a Soviet manager, and demands to know how long it would take the man to alter his job. The hapless Alex, conspicuous in a front-row seat, answers, 'It's difficult to say.' But Mr. Erhard persists: 'Say three weeks. Say it, say it.' Alex finally submits, and Mr. Erhard says triumphantly, 'he creates the possibility of finding new approaches to his work in three weeks!' " Robert Greenberger, "East Meets Est: The Soviets Discover Werner Erhard," *The Wall Street Journal,* 3 December 1986.

29. Mark Dowie suggested eerily that an estimated 500,000 est graduates, many of them "rising to powerful positions in the corporate world [a]nd through his well-maintained mailing list, Erhard knows where they are," might explain the attraction for TransTech among large U.S. corporations. Mark Dowie, "The Transformation Game"; Robert Greenberger, "East Meets Est: The Soviets Discover Werner Erhard."

30. "11 million U.S. workers...were 'dislocated' between 1979 and 1984 by the megamergers, regionalizations, 'downsizings,' acquisitions and outright failures that form the warp and weft [sic] of an economy in transition." Daniel Rosenheim, "Job Hopping is New Trend for Workers in the '80s," *San Francisco Chronicle,* 16 March 1987. In 1987, Jonathan Kozol gauged "the loss of traditional jobs in industry" at "2 million every year since 1980." Jonathan Kozol, "Distancing the Homeless," *Yale Review,* Winter 1988.

31. *U.S. News & World Report,* 17 March 1986. In 1986, a spokesman for the President's Council of the American Institute of Management predicted "Up to one-half of all middle management jobs in the United States will disappear in

the next five years." Wanda Cavanaugh, "Cutting Back: Middle Management Shrinks as Firms Tighten Belts," *San Jose Mercury News*, 12 January 1986.

32. John McCormick and Bill Powell, "Management for the 1990s."

33. "Almost 30 percent of the county's workforce spends 41-50 hours a week at work, and another 10.4 percent works 51 hours or more. Nationally only 19% of the workforce works 41-50 hours on the job." Alan Gathright and Pete Carey, "For Workaholics, A Never-ending Labor of Love," *San Jose Mercury News*, 19 February 1985. The Silicon Valley figures included "high-tech" and "non-high tech" workers, and therefore probably understated "overtime" by people employed in the electronics industry.

34. Wage workers enjoy precious little of the heralded Silicon Valley workday flexibility, and even less of the fitness courses and running tracks. They are constrained by brief (30 to 45 minute) lunch times and much shorter breaks, often at preset times. One microchip fabrication worker, a single parent of three, had to quit her job at Signetics when her employer rescheduled her shift: "The new shift ended at 1:30 (a.m.) and the day care center closed at 12:30." She subsequently found work helping elderly people for $4.63 an hour. The Signetics worker's plight is not uncommon. In addition, assemblers and clean room workers are expected to report to work more punctually than salaried workers. "Surviving at the Bottom of the Ladder," *San Jose Mercury News*, 5 November 1984.

35. Brandon Bailey, "Silicon Valley's Job Losses Continue," *San Jose Mercury News*, 28 December 1985.

36. Ray Alvareztorres, "The End of the No-Layoff Policy," *San Jose Mercury News*, 19 August 1986; Christopher Schmitt, "AMD Abandons its Policy of No Layoffs," *San Jose Mercury News*, 12 August 1986; Evelyn Richards, "Computer Maker Drops 'No Layoff' Policy, cuts 500," *San Jose Mercury News*, 14 August 1986. As it was, the "no layoff" policies at most electronics corporations, including IBM and Hewlett Packard, were bogus; see Chapter 2. For a summary of IBM's "restructuring" (as of July, 1988), see Don Clark, "Vast IBM Cutback in Operations," *San Francisco Chronicle*, 30 June 1988.

37. Robert Levering, Milton Moskowitz, and Michael Katz, *The 100 Best Companies to Work for in America* (New York: New American Library, 1985, by arrangement with Addison-Wesley, 1984).

38. Andrew Grove, "High Output Management," *San Jose Mercury News*, 16 January 1985.

39. Author's clean room interviews, 1985.

40. Even Levering, Moskowitz, and Katz, who advertise Intel to prospective employees, note that "Intel is not for everyone. In general, it's for high achievers who don't mind being measured, because at Intel you are always being measured...some have left because they didn't like working in a pressure cooker." Robert Levering, Milton Moskowitz, and Michael Katz, *The 100 Best Companies to Work for in America*, pp. 160-61.

41. UPI, "GE's Welch, Intel's Grove rated as Toughest Bosses," *San Jose Mercury News*, 19 July 1984.

42. ROLM Corporation Annual Report, 1983, p. 26.

43. Internal ROLM memorandum to employees, 11 May 1988. ROLM was a subsidiary of IBM until 1988.

44. Daniel Rosenheim, "Job Hopping is New Trend for Workers in the '80s," *San Francisco Chronicle,* 16 March 1987; Gary Dessler, "Jumping Jobs Could Be Step to the Fast Track," *San Jose Mercury News,* 1 June 1986.

45. "In the age of the Me Generation, job-switching has become something of a national pastime." Daniel Rosenheim, "Job Hopping is New Trend for Workers in the '80s."

46. Throughout I use *professionalism* in the sense assigned by *Webster's Ninth New Collegiate Dictionary:* "the conduct, aims, or qualities that characterize or mark a profession or a professional person." *Webster's* second and only other definition: "the following of a profession (as athletics) for gain or livelihood." The "athletics" *profession* example befits the surfboard imagery of AMD's 1980 recruitment ad. In fact, the *Webster's* listings for the slightly archaic profession (13th century) and for the modern *professional* (15th century) illustrate the evolution. *Webster's Ninth New Collegiate Dictionary* Ninth Edition (Springfield, Massachusetts: Merriam-Webster, 1987), p. 939.

47. For the preponderance of salaried design, development, communications, sales, and business employees in Silicon Valley, see Chapter 2.

48. Robert Levering, Milton Moskowitz, and Michael Katz, *The 100 Best Companies to Work for in America* (Menlo Park, California: Addison-Wesley, 1984); *Everybody's Business: An Almanac* (New York: Harper & Row, 1980).

49. The authors introduce *100 Best* by accurately noting that "American companies are rarely examined from the standpoint of their employees." Though emphatic about conveying employees' perceptions of the workplace, Levering, Moskowitz, and Katz's information-gathering techniques seem to have undermined their stated goal. They interviewed manager and managed at 135 companies. The authors allowed employers to set up employee interviews, conducted mainly in groups on corporate premises, all of which is hardly conducive to the whistle-blowing and anger that might have emerged elsewhere (e.g., in a bar after work) by employees not hand-picked by their employers for interviews. As a result, *100 Best* is rife with the kind of sanguine and gushy appraisals of corporate culture that fill annual reports to stockholders.

50. The jacuzzi-and-fern-bar "ROLM Culture" is a far cry from the sweatshops and company barracks of Silicon Valley firms' Far-Eastern operations, which supply chips for ROLM computers. (The authors do not review the brutalities practiced at some of the "offshore" corporate worksites of AMD, Intel, and other *100 Best* firms.)

51. The authors suggest that for prospective ROLM recruits, answers to such questions as "How do you look in a bathing suit?" outweigh the social implications of building ROLM's MIL-SPEC (Military Specification) Hawk/32-bit computer. The Hawk is used for "command, control, communications, intelligence, signal processing and weapons control" applications (*ROLM Corporation Annual Report,* 1983), but is misleadingly referred to in *100 Best* as an "all-weather minicomputer." In fact, the authors omit all but a single passing reference to ROLM's considerable military hardware pipeline, which also includes its proprietary *Ada* compiler and *"Ada* Development Environment"

hardware (*ibid.*) (*Ada* is the Pentagon's official computer language; ROLM pioneered *Ada* hardware R&D). Since publication of *100 Best,* ROLM's Mil-SPEC division has been acquired.

52. See note 49.

53. Robert Levering, Milton Moskowitz, and Michael Katz, *The 100 Best Companies to Work for in America,* p. xiv.

54. Initially religious in connotation, *profession* and *professional* emerged in the Middle Ages (thirteenth and fifteenth centuries, respectively). The quasireligious guilds of carpenters, weavers, physicians, and merchants offered members protection from an impersonal labor market by cornering local supplies of skilled labor. As self-employed craft and merchant collectives, the guilds also protected the professional's control over the process, conditions, and materials of work. The guilds indirectly played something of a historic role in the consolidation of a "free" and cheap capitalist labor market. In England, for example, Maurice Dobb notes: "Coincident with the influence of enclosures in the Tudor age was the growing exclusiveness of the guilds which barred the way to any urban occupation except as a hired servant. The tightening of entrance requirements, the exaction of fees and payments as the price of setting up as a master, the elaborate requirements of a 'masterpiece', all served to bar the man without means from ever rising above the rank of journeyman...So it was that the regime of guild monopoly, while it was ultimately to prove an obstacle to capitalist industry, in its time performed the unwitting function for capitalism of swelling the ranks of those whose condition made them pliable to a master's will." (See note 61.) Maurice Dobb, *Studies in the Development of Capitalism* (New York: International Publishers, 1947, 1976), p. 229.

55. Burton Bledstein, *The Culture of Professionalism: The Middle Class and the Development of Higher Education in America* (New York: Norton, 1976, 1978).

56. *Ibid.*

57. In the study, Santa Clara Valley ranked eighteenth in effective buying income but fell to 47th in charitable contributions. The tight-fisted computer professional was blamed by a variety of disinterested observers. Intel Chairman Gordon Moore: "In the electronics industry, we've found that it's the lower-paid people who make the larger contributions. Many of the young engineers haven't seen some of the problems that are out there and they haven't yet developed social consciences." Santa Clara United Way chief fund raiser Tom Vais, agrees. "With a few notable exceptions, the people who have gotten rich in Silicon Valley still don't believe it...There is no tradition of philanthropy, as there is in many of the old Eastern families." Another Santa Clara County United Way manager on the computer professional's stinginess: "Take a fellow who lives in Cupertino, which is a nice town. He gets on I-280, the world's most beautiful freeway, and drives to Hewlett-Packard, which almost looks like a college campus. Where's the poverty? He doesn't see it. Few of these people have reason to go into East San Jose. In most Eastern or Mid-Western cities, you at least drive past poor areas when you go to work or even go shopping." Dale Lane, "Silicon Valley's Newly Rich Don't Believe Their Wealth—and Aren't Apt to Share," *San Jose Mercury News,* 13 October 1985.

58. Daniel Rosenheim, "Job Hopping is New Trend for Workers in the '80s."

59. The figures are from Judith Larsen and Cognos Associates. David Early, "The Career Usually Wins in Job-Family Tug of War, Researcher Says."

60. Lenore Weiss, "Notes from a Desktop Publisher," *Computer Currents,* 21 April-7 May 1987.

61. The autonomy of the old professional was fought for and in many cases upheld by common law or statute; the autonomy of the programmer and engineer is inscribed nowhere (much less grounded in a code of social responsibility). It exists because the marketplace currently rewards a scarcity of skills in high demand and because programming, engineering, and technical writing resist rationalization (see Chapter 4), not because programmers, engineers, and technical writers *as groups* have fought for the privileged status they can claim.

62. See Chapters 4 and 5.

63. Burton Bledstein, *The Culture of Professionalism,* p. 92. An unhealthy dependence on the professional's expertise emerged as a source of public concern in the nineteenth century. (*Ibid.* pp. 99, 102). What if the doctor, the lawyer, the accountant, upon whose expertise the lay person depended, was bilking the client? This was the context for the George Bernard Shaw quip that introduces this chapter.

64. Mills was concerned mainly with the clerical, professional, and manager's "bureaucratization," a process that had begun in the U.S. in the mid-nineteenth century. In *White Collar,* Mills insisted that "The main trend is for the bureaucratic organization of businessmen and of professionals to turn both into bureaucrats, professionalized occupants of specified offices and specialized tasks," and elsewhere "Even on managerial and professional levels, the growth of rational bureaucracies has made work more like factory production." C. Wright Mills, *White Collar,* (New York: Oxford University Press, 1951), pp. 137-38, 226-27. On the bureaucratization of clericals, see Harry Braverman, who, like Mills, was not enthusiastic about the oppositional political capacities of the professional "stratum." Braverman observed that the professional, like the clerical working class, experiences "alienation." However, the clerical "white collar" worker had been "enlarged into a mass of working-class employment, and in the process divested of all its privileges...it is not necessary to anticipate here a similar evolution of the specialized and lower-managerial employees in any near-term future." Harry Braverman, *Labor and Monopoly Capital: The Degradation of Work in the Twentieth Century* (New York: Monthly Review Press, 1974).

65. Gary Dessler, "Jumping Jobs Could Be Step to the Fast Track."

66. For example, in a Control Data Corporation's *Policies and Procedures* manual, managers are apprised of "[i]nformation not to be given to non-managerial employees:...overall performance ratings, salaries, or salary increase amounts of other employees...planned or forecasted increases." The manual cited in text also forbids revealing "[w]age and salary *survey information*" [emphasis added] to employees. Corporations routinely conduct secret industry-wide surveys to determine salary ranges. The results are then shared at conferences and in reports among participating corporations. The surveys are

considered especially sensitive since they reveal—and constitute legal evidence of—the widely varying rates at which the industry compensates workers of comparable experience and skill. Workers are constrained from conducting their own surveys; at some firms, discussing or comparing pay levels is considered worse than bad form—it is also grounds for dismissal. At IBM, a black worker sought to expose company-wide discrimination by distributing a confidential IBM document on wage guidelines; for this indiscretion he was fired. The National Labor Relations Board upheld IBM's dismissal on the grounds that its "legitimate" need to maintain wage secrecy outweighed workers' right to know. A front-page *Electronic Engineering Times* article reported on an "informal cartel" of 29 firms and labs that had been meeting since the 1950s to, among other things, "swap salary data" with a view to prevail during pay negotiations with engineering employees.

67. See note 33.

68. Gary Dessler, "Jumping Jobs Could Be Step to the Fast Track."

69. F. Milene Henley, "Stay Cool in Heat of Quitting," *San Jose Mercury News,* 26 May 1985.

70. Steve Early and Rand Wilson, "High Tech Professionals are Hard to Organize," *Labor Research Review,* Spring 1986, p. 66. The professional associations and societies cannot legally take collective action on behalf of their members, because they are not certified under the National Labor Relations Act. When work problems emerge, professionals (who have colleagues, not fellow workers) don't call strikes; they are more likely to call lawyers to instigate individual damages claims. ASPEP distinguishes itself among the computer professional associations in advocating a semblance of collective bargaining for its members. The ASPEP executive director apologetically declines any resemblance to working-class organizing, however, and emphasizes that concessions from employers should be "obtained through continuous negotiation, not confrontation." The National Writers Union (NWU) probably exhibits the most corporate independence, but the technical writers (in NWU Local 3) organize themselves mainly as a contractor network and lobby against tax laws threatening their self-employed status.

71. Ken Gordon, "Guest Editorial," *STC Intercom* (31: 7), March 1986.

Chapter Seven

1. Jill Wolfson, "Body Business," *San Jose Mercury News,* 15 October 1984.

2. Mary Gottschalk, "When Spending Costs [sic] Their Control," *San Jose Mercury News,* 3 April 1985.

3. Susan Faludi, "A Separate Peace," *West,* a Sunday supplement to the *San Jose Mercury News,* 4 May 1986.

4. A *San Jose Mercury News* article laments the absence of neighborliness and offers a primer on how to make neighbors. Doris, a single parent who has lived in the same two bedroom apartment in a quiet, multiracial Sunnyvale

neighborhood for over ten years and still drives her car three blocks to a convenience store, registered an emphatic "No" when I asked her if she felt like she lived in a neighborhood: "I'm a foreigner...I don't feel safe or secure." On the decline of neighborliness in the new U.S. habitats: Betsy Morris, "Shallow Roots: New Suburbs Tackle City Ills While Lacking A Sense of Community," and "Shallow Roots: Young and Old Alike Can Lead Lonely Lives in New U.S. Suburbs," *The Wall Street Journal,* 26-27 March 1987.

5. Silicon Valley's development strategy of courting electronics workplaces over housing, especially over lower income housing, forces workers into outlying bedroom communities and thus structures the automobile commute into daily life. By late 1987, San Jose had spent roughly $1 billion on office towers, a light-rail trolley (between downtown San Jose and an outlying and largely vacant industrial park—not a strategic investment in thinning the commute), and $28 million toward a luxury hotel. As a journalist noted, "the city now is limiting residential development and is opening up new areas for industry and offices." Steve Massey, *San Francisco Chronicle,* 6 October 1987. A housing developer complained of San Jose's housing policy, "You bring these people into your community to work during the day and they go home 40 miles away at night. They develop no allegiance to the community." The mayor of San Jose, who has crusaded to redevelop the old downtown core at the expense of housing and residential services, acknowledges, "I don't think you're ever going to meet the demand for housing" in San Jose. Ray Tessler, "Facelift Has San Jose Jittery," *San Francisco Chronicle,* 27 April 1988.

6. In 1957, 13 percent of Americans had seen some kind of psychological counselor. By 1985, the number was nearly 30 percent—or 80 million people. Nikki Meredith, "Psychotherapy: Everybody's Doin' it, But Does It Work?" *Utne Reader,* March/April 1987 (excerpted from *Science 86,* June 1986). Among many Silicon Valley electronics employees, who experience some of the nation's highest divorce rates and most stressful work, 60 percent or more are in therapy. See chapter 6.

7. A 1984 Santa Clara County survey of blue collar, office, professional, technical, and managerial workers in high-tech and non-high-tech fields found that over 59 percent were "very satisfied" with their jobs; over 38 percent said that "my main satisfaction in life comes from my work." Pete Carey & Alan Gathright, "By Work Obsessed: The Silicon Valley Ethic," *San Jose Mercury News,* 17 February 1985.

8. "Americans filed a record number of stress-related workers' compensation claims last year [1987], citing everything from surly supervisors to unsafe offices. In all, they accounted for 14 percent of occupational-disease claims, up from less than 5 percent in 1980. In California...the number of cases has increased five-fold since 1980." Annetta Miller et al., "Stress on the Job," *Newsweek,* 25 April 1988.

9. Surveying adults in 1,119 households, *American Health* magazine asked why they exercised. Only 18 percent said they exercised for "fun or enjoyment." Robert Johnson, "Mind Games: Weekend Athletes Seek Help From Sports Psychology," *The Wall Street Journal,* 11 August 1987.

10. Robert Bellah *et al., Habits of the Heart: Individualism and Commitment in American Life* (Berkeley: University of California Press, 1985), p. 335.

11. Claudia Morain, "Your Life in Her Hands," *San Jose Mercury News,* 8 April 1987. "More often, it's the personality of the [aerobics] teacher that brings 'em in or drives 'em out...Charm and pizazz are so important to [aerobics] students that instructors are no longer called instructors or teachers or leaders. They are called stars." Jill Wolfson, "Body Business."

12. The $500 million estimate is attributed to San Jose's Sheriff in a documentary by Michael Malone, author of *The Big Score* (New York: Doubleday & Co., 1985) in which the author writes, "The Drug Enforcement Agency has called Silicon Valley one of the biggest cocaine users in the United States." (p. 398) The San Jose Police Department told the McNeil-Lehrer Report 60-80 percent of Silicon Valley employees, from assembly line to top management, use drugs. (McNeil-Lehrer Report, 19 April 1984.) The 1984 *San Jose Mercury News* survey found that over 35 percent of respondents said they "frequently or occasionally" worked "under the influence of drugs (like marijuana or cocaine)." This approached the proportion (slightly under 44 percent) of those who worked under the influence of alcohol. Pete Carey and Alan Gathright, "By Work Obsessed," *op. cit.*

13. Marj Charlier, "Overdoing It: In the Name of Fitness, Many Americans Grow Addicted to Exercise," *The Wall Street Journal,* 1 October 1987; see also Eleanor Grant, "Hooked on Exercise: What happens to Fitness Fanatics Who Can't Say No?" in *This World,* a Sunday supplement of the *San Francisco Examiner,* 28 February 1988.

14. Eleanor Grant, "Can't Eat, Gotta Run," *This World,* 28 February 1988. Among the shared symptoms were loneliness, emotional withdrawal, and difficulty expressing anger. See also Charlier, "Addicted to Exercise," *op. cit.*

15. L. De Villers & R.M. Podell, "How Do You Feel About Your Body?" *Shape,* April 1988.

16. For the revival of the work ethic, see Chapter 6.

17. See for example the *University of California, Berkeley Wellness Letter* ("The Newsletter of Nutrition, Fitness, and Stress Management") and the *Tufts University Diet and Nutrition Letter.*

18. De Villers & Podel, "How Do You Feel" *op. cit.*

19. "Stress is...eroding the bottom line...some experts put the overall cost to the economy as high as $150 billion a year—almost the size of the federal deficit. Dr. Kenneth R. Pelletier, a specialist in executive health at the University of California, San Francisco, notes that many large corporations spend more than $200 million a year on medical benefits for their employees." Annetta Miller et al., "Stress on the Job" *op. cit.* p. 40-41.

20. Silicon Valley hosted one of the first of several "runner's" magazines in the 1970s. Running and jogging are used tirelessly to convey electronics industry ad copy, such as 3COM's "You're finally over the last hurdle" brochure introducing new computer software products. The presumption is that electronics professionals, who jog in densities at least as thick as any other occupational group, will find the iconography appealing.

21. "Perks like Parcourses tell the employee that the company cares about them and their health. It increases morale and productivity." R.C., *San Jose Mercury News,* 29 March 1984.

22. Judith Neuman, *San Jose Mercury News,* 2 November 1985.

23. Claudia Morain, "Body Worship," *San Jose Mercury News,* 1 July 1987.

24. Diane Lesniewski, "Holly Gagnier: Exercise Keeps Me Focused," *Diet & Exercise,* Spring 1988.

25. "Looking Good While Shaping Up," *Shape,* April 1988.

26. "Lose the fat, keep the muscle," was the voice-over jingle for a 1988 *Special K* cereal television commercial. The ten-second spot featured a well-chiseled woman in swim attire swimming in slow motion; the model's face was never shown.

27. Health & Fitness section, *San Jose Mercury News,* 1 July 1987.

28. Dana Ullman, "Getting Beyond Wellness Macho: The Promise and Pitfalls of Holistic Health," *Utne Reader,* January/February 1988; Miller *et al.,* "Stress on the Job" *op. cit.* See also Christopher Lasch, who notes in passing "the shift from an authoritative to a therapeutic mode of social control—a shift that has transformed not only industry but politics, the school, and the family." *The Minimal Self: Psychic Survival in Troubled Times,* (New York: Norton, 1984), p. 47.

29. Peter Gambaccini, "Get It In Gear: There Are As Many Ways to Stay Motivated As There Are Reasons To Run," *Runner's World,* May 1987, p. 85.

30. " 'We have people who are in here three times a day,' says Max Morton, manager of Adolph Coors Co.'s Wellness Center. He tells Coors' employees who exercise more than an hour and a half a day that they need to examine why they are doing it. 'We're certainly trying to steer them to a more moderate approach,' he says." Charlier, "Overdoing It," *op. cit.*

31. Grant, "Hooked on Exercise," *op. cit.*

32. Charlier, "Overdoing It," *op. cit.*

33. Johnson, "Weekend Athletes Seek Help," *op. cit.*

34. At the Palo Alto Sports Medicine Clinic, which treats mainly amateur but also college and professional athletes including Major League baseball pitchers, the waiting period for a physical therapy appointment in 1987 was often over a week.

35. Morain, "Your Life in Her Hands," *op. cit.*

36. Charlier, "Overdoing It," *op. cit.*

37. *Ibid.*

38. Miller et al., "Stress on the Job," *op. cit.*

39. Thorstein Veblen, *Theory of the Leisure Class* (New York: Mentor, 1953), pp. 60 ff.

40. Lasch, Christopher, *The Minimal Self, op. cit.*

41. Compulsive shopping is not peculiar to Silicon Valley, although it was here that marketing developed the most widely used modern advertising techniques.

42. William Ecenbarger, "You Can't Leave Home Without It," *This World,* 20 March 1988.

43. "When asked how much they would pay for an item like a toaster, the participants were consistently bigger spenders when a credit card was pictured nearby (as it is on many cash registers). They would spend $67.33 for the toaster, for instance—three times as much as when credit cards weren't in sight. They were also bigger tippers and more generous charity donors when they saw pictures of credit cards." Richard Feinberg, a Purdue University consumer-sciences and retailing professor, conducted the study. Betsy Morris, "Shopping Ranks High," *op. cit.*

44. William Ecenbarger, "You Can't Leave Home Without It," *op. cit.*

45. Another Pavlovian association: when consumers stop paying off their entire credit card balances each month, thereby incurring finance charges, credit lines are extended and preapproved loans and credit cards arrive via mail. Even the monthly payment has become a shopping occasion. Enveloping the credit card bill are mini-shopping catalogs toward which cardholders accumulate discount coupons. Banks also issue "superchecks" with balances tied to card accounts—the cost of writing each check is many times higher than that of issuing a personal check. In 1988, one bank card service announced a sliding scale of weekend to week-long luxury travel for those who charged between $2,500 and $15,000—*over a four month period.* The bank simultaneously offered to deduct insurance premiums against the day when monthly payments could no longer be made.

46. V. Kershner and Kathleen Pender, "Valley Fair Winning South Bay Mall War," *San Francisco Chronicle,* 14 December 1987.

47. Peter Freundlich, "Notes on the Higher Shopping," *Harper's,* December 1987.

48. Peter Zollo, executive vice president of Teenage Research Unlimited, claims teens are spending more time shopping (two hours for boys, four hours for girls per week) and enjoying it more. "Teen-age males are becoming extremely fashion conscious," confides Zollo who says that 27 percent wear designer jeans and 23 percent use hair-styling mousse. Morris, "Shopping Ranks High," *op. cit.*

49. The 70 percent figure is from a national survey for the International Council of Shopping Centers. (Morris, "Shopping Ranks High," *op. cit.*) The still evolving political economy of shopping centers: proprietors now measure performance in sales-per-square-foot. The higher the transaction density, the more the mall can charge its tenants. "With strong lead tenants in Macy's, Nordstrom, Emporium-Capwell and I. Magnin, [Silicon] Valley Fair reports sales of $325 to $330 a square foot, compared with the $196 national average, according to [mall] marketing director Warren Chaumont." Kershner and Pender, "Valley Fair Winning South Bay Mall War," *op. cit.*

50. "Malls are the new Main Streets of America," says Lawrence Sherman, a University of Maryland criminologist. "With video-game arcades, fast-food restaurants, movie theaters and parking-lot cruising scenes, malls also have become teen-age hangouts." (Ann Hagedorn, "Shoppers Beware: Malls May Look Safe, But Some Lure Crooks as well as the Crowds," *The Wall Street Journal,* 10 September 1987.)

51. Karl, Marx, *Capital,* vol 1., Moscow: Progress Publishers, based on 1887 English edition, p. 671.

52. The time studies are from University of Maryland sociologist John Robinson and are cited with similar surveys in Morris, "Shopping Ranks High," *op. cit.*

53. *Ibid.*

54. Betsy Morris, "Big Spenders: As a Favored Pastime, Shopping Ranks High With Most Americans," *The Wall Street Journal,* 30 July 1987.

55. *Ibid.*

56. *Ibid.*

57. University of Southern California study of 133 people. "Mall Mania," *University of California, Berkeley Wellness Letter,* February 1988.

58. A University of Minnesota study, cited in *ibid.,* found that "40% of those who defined themselves as compulsive shoppers said they were most likely to buy something when 'feeling bad' about themselves. About the same number of people also admitted that their closets were filled with unopened items."

59. Author's interview with Anthony Gonzales of Consumer Credit Counselors of Santa Clara Valley, 5 May 1988.

60. Morris, "Big Spenders," *op. cit.*

61. *Ibid.*

62. *Ibid.*

63. Gonzales interview and Gottshalk, "When Spending Costs Control," *op. cit.*

64. Morris, "Big Spenders," *op. cit.*

65. "Mall Mania," *op. cit.*

66. Joanne Grant, "San Jose Leads Nation in Crime War," *San Jose Mercury News,* 19 April 1984.

67. Another testimonial: "Holly Tappen, like many working women at times, considers shopping a pleasant, mind-numbing narcotic. 'It's a little vacation from your daily tasks...It is absolutely mindless behavior.' " Morris, "Big Spenders," *op. cit.*

68. Demographics distinguishes population groups by age, income, and other vital traits, from which marketing constructs consumer profiles.

69. Excerpts from the report are cited in Joel Makower, *Office Hazards* (Washington D.C.: Tilden Press, 1981), pp. 102-3; see also chapter 6.

70. Arnold Mitchell, *The Nine American Lifestyles* (New York: Warner Communications, 1983).

71. "Advertisements have fueled the increasing tendency of consumers to value objects for what they stand for instead of what they can do." Morris, "Big Spenders," *op. cit.*

72. The quotes from senior SRI researcher James Ogilvy are found in Brad Edmondson, "Skirmishes Along the Marketing Front," *Whole Earth Review,* Spring 1987.

73. *Ibid.*

74. Esprit advertising brochure, 1987.

75. Jordache ad, 1987.

76. The Jordache ad, along with Bugle Boy fashion copy, depicts those who recognize and identify with the alienation or, as Adam Cornford put it, the "pseudocommunity of the consciously but passively alienated." Another approach is reflected in the 1988 AT&T ads featuring testimony by responsive, honest, and folksy computer professionals. The professionals exemplify those who disavow and consciously escape alienation to the pressures and responsibilities of a career. See chapter 6.

77. Christopher Lasch, *The Minimal Self.*

78. Andrew Sullivan, "Advertising Goes Soft-Core: Today's Marketing Campaigns Peddle Titillation with a Twist," reprinted from *New Republic* in *This World,* a Sunday supplement of the *San Francisco Examiner,* 3 April 1988.

79. Here and there, the shabby trappings of popular culture have emerged around the shopping experience. The bumper stickers ("I'd rather be shopping," "I shop, therefore I am," "Born to Shop") and the unabashed vanity of new game shows capture the spirit of compulsive shopping. One such show debuted in 1988. "Double Dare" is a teen consumer game show based apparently on an episode from the Max Headroom pilot series in which "Wackets," an intolerably lame game show, conveyed an unconscious hexadecimal opiate to viewers. Scheduled for after school, before-dinner consumption, "Double Dare" features relay teams racing through a humiliating obstacle course. The faster they go, the more calculators, TV sets, midget automobiles, etc. they win. An announcer "calls" the race in studied caricature of the race track announcer. A family version of "Double Dare" airs separately.

80. The Lawrence Livermore National Laboratory, due east of Silicon Valley, is one of two U.S. nuclear weapons design facilities and the target of frequent political demonstrations as well as a major drug scandal among scientists and technical workers. For more on the Livermore Labs and scientists, see William Broad, *Star Warriors: A Penetrating Look into the Lives of the Young Scientists Behind Our Space Age Weaponry* (New York: Simon and Schuster, 1985). Reports of the drug scandal, which involved widespread cocaine use by lab employees, were spiked after an initial front-page story in the newsprint media, then reappeared as the topic of congressional probes. See Edward Iwata, "U.S. Officials Accused of Drug Coverup at Lab," *San Francisco Chronicle,* 24 May 1988; Josh Meyer, "High-Level Drugs Cover-up at Livermore Lab Charged," *San Francisco Examiner,* 15 June 1988; Coimbra Sirica, "Livermore Lab was Drug Haven, Investigators Say," *San Francisco Chronicle,* 16 June 1988; Sharon McCormick, "Livermore Lab Now Faces Probe Over Missing Precious Metals," *San Francisco Chronicle,* 14 July 1988.

81. Ken Garcia, "A Monument to Peace," *San Jose Mercury News,* 23 June 1984. The reporter describes the peace monument: "The two-piece teak monument mixes a series of curves, slopes and gaping holes, which Homan said reflect the serenity of the hills above Livermore where he lives." Explains Homan, "I wanted to make it abstract because peace is abstract."

82. Author's Kincholoe interview and correspondence, March 1985.

83. Author's Lockheed interviews, July 1985.

84. Notably, CPSR's focus on Star Wars, and PSR's on Nuclear Winter. CPSR in particular has sought to limit its critique of military electronics. CPSR leaders,

it seems, consciously restrict the depth and scope of their political critique in an effort to remain respectable and legitimate in the eyes of the opinion makers whom CPSR leaders seek to influence. CPSR's efforts to expose the fairytale "science" on which much of advanced weaponry is based are admirable. But there are at least two problems with CPSR's narrow approach. By stifling political discussion within CPSR (as leader Severo Ornstein did at the 1986 CPSR annual conference in Palo Alto), CPSR accepts the Pentagon's terms of debate over Star Wars, and the debate becomes one of technical feasibility, rather than political desirability. Thus, CPSR makes much of the debate inaccessible to those of us who aren't experts. The second problem is that by seeking legitimacy in the ideology of "professionalism," CPSR poses no viable alternative context to which computer workers can turn. (For contemporary professionalism, see chapter 6; for more on the CPSR's narrow conception of "responsibility," see chapter 4.)

85. Christopher Lasch, *The Minimal Self, op. cit.,* pp.17-18.

86. Faludi, "Separate Peace," *op. cit.*

87. Consider the biographies of the following Beyond War leaders: Dean and Donna Richeson: Dean met Donna in the CIA, where both worked throughout the 1960s, Dean as the agency's Chief Systems Engineer. Dean tired of launching surveillance satellites, and moved to Silicon Valley to co-found ROLM Corporation (the "R" is for Richeson), initially, an exclusively military contractor. Dean worked there as Vice President of Marketing. Both joined what is now Beyond War over eighteen years ago. Wayne Mehl: a former Navy nuclear weapons specialist in the 1960s, Wayne had become VP of ROLM's telecommunications division by the time he joined Beyond War. Wayne, who left ROLM to work as Beyond War's national staff director, said he "felt guilty" paying taxes for Pentagon projects, but not about working at management level for a company that makes nuclear weapons guidance systems and military computers. Ed Kyser: Ed has a Ph.D. in Applied Mechanics from Berkeley and is a former Lockheed Missile and Space Co. engineer. He left Lockheed to co-invent an ink-jet printer later sold by Siliconics Corp. In 1985, Ed was living off royalties and chose to devote his life "to the movement." Of Beyond War's demographics, Ed acknowledged "we do have a lot of contacts with business. We come from that milieu." Author's Beyond War interviews, 1985.

88. Beyond War's roots, according to former member Bob Kincholoe, go back to the Sequoia Seminar. Founded in the 1950s by the Rathbuns—Harry, an engineer and Stanford business law professor, and his wife Emelia—the Sequoia Seminar was an intensive non-sectarian study of the teachings of Jesus at a mountain retreat in the redwoods near Ben Lomond, a sleepy town in the Santa Cruz Mountains south of Silicon Valley. According to Kincholoe, many people discovered a deep personal meaning and had their lives changed while attending these seminars. The Sequoia Seminar spawned new groups, known sequentially as "The Community," "New Sphere," and "Creative Initiative." Each "explored a number of ways to reach people and help them grow." "Jesus as Teacher" groups were continued and techniques such as "T-Groups," and encounter and sensitivity groups were investigated as these became popular during the 1960s. Creative Initiative gave birth to Beyond War in 1981-82.

Author's Beyond War interviews, 1985, and the Kincholoe interview and correspondence, March 1985.

89. Beyond War member Ed Kyser likened social evolution to a scientific search for "pre-existing order, laws. From that level of science you reduce it to engineering and you actually make use of these laws and you shape your environment." When I asked about the "laws," Ed responded: "acting out of goodwill is a law. If you and I act out of goodwill there's a good chance that our interactions will be mutually satisfying...that means we're on the same team—I'm concerned about your well-being and you're concerned about my well-being. What we have to do is to take those universals and develop the engineering aspect of it." Author's Beyond War interviews, 1984.

90. Beyond War staff Norm Alquist, who left his electronics engineer career to work with Beyond War, comments on Beyond War's "unity principle," also known as "we are one" philosophy. "You can see it here in the Valley, some of the companies that I work for see that everyone in the corporate structure has to see that we are part of that corporation. We're pulling for that corporate goal. Companies that instill that belief in their employees are generally very successful in managing their company." Norm suggested that internationally, businesses, especially in Silicon Valley, are coming to more rationally plan their production in line with global needs and regardless of differences in economic systems. *Ibid.*

91. The "unity principle" is Beyond War's all encompassing epistemology that girds its "new mode of thinking." Beyond War literature goes cosmic, and a little mushy, when discussing the unity principle: "Lift your little finger and the stars move—ever so slightly, but they move. When the stars move, you are affected—ever so slightly, but you are affected. The same law of gravity that governs planetary motions and the formation of galaxies is present down to the subatomic level. The unity principle is present in its very name, the law of *universal gravitation." Beyond War: A New Way of Thinking* (Palo Alto: Creative Initiative, 1984) p. 14. See the immediately preceding note for an application of the unity principle to the Silicon Valley corporation.

92. Author's Beyond War interviews, 1984.

93. Martin Hellman, "A World Beyond War: the New Manner of Thinking," *The Stanford Daily,* 13 February 1984.

94. Author's Beyond War interviews, 1984; see also Faludi, "A Separate Peace," *op. cit.*

95. Speech before World Affairs Council, Spring, 1985.

96. Bill Workman, "Silicon Valley Fights Anti-Nuclear Move," *San Francisco Chronicle,* 31 October 1987.

97. Author's election eve Beyond War interview, 1987.

98. Author's Beyond War interviews, 1984.

99. Under the heading, "Action: Building Agreement" in *Beyond War: A New Way of Thinking,* the following passage appears: "We have not always lived up to the highest expression of our [U.S. Declaration of Independence] founding principles. For example, the principal that 'all men are created equal' originally meant only white, tax-paying, property-owning males. Clearer understanding of these principles has resulted in creative change. When enough of us agreed

that 'all men are created equal' meant black and white, we abolished slavery. When enough of us agreed that it meant women and men, we instituted woman suffrage [sic]. When enough of us agreed that it meant more than 'separate but equal,' we recognized civil rights." No where does Beyond War acknowledge the violent and valiant struggles and confrontation that forced these "agreements," such as they have been.

100. Author's Beyond War interviews, 1984.

101. Faludi, "A Separate Peace," *op. cit.*

102. This is one of several versions of the Beyond War pledge. See *Beyond War: A New Way of Thinking,* (Palo Alto: Creative Initiative, 1984).

103. For Beyond War origins in small group therapy, see note 88.

104. Author's Beyond War interviews, 1984.

105. See note 87.

106. Author's Beyond War interviews, 1984.

107. Hillel Zeitlin is a licensed clinical psychotherapist and director of Options for Personal Transition (OPT), a Berkeley counseling service specializing in cults and new religious groups. A critic of 'religious coercion,' Zeitlin said OPT was founded to provide an alternative to forcible 'deprogramming' practices. At my request, Zeitlin reviewed Beyond War literature. (While analyzing Beyond War literature, Zeitlin had no knowledge of the group's history.) The Zeitlin interviews and correspondence, 1985.

108. Faludi, "A Separate Peace," *op. cit.*

109. George Orwell, "Charles Dickens," *A Collection of Essays by George Orwell* (New York: Harcourt Brace Jovanovich, 1946).

110. Christopher Lasch, *The Minimal Self, op. cit..* p. 17.

111. *Ibid.* p. 33.

112. Tim Hunter, *River's Edge,* Hemdale Film Corporation, 1986.

113. *San Jose Mercury News,* 17 May 1987.

114. The "rebellion" of Silicon Valley youth depicted in *River's Edge* was unlike that of previous generations of outsiders, whose rebellion consisted in tension between themselves and a cohesive, if hostile, community (*The Wild One,* 1953) or family (*Rebel Without A Cause,* 1955) or both (*Five Easy Pieces,* 1970).

115. Raymond McLeod, "Milpitas Leads Bay Rise in Household Incomes," *San Francisco Chronicle,* 13 October 1987.

116. Joe Mannina, "Ozone Depletion: Study Points to Silicon Valley," *Silicon Valley Toxics News,* Spring, 1988; Elliot Diringer, "Foes of Toxics Sic New Law On Silicon Valley Firms," *San Francisco Chronicle,* 3 August 1988.

117. Martin Halstuk and Ray Tessler, "Hundreds Ordered Away From San Jose Toxic Fire," *San Francisco Chronicle,* 13 August 1988.

Index

About South End Press

South End Press is a nonprofit, collectively run book publisher with over 150 titles in print. Since our founding in 1977, we have tried to meet the needs of readers who are exploring or are already committed to the politics of radical social change. Our goal is to publish books that encourage critical thinking and constructive action on the key political, cultural, social, economic, and ecological issues shaping life in the United States and in the world. In this way, we hope to give expression to a wide diversity of democratic social movements and to provide an alternative to the products of corporate publishing.

If you would like to receive a free catalog of South End Press books or get information on our membership program—which offers two free books and a 40% discount on all titles—please write us at South End Press, 116 St. Botolph Street, Boston, MA 02115.